UCSD PASCAL T.M.:
A BEGINNER'S GUIDE
TO PROGRAMMING
MICROCOMPUTERS

J.N.P. Hume

R.C. Holt

Department of Computer Science
University of Toronto

RESTON PUBLISHING COMPANY, INC., Reston, Virginia
A Prentice-Hall Company

Library of Congress Cataloging in Publication Data

Hume, J. N. P.
  UCSD Pascal.

  Includes index.
  1. PASCAL (Computer program language)
  2. Microcomputers—Programming.   I. Holt, R. C.
  (Richard C.).   II. Title.
  QA76.73.P2H85   001.64'24   81-10590
  ISBN 0-8359-7915-6   AACR2
  ISBN 0-8359-7913-X (pbk.)

46,494

© 1982 by
Reston Publishing Company, Inc.
A Prentice-Hall Company
Reston, Virginia 22090

This book describes UCSD Pascal™ and the UCSD p-System™, which are distributed and licensed for distribution by SofTech Microsystems, Inc., 9494 Black Mountain Road, San Diego, CA 92126. The UCSD Pascal language and UCSD p-System facilities as represented in this book are, with minor exceptions, correct for Version II.0 of the UCSD p-System. The Turtlegraphics procedures which are described are specific to those distributed by Apple Computer™ Corporation.

UCSD Pascal and UCSD p-System are trademarks of the Regents of the University of California.

Apple Computer is a trademark of Apple Computer Corporation.

10   9   8   7   6   5   4   3   2

Printed in the United States of America.

PREFACE

This book is intended to introduce the reader to computer programming. No particular mathematical background beyond basic arithmetic is needed; examples are taken largely from everyday life. It is our strong conviction that the foundation of computer programming must be carefully laid. Bad habits once begun are hard to change. Computer programming provides excellent experience in the systematic analysis of problems from the statement of "what is to be done" to the final algorithm for "doing it". This can be very helpful in encouraging logical thinking.

The programming language presented here is UCSD Pascal, a high-level language that encourages good programming style. The language Pascal was devised by Niklaus Wirth and his book "Pascal User Manual and Report" with Kathleen Jensen contains the definition of what is called Standard Pascal. UCSD Pascal was developed at the University of California San Diego. It contains a number of extensions to Standard Pascal particularly ones to handle graphics and character strings. One of the great advantages of Pascal over other high-level languages is that it is not a language with a very large number of language constructs. It was possible because of this for UCSD to implement it even on microcomputers. These include the LSI-11 of the Digital Equipment Corporation, the Apple computers, and the Zilog Z80.

In this book, Pascal is introduced in a series of subsets that we call PS/1, PS/2, PS/3, and so on. The PS stands for Pascal Subsets. The book is about structured programming and that is what we hope you will be learning by following this step-by-step presentation of Pascal subsets.

Just as a program provides a list of instructions to the computer to achieve some well-defined goal, the methodology of structured programming provides a list of instructions to persons who write programs to achieve well-defined goals. The goals of structured programming are to get a programming job done correctly and in such a form that later modifications can be done easily. This means that programs must be understood by people other than their authors.

As each Pascal subset is learned, new possibilities open up. Even from the first subset PS/1, it is possible to write programs that do calculations and display results. By the time the subset PS/5 is reached, you will have learned how to handle alphabetic information, as well as to do numerical calculations and structure the control flow of the program.

Structured programming is especially important when working on larger programs; a detailed discussion of the techniques of modular programming and top-down design accompanies the introduction of Pascal subprograms in PS/6. Many examples in the book are from data processing, and in PS/8 the ability to handle files and records is introduced.

At all times we have tried to present things in easy to understand stages, offering a large number of program examples and exercises to be done on your microcomputer. Each chapter has a summary of the important concepts introduced in it.

The subsets PS/1, PS/2, PS/3, ..., referred to as a group by the name PS/k, are based on subsets for PL/1 called SP/k designed by Richard Holt and David Wortman of the University of Toronto.

This book was prepared using a type setting system on a computer. Each program was tested using a UCSD Pascal compiler by Mark Hume. The job of transcribing the authors' pencil scrawls into the computer and supervising the computer type setting process was done with great care and patience by Inge Weber assisted by Vicky Shum.

The time taken to write a book comes at the expense of other activities. Since most of the time was in the evenings or weekends we must end with grateful thanks to our wives Patricia and Marie.

J.N.P. Hume

R.C. Holt

CONTENTS

Chapter 1

INTRODUCTION TO STRUCTURED PROGRAMMING

We hope that it is no secret that the book has to do with *computers* and particularly with the *use* of computers rather than their design or construction. To use computers you must learn how to speak their *language* or a language that they can understand. We do not actually speak to computers yet, although we may some day; we write messages to them. The reason we write these messages is to instruct the computer about some work we would like it to do for us. And that brings us to *programming.*

WHAT IS PROGRAMMING?

Programming is writing instructions for a computer in a language that it can understand so that it can do something for you. You will be learning to write programs in one particular *programming language* called Pascal. When these instructions are entered into a computer directly by means of a keyboard input terminal they go into the part of the computer called its *memory* and are recorded there for as long as they are needed. The instructions could then be *executed* if they were in the language the computer understands directly, the language called machine language. If they are in another language such as Pascal they must first be *translated*, and a program in machine language *compiled* from the original or *source* program. After compilation the program can be executed.

Computers can really only do a very small number of different basic things. For example, an instruction which says, STAND ON YOUR HEAD, will get you nowhere. The repertoire of instructions that any computer understands usually includes the ability to move numbers from one place to another in its memory, to add, subtract, multiply, and divide. They can, in short, do all kinds of *arithmetic calculations* and they can do these operations at rates of up to a million a second. Computers are extremely fast calculating machines. But they can do more; they can also handle alphabetic information, both moving it around in their memory and comparing different pieces of information to see if they are the same. To include both numbers and alphabetic information we say that computers are *data processors* or more generally *information processors.*

When we write programs we write a sequence of instructions that we want executed one after another. But you can see that the computer could execute our programs very rapidly if each instruction were executed only once. A program of a thousand instructions might take only a thousandth of a second. One of the instructions we can include in our programs is an instruction which causes the use of other instructions to be repeated over and over. In this way the computer is capable of repetitious work; it tirelessly executes the same set of instructions again and again. Naturally the data that it is operating on must change with each repetition or it would accomplish nothing.

Perhaps you have heard also that computers can make *decisions.* In a sense they can. These so-called decisions are fairly simple. The instructions read something like this:

IF JOHN IS OVER 16 THEN PLACE HIM ON THE HOCKEY TEAM
       ELSE PLACE HIM ON THE SOCCER TEAM

Depending on the *condition* of John's age, the computer could place his name on one or other of two different sports teams. It can *decide* which one if you tell it the decision criterion, in our example being over sixteen or not.

Perhaps these first few hints will give you a clue to what programming is about.

WHAT IS STRUCTURED PROGRAMMING?

Certain phrases get to be popular at certain times; they are fashionable. The phrase, "structured programming" is one that has become fashionable. It is used to describe both a number of techniques for writing programs as well as a more general methodology. Just as programs provide a list of instructions to the computer to achieve some well-defined goal, the methodology of structured programming provides a list of instructions to persons who write programs to achieve some well-defined goals. The goals of structured programming are, first, to get the job done. This deals with *how* to get the job done and how to get it done *correctly.* The second goal is concerned with having it done so that other people can see how it is done, both for their education and in case these other people later have to make changes in the original programs.

Computer programs can be very simple and straightforward but many applications require that very large programs be written. The very size of these programs makes them complicated and difficult to understand. But if they are well-structured, then the complexity can be controlled. Controlling complexity can be accomplished in many different ways and all of these are of interest in the cause of structured programming. The fact that structured programming is the "new philosophy" encourages us to keep track of everything that will help us to be better programmers. We will be cataloguing many of the elements of structured programming as we go along, but first we must look at the particular programming language you will learn.

WHAT IS PASCAL?

Pascal is a language that has been developed to be independent of the particular computer on which it is run and oriented to the problems that persons might want done. We say that Pascal is a *high-level language* because it was designed to be relatively easy to learn. As a problem-oriented language it is concerned with problems of numerical calculations such as occur in scientific and engineering applications as well as with alphabetic information handling required by business and humanities applications.

Pascal is a reasonably extensive language, so that although each part is easy to learn, it requires considerable study to master. Many different computers, ranging in size from large computers to microcomputers, have available the facilities to accept programs written in Pascal. This means that they have a *Pascal compiler* that will translate programs written in Pascal into the language of the particular machine that they have.

It has been the experience over the past years that a high-level language lasts much longer than machine languages, which change every five years or so. This is because once an investment has been made in programs for a range of applications, you do not want to have to reprogram when a new computer is acquired. What is needed is a new compiler for the high-level language and all the old programs can be reused.

Because of the long life-span of programs in high-level languages it becomes more and more important that they can be adapted to changes in the application rather than completely reconstructed.

A high-level language has the advantage that well-constructed and well-documented programs in the language can be readily modified. Our aim is to teach you how to write such programs. To start your learning of Pascal we will study subsets of the full Pascal language called PS/k.

WHAT IS PS/k?

The PS in the name PS/k stands for "*Pascal Subset*". There really is a series of subsets beginning at PS/1, then PS/2, and going on up. The first subset contains a small number of the language features of Pascal, but enough so that you can actually write a complete program and try it out on your computer right away. The next subset, PS/2, contains all of PS/1 as well as some additional features that enlarge your possibilities. Each subset is nested inside the next higher one so that you gradually build a larger and larger vocabulary in the Pascal language. At each stage, as the special features of a new subset are introduced, examples are worked out to explore the increased power that is available.

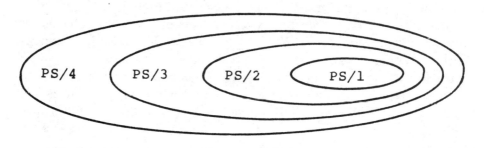

THE PS/k SUBSETS

In a sense, the step-by-step approach to learning Pascal is *structured* and reflects the attitude to programming that we hope you learn.

There is no substitute for practice in learning to program, so as soon as possible and as often as possible, submit your knowledge to the test by creating your own programs and running them on your computer.

WHY LEARN JUST A SUBSET?

The Pascal language is reasonably extensive; some features are only used rarely or by a few programmers. If you know exactly what you are doing, then these features may provide a faster way to program; otherwise they are better left to the experts. A beginner cannot really use all the features of the complete Pascal language and will get lost in the complexity of the language description. With a small subset it is much easier to pick up the language and then get on with the real job of learning programming.

CORRECTNESS OF PROGRAMS

One of the maddening things about computers is that they do exactly what you tell them to do rather than what you want them to do. To get correct results your program has to be correct. When an answer is displayed by a computer you must know whether or not it is correct. You cannot assume, as people often do, that because it was given by a computer it must be right. It is the right answer for the particular program and data you provided because computers now are really very reliable and rarely make mistakes. But is your program correct? Are your input data correct?

One way of checking whether any particular answer is correct is to get the answer by some other means and compare it with the displayed answer. This means that you must work out the answer by hand, perhaps using a hand calculator to help you. When you do work by hand you probably do not concentrate on exactly how you are getting the answer but you know you are correct (assuming you do not make foolish errors). But this seems rather pointless. You wanted the computer to do some work for you to save you the effort and now you must do the work anyway to test whether your computer program is correct. Where is the benefit of all this? The labor saving comes when you get the computer to use your program to work out a similar problem for you. For example, a program to compute telephone bills can be checked for correctness by comparing the results with hand computation for a number of representative customers and then it can be used on millions of others without detailed checking. What we are checking is the method of the calculation.

We must be sure that our representative sample of test cases includes all the various exceptional circumstances that can occur in practice, and this is a great difficulty. Suppose that there were five different things that could be exceptional about a telephone customer. A single customer might have any number of exceptional features simultaneously. So the number of different types of customers might be 32, ranging from those with no exceptional features to those with all five. To test all these combinations takes a lot of time, so usually, we test only a few of the combinations and hope all is well.

Because exhaustive testing of all possible cases to be handled by a program is too large a job, many programs are not thoroughly tested and ultimately give incorrect results when an unusual combination of circumstances is encountered in practice. You must try to test your programs as well as possible and at the same time realize that with large programs the job becomes very difficult. This has led many computer scientists to advocate the need to *prove* programs correct by various techniques other than exhaustive testing. These techniques rely partly on reading and studying the program to make sure it directs the computer to do the right calculation. Certainly the well-structured program will be easier to prove correct.

WHAT IS UCSD PASCAL?

UCSD Pascal is a version of Pascal that was designed (at the University of California San Diego) particularly for microcomputers. It incorporates a number of extensions to the Pascal language, extensions that allow you to manipulate graphic images and strings of alphabetic information more easily than you can with Standard Pascal. A whole UCSD Pascal system has been developed to allow users to run Pascal programs on a variety of the small single-user computers we call microcomputers. These include the LSI-11 of the Digital Equipment Corporation, the Apple Computers, and the Zilog Z80.

In order that a microcomputer can accept programs in Pascal and run them it must already have programs inside it. These are called *systems programs*. One of these systems programs is a Pascal compiler. Another is called its *operating system*. The operating system permits you to enter your program through the keyboard, make any alterations in it that are necessary (*edit* it), store it away in the secondary memory of the computer (*file* it), initiate compilation and execution (*run* programs), initiate printed output (prepare *hardcopy*), and so on.

In order to get the UCSD operating system to accept, edit, file, compile, or execute your Pascal program you must give it instructions through the keyboard. These are called *system commands*. So, in addition to learning the Pascal language for writing Pascal programs, you must also learn the UCSD Pascal *command language*. This command language, like the Pascal language, is extensive and we will be introducing only as much as you will need at any time. It is a good idea to learn a few commands at a time and become confident in their use before learning more.

CHAPTER 1 SUMMARY

The purpose of this book is to introduce computer programming. We have begun in this chapter by presenting the following programming terminology.

Program (or computer program) - a list of instructions for a computer to follow. We say the computer "executes" instructions.

Programming - writing instructions telling a computer to perform certain data manipulations.

Programming language - a language used to write programs that direct the computer to do work for us.

Pascal - a popular programming language devised by Professor Niklaus Wirth. PL/1, Fortran, Cobol, Basic, and APL are some other popular programming languages.

UCSD Pascal - a version of Pascal that contains extensions to the standard Pascal that permit easy manipulation of graphic images and strings of characters. These extensions were devised at the University of California San Diego.

PS/k - the part of the Pascal programming language used in this book. PS/k is a subset of the UCSD Pascal programming language, meaning that every PS/k program is also a Pascal program, but some Pascal programs are not PS/k programs. PS/k is itself composed of subsets PS/1, PS/2, and so on. This book teaches PS/1, then PS/2, and so on up to PS/8.

High-level language - a programming language that is designed to be convenient for writing programs. Pascal is a high-level language.

Compiler - a systems program that translates a program written in a high-level language, such as Pascal, into a language that can be executed on a computer. Compilers vary from one computer to another.

Structured programming - a method of programming that helps us write correct programs that can be understood by others. The Pascal language has been designed to encourage structured programming. This book presents a structured approach to programming.

Correctness of programs - the validity of programs should be checked. This can be attempted by comparing test results produced by the computer with the results of calculations made in another way, e.g. by using a hand calculator. Although the ideal is to try to prove a program correct by mathematical means, it is often extremely helpful to read and study the program to see that your intentions will be carried out.

Operating system - a program that is kept in the computer and which permits users to operate. It lets them submit programs, edit them, file them, compile them, and execute them.

Command language - a set of commands that cause the operating system to perform certain functions for you. These are used to submit, edit, file, compile, and execute programs.

UCSD command language - the particular set of commands that are used with the UCSD Pascal operating system.

Chapter 2

THE COMPUTER

The things we want to talk about in this chapter have to do with getting to know a little bit about computers and how they are organized. A computer is a complex object composed of wires, silicon chips with electronic circuits on them, and so on, but we will not be trying to follow circuit diagrams and worrying about how to build a computer. What we will be interested in is the various main parts of a computer and what the function of each is. In this way your programming will be more intelligent; you will understand a little of what is going on inside the computer.

PARTS THAT MAKE THE WHOLE

We have already mentioned a number of things about computers. They have a *memory* where programs, numbers, and alphabetic information can be recorded. They can add, subtract, multiply, and divide. This means they have a part called the *arithmetic unit*. They can read information from a keyboard input and output results on a screen. They may also have a printer. The printer may output a whole line at a time or just one character at a time, like a typewriter. We say they have an *input* (for example, keyboard) and an *output* (a screen). The input-output unit is often referred to as the I/O. Computers execute instructions in sequence. The part of the machine that does this is called the *control unit*. The arithmetic unit and the control unit are usually grouped together in a computer and called the *central processing unit* or CPU. So then the computer is thought of as having three parts, memory, I/O and CPU.

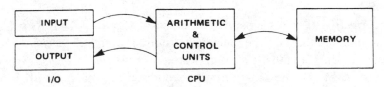

MAIN PARTS OF A COMPUTER

We will look at these different parts in turn and see how they work but first we must see how numbers and alphabetic information can be represented in a computer.

CODED INFORMATION

You are all familiar with the way that information used to travel over telegraph wires in the form of Morse Code. Perhaps you know that each letter or number is coded as a pattern of dots and dashes. For example, the letter A is a dot followed by a dash, E is one dot, V is three dots and a dash. The letters are separated from each other by a pause with no dots or dashes. The famous signal SOS is

    · · ·   _ _ _   · · ·

This is an easy one to remember in emergencies. The Morse Code was designed so that the signal could activate some noise-making device and the listener could then translate the coded message back into letters. Modern teletype machines can send messages much faster because the machines themselves can be used to decode the messages. For these, a character is represented by a pattern of pulses, each pattern being of the same length. Instead of dots and dashes, which are two different lengths of electric pulses, they use one basic time interval and in that time interval have either a pulse or a pause. Each character requires 5 basic time intervals and is represented by a sequence of pulses and pauses. We often write down a pulse as a 1 and a pause as 0, and then the pattern for B is 10011, I is 01100, L is 01001. The word BILL would be transmitted as

    10011011000100101001

Strings of ones and zeros like this can be associated with numbers in the *binary system*. In the decimal system the number 342 means

$$3 \times 10^2 + 4 \times 10^1 + 2 \times 10^0$$

where 10^2 stands for 10 squared, 10^1 for 10 to the first power, that is 10, and 10^0 for 10 to the power zero, which has a value 1. In the binary system of numbers 1101 means

$$1 \times 2^3 + 1 \times 2^2 + 0 \times 2^1 + 1 \times 2^0$$

In the *decimal system* this binary number has a value $8+4+0+1=13$. We say that this number in the decimal system requires 2 *decimal digits* to represent it. In the binary system it requires 4 *binary digits*. We call a binary digit a *bit*. So the binary number representing the word BILL has 20 bits, each letter requiring 5 bits. Sometimes we take the number of bits required to represent a character as a group and call it a *byte*. Then the word representing BILL has four bytes. In a computer we must have a way of recording these bits, and usually the memory is arranged into *words*, each capable of holding a whole number of bytes.

In some machines a single letter is represented by a byte of six bits and the word length is 6 bytes or 36 bits. Most minicomputers and micro-computers have 2 bytes in a word and 8 bits in each byte. There are many different combinations of byte length and word length in different comput-ers. This is something the machine designer must decide.

MEMORY

Most machines record letters and numbers in the binary form because it is possible to have recording devices that can record, read, and hold such information. Most recording devices involve a recording something like that on the tape of a magnetic tape recorder. There is a big difference, though, in the recording. On audio tape we have a magnetic recording that varies in intensity with the volume of the sound recorded. The frequency of the variations gives the pitch of the sound. For a computer, the record-ings vary between two levels of intensity which you might think of as "on" and "off". If in a particular region there is an "on" recording it could indi-cate the binary digit one and if "off" the digit zero. So on a strip of mag-netic tape there would be designated areas that are to hold each bit of infor-mation.

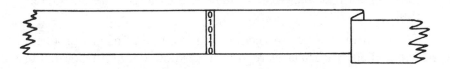

BITS RECORDED ON MAGNETIC TAPE

Binary digits can thus be recorded on reels of magnetic tape. In a similar way they can be recorded on tracks of a magnetic disk. To read or record information on a magnetic disk the recording/reading head moves to the correct track of the disk and the disk is set spinning so that the infor-mation on the track can be accessed.

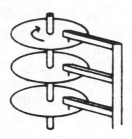

MAGNETIC DISK MEMORY

Tape reels and disks can be removed from the machine and stored if you need to keep information for long periods of time. Small disk memories are often used on microcomputers where individual disks are inserted into the reader by the user. These disks are often limp and are called *floppy disks* or *diskettes*. Diskettes are kept in paper envelopes to protect them. They are *not* removed from the envelope even during use. Tape reels on regular audio-type cassettes can also be used as secondary memory.

Both tape and disk secondary memories require the movement of objects, a reel of tape, a spinning disk and sometimes read/write heads. These mechanical devices can never give really high-speed access to information. We need memory devices with no moving parts so we can perform operations at rates of the order of a million a second. The only things that move in a really high-speed memory device are the electric signals. As you know, electric signals can move very rapidly, at nearly the speed of light. A very common form of high-speed memory uses large scale integrated circuits (LSI).

The main memory of the computer is a number of bits grouped into words; to find any particular word you must know where it is located in the array of words. You need to know its *address*. Every word (which, remember, is just a group of bits) has its own address which is a number. An address may, for example, be 125. Words that are neighbors in the array have consecutive addresses, such as 125 and 126, just like houses on a street. The addresses themselves do not have to be stored in the computer. You can tell what address a word has from its location in the array. This is not always possible for houses on the street because the numbering is not completely systematic.

125						3	1	2
126					5	2	8	7

THE CONTENTS OF WORDS IN MEMORY

Since the development of microminiaturized electronic circuits on silicon chips, high-speed memory devices holding thousands of bits can be produced using as little as a single chip.

ARITHMETIC UNIT

All computers have a part where arithmetic can take place. This is the *arithmetic unit*. When a new number is written in a memory location, the old number stored there is automatically erased, just as any old recording is erased as a new recording is made on a magnetic tape recorder. Just reading a number, like playing an audio recording, does not damage the recording no matter how often you do it. If you want to combine numbers, say add them, it is usually done in a special location in the arithmetic unit called the *accumulator*. On some machines, the size of the accumulator is the same as the size of a word in memory. Words, or rather the information stored in memory locations, can be loaded into the accumulator. In a simple machine language, the instruction

LOAD 125

would cause the number recorded in location 125 to be placed in the accumulator. Whatever was recorded in the accumulator before would be erased before the load takes place. If we want to add another number we would write

ADD 126

This would add the number stored in 126 to what was already in the accumulator and the sum of the two numbers would then be in the accumulator. This total could be recorded in the memory for later use by the instruction

STORE 127

The result of the addition would now be in location 127 but would also remain in the accumulator.

The accumulator can also be used for subtraction, multiplication, and division. In a high-level language like Pascal you never need to think about the accumulator. You merely indicate that you want numbers in two locations, say A and B, to be added and name the location, say C, where you want the answer to be stored. You write this all in one statement, namely

C:=A+B

This Pascal statement says: add the number stored in location A to the number stored in location B and place the result in location C. In the machine all location addresses are numbers. In Pascal we give the locations names which are called *identifiers*. The compiler changes these names to numerical locations and changes the single Pascal instruction

C:=A+B

to the three machine instructions.

LOAD A
ADD   B
STORE C

CONTROL UNIT

You have just seen examples of machine language instructions. They each consist of two parts: the operation part, for example LOAD, and the address part, A. Each part can be coded as a binary number, then the whole instruction will just be a string of bits. Suppose that you have a machine with a word length of 36 bits. Then an instruction might be itself stored in such a word with, say, 18 bits for the operation part and 18 bits for the address part. With 18 bits you can represent binary numbers that go from 1 up to 2 to the power 18, which is 262,144. You can refer to any one of over a quarter of a million different memory locations.

Consecutive instructions in a machine language program are stored in consecutive locations in the memory and are to be executed one after the other. The control unit does two things. It uses a special location called the *instruction pointer* to keep track of what instruction is currently being executed. It places the instruction to be executed in a special location called the *control register*. In the control register the instruction is decoded and signals are issued to the different parts of the computer so that the operation requested is actually carried out. As each instruction is executed, the instruction pointer is increased by one to give the address of the next instruction in the program. This next instruction is then fetched from the memory, placed in the control register, and executed. This process continues, with instructions being executed sequentially unless a special instruction is encountered, which resets the instruction pointer and causes a *jump* from the normal sequence to a different part of the program.

In brief, the control unit controls the sequence of execution of instructions and determines the effect that execution has on the information stored in the memory.

Computers were originally referred to as *stored program calculators* because the instructions as well as the numbers or characters they operate on are stored in the memory. They were also referred to as *sequential machines*, because normally they followed a sequence of instructions one after another unless a jump instruction directed them to do otherwise.

We have said that the memory of a computer can be contained on a single silicon chip. This is true also of the parts of the computer that make up the central processing unit. If the CPU is all on a single chip we call the computer a *microprocessor.*

INPUT AND OUTPUT

We have spoken of putting both data and instructions in the memory of the machine and changing the data by the execution of instructions. But how do we get data or instructions into the computer, and how do we get data out of the machine after it has been operated on? That is the function of the *input and output units.* We must have instructions that cause the machine to *read* information into its memory and to *write* information out from its memory. And we must have parts of the computer, the input and output units, that respond to these instructions. Most small computers use individual input/output terminals at which information can be entered through a keyboard and output is produced as a display on a cathode ray tube (CRT) screen. Sometimes there is also a printer for obtaining *hard copy* of what can be seen on the screen. Because each user enters his program and data directly into the computer and receives the results rapidly, the system is often said to be an *interactive* system.

The keyboard of a computer is similar to that of a standard typewriter, so it helps if you can type. But hunt-and-peck methods will get you there too. In addition to the ordinary typewriter keys, there are special keys for indicating that you want the computer to take certain actions. These keys are not the same from one kind of microcomputer to another. The hard copy output units can be line-at-a-time printers or typewriters. Across a displayed page there are often positions to output 120, 132 or more characters although some printers output only 72 characters on a line. The paper is continuous but may be divided by perforations into pages, each capable of holding about 60 lines of output.

PROGRAM TRANSLATION

We have said that three machine language instructions, namely,

LOAD   A
ADD   B
STORE   C

correspond to what is written in Pascal as

$$C := A + B$$

Instructions in the high-level language Pascal are very much simpler to write than instructions in machine language. For one thing, you do not have to be aware of the accumulator; for another, the notation is very similar to the one used in simple mathematical expressions and should be easy for you to get used to. The Pascal language is more powerful in that a single Pascal instruction can correspond to many machine language instructions. We will see later that if you are working in a high-level language, the machine can detect when you make certain kinds of mistakes in your program.

In summary, high-level languages are designed to suit *you* rather than suit a computer. And in being that way they make the job of programming less difficult.

A Pascal program cannot execute directly on a computer but must be translated into the language for the particular computer you have. This is accomplished after the Pascal program has been entered into the memory. The translation is performed by another program, called the compiler, that is already stored in the computer memory. The compiler reads your Pascal program and produces the appropriate sequence of machine language instructions from your Pascal statements. After compilation, execution of the machine language program is initiated provided you have not made any errors in your Pascal program that the compiler can detect. The kind of errors that are detectable are mostly in the *form* of the statements. If they are not proper or grammatical statements in the Pascal language the compiler will report an error to you on your screen. Errors in grammar are called *syntax errors*. In English you know there is an error in the sentence,

THE BOYS IS WALKING.

A machine can spot this kind of error but it cannot easily spot an error in meaning. It might never determine that the sentence,

THE HOUSE IS WALKING.

is not a meaningful sentence; it would accept it as syntactically correct.

Well, that is enough of an introduction now; let us get down to actually writing programs.

CHAPTER 2 SUMMARY

In this chapter we presented the main parts of a computer and showed how information is stored in the memory. We explained briefly how a high-level language such as Pascal is translated, or compiled, into machine language before being executed by a computer. The following important terms were introduced.

Memory - the part of a computer that stores information, such as data or a program. Magnetic tapes and disks are called secondary memory; they require mechanical motion to access information stored on them. Main memory can be immediately accessed by the computer; main memory is usually in the form of a microminiaturized circuit on a silicon chip. We say the memory is a solid state one. The computer can transfer information between secondary memory and main memory.

CPU (central processing unit) - composed of the arithmetic unit and the control unit. The arithmetic unit carries out operations such as addition and multiplication. The control unit directs other parts of the computer, including the arithmetic unit, to carry out a sequence of instructions that is in the main memory.

Input and output - ways of getting information into and out of a computer. An output device called a printer takes information from main memory and outputs it on paper. This is referred to as hard copy. An input/output device suitable for use by individual users is often a keyboard and a cathode ray tube display screen attached to the computer.

Screen - a cathode ray tube used to display the output from a computer.

Keyboard - the array of keys used to enter data and instructions into a computer.

Bit - a digit in the binary system of numbers, usually written as a 0 or a 1.

Byte - a sequence of bits treated as a unit, e.g. the number of bits used to represent an alphabetic character.

Word - a number of bits grouped as a unit for holding information in the memory of a computer. Each word has an address which indicates its location in the array of words in memory. A word often consists of four bytes.

Coded information - before information can be entered into a computer, it must be coded in a convenient form for the computer's circuitry. The circuitry recognizes "off" and "on" which we can think of as 0 and 1.

Translation (or compilation) - before a program written in a language like Pascal can be executed by a computer, it must be translated into a language that can be interpreted by the computer. The program as written in Pascal is called the source program. The translated program is placed in words in the main memory and is executed by the computer's CPU.

Microprocessor - a computer in which the entire CPU is contained on a single silicon chip.

Syntax error - an error in the form (or grammar) of instructions.

Semantic error - an error in the meaning of a program.

Accumulator - the part of the CPU where arithmetic operations are performed.

Control unit - the part of the CPU that determines the sequence of execution of instructions.

Chapter 3

PS/1: PROGRAMS THAT CALCULATE AND OUTPUT

This is the chapter where we set the stage for programming and you meet the cast of characters in the play. Nothing very much is going to happen in this first subset, PS/1, but you will be able to go through the motions of writing a complete program, entering it into a computer and having it executed. This will let you get used to the keyboard. Also you will see what kind of output to expect. Things will happen, though what the computer is actually doing for you will not be very exciting yet. But remember you will go through the same motions as are necessary when your programs do have more content.

CHARACTERS

You will be learning the programming language Pascal a little bit at a time. Any language consists of words and the words are made up of *symbols* that we call *characters*. These characters are put together in *strings*. In English the word

ELEPHANT

is a string of characters of length eight. It contains only seven different characters, the character E being used twice. We can tell that it is a word because it has a blank in front of it and one at the end. In a way the blank is also a character, but a *special character* for separating words. We sometimes denote the blank by b when we output programs in this book so that you can see how many blanks are present.

In English, we group words into sentences and we can tell the end of a sentence because of a special mark, the period. We also have a different kind of sentence that ends with a question mark, don't we? In addition to periods and question marks, we have other *punctuation marks* which serve to make sentences in the language easier to read. They also serve to remove ambiguity in a sentence. There is some doubt about the meaning of the sentence,

THE STUDENT CLAIMS THE TEACHER UNDERSTANDS.

The doubt is removed if it is written with commas, as,

THE STUDENT, CLAIMS THE TEACHER, UNDERSTANDS.

It is important that statements in a programming language be *unambiguous*, so punctuation is used a great deal. Instead of a sentence, the basic unit in the main part of a program is a *statement*. Statements are separated by semicolons. This serves to separate them just as periods separate sentences in English. The comma is used to separate items in any list of similar items, and parentheses are used to enclose things that belong together.

We will have words in Pascal that are made up of letters of the alphabet and might also have digits in them. When we are writing a Pascal program we want it to be understandable. So we choose words like English words. We use words like NAME, COST, INCOME, TAX, INVOICE, SUM, or words like PAGE1, TABLE6, ITEM35, and so on. Most of these words are invented by you. You are not allowed to use words that do not at least have one letter at the beginning. If the Pascal compiler sees a digit at the beginning of a word it assumes that it is a *number*. For example, 317 is taken as a number. This means that words like 3RDPAGE are illegal and will not be accepted by the Pascal compiler.

Before we leave characters we should perhaps list them. A *character* is a letter, or a digit, or a special character. The *letters* are

A B C D E F G H I J K L M N O P Q R S T U V W X Y Z
a b c d e f g h i j k l m n o p q r s t u v w x y z

In this book we will use capital letters only, in our programs. In general, lower case letters may be used instead of upper case letters. Matching upper and lower case letters are equivalent.

The *digits* are

0 1 2 3 4 5 6 7 8 9

The *special characters* are

: + - * / ( ) = , . ' [ ] < > ; { } ↑
b blank

Pairs of special characters are often used as *special symbols* in the language. For example, each of the following pairs has a fixed meaning

:= <> <= >= ..

Various other special characters are often available on different computer systems.

NUMBERS

Computers can do arithmetic calculations and they can do them extremely rapidly. When you learned arithmetic you first learned to handle numbers that are whole numbers, or integers. You learned that $5+6=11$ and $2x3=6$. In Pascal numbers like 2, 3, 512, 809, and 46281 are called *integer constants*. Any string of digits is an integer constant. You will remember that we will be storing numbers in the computer and representing them as a string of bits in some coded representation. The largest integer we can represent will be limited by the length of the string of bits that are in a word in our computer. Word lengths vary from one computer to another and different Pascal compilers have different maximum lengths for the digit strings that represent integer numbers. You will be safe in expecting at least four decimal digits to be within the maximum.

If you have integers requiring longer digit strings, for instance the population of the world, you must use the other form of numbers which is the *real* form.

If you have a large number like

635,642,000

you can write it as

6.35642×10^8

Perhaps you recognize this as what is called scientific notation. In Pascal the form of a *real constant* such as our example is

6.35642E8

The first part is called the *fraction part* or *mantissa*, the second part the *exponent*. The exponent part is written using the letter E followed by the power of 10 that is to multiply the fraction part. Maybe you learned this notation before in a science course where very big numbers, like the mass of the moon, often occur. *Real* notation is also used for numbers that are not integers. These are either *fractions* or *mixed numbers*. We write either of these in decimal notation where a point called the decimal point separates the integer from the fraction part. Examples of fractions are

.5   .0075   .0000023

Mixed numbers are

5.27   889.6   6.0216

When we write fractions or mixed numbers in exponent notation we usually standardize the form by putting the first non-zero digit followed by a decimal point then the remaining digits. Then the power of 10 is computed to make it right. The fraction .0000023 is written as 2.3×10^{-6}. In Pascal this then is 2.3E-6. It could also be written as 0.23E-5, or 23.0E-7, or even as 23E-7.

An integer constant must *not* have a decimal point. A real constant can be written either as a mixed number with at least one digit to the left of the decimal point *and* one digit to the right, e.g. 0.02, or in the exponent form. In the exponent form it usually has a decimal point (with exceptions like the example 23E-7) and *must* have an exponent part. There must be digits on both sides of the decimal point if there is one. The exponent part is the letter E followed by an optional plus or a minus sign followed by one or more digits.

CHARACTER STRINGS

We have said that computers can handle both numbers and strings of characters. We have seen that there are two forms for numbers, integers and reals.

A character string can consist of any of the characters that we have specified: letters, digits and special characters. Very often, when displaying the results of a computer calculation, we want the results labeled. What we want is to output a string of characters on the screen. In the statement that specifies what we want the computer to output, we include the actual string that we want displayed enclosed in single quotation marks. These strings enclosed in quotation marks are called *literals* or *character string constants*.

Examples of literals are

'BILL JONES', 'BALANCE IN ACCOUNT', 'X='

If the literal you want to use contains a quotation mark or an apostrophe, which is the same character, then you must put two quotes rather than a single quote. For example, the literal corresponding to the short form of 'CANNOT' is 'CAN''T'.

EXPRESSIONS

One of the important concepts we have in Pascal is that of an *expression*. The way that we explain what a word like expression means is basically to give examples and then generalize these examples.

First of all 32, 5, 6.1E2 and 58.1E6 are all expressions. So the general statement is that integer constants and real constants are expressions. So are literals like

'THIS IS AN EXPRESSION'

Any expression may be enclosed in parentheses and still be an expression. For example (32) and (6.1E2) are also expressions. The expressions that are integer or real constants can be combined into compound expressions using the signs of arithmetic for adding, subtracting, multiplying, and dividing. These expressions are called *arithmetic expressions*. We use the standard signs for adding and subtracting, namely the plus and minus. For multiplication we use the asterisk (*) because there is no times sign. For division we use the slant or slash symbol (/). Examples of arithmetic expressions are

2+3, 5.2E1*7.8E5, 6E0/2E0, 10-15

Integer and real values may be combined in a single expression, and when they are the result is a real value. For example, 2+3.0E1 has the value 3.2E1.

If two numbers are to be divided using the slant operator, the result will be a real value even if both numbers are integers. For example, 6/2 gives the real result

3.0E0

Two integers may be divided to produce an integer value using the operator DIV. For example, 5 DIV 2 would give the integer 2. The result is truncated. If you want to find the remainder in an integer division, use the operator MOD. The result of 5 MOD 2 is the integer 1, the remainder when 5 is divided by 2.

Here is a very complicated arithmetic expression

2*5+8-3*5/2+6

In evaluating this you have to know what to do first because you really can only add, subtract, multiply, or divide numbers two at a time. The rule is to do the multiplications and divisions first, then the additions and subtractions. Also you start at the left-hand side of the expression and work to the right. We are using here *rules of precedence*, that the operations multiply and divide have precedence over add and subtract. Parentheses can be used to guide the sequence of evaluation. For example, you write 3*(5+8) instead of 3*5+8 if you want the addition to take place before the multiplication. Expressions in parentheses take precedence.

EXAMPLES OF ARITHMETIC EXPRESSIONS

The following examples illustrate the rules for performing arithmetic in the Pascal programming language.

72+16   Value is 88.

8*5+7   Value is 47. Note that * means multiply.

2+10*4   Value is 42. Note that multiplication is done before addition.

(2+10)*4   Value is 48. The parentheses cause the addition to be done before the multiplication.

1/3   This division will produce the real value 3.33333E01. We can use integers and real values with / and we always get a real value as the result.

72E0+16E0   Value is 88E0, which can be written in other forms such as 8.8E1 and 8.80000E+01.

(9.83E0+16.82E0)/2.935E0

This expression is equivalent to the following

$$\frac{9.83+16.82}{2.935}$$

Real numbers may be written in the exponent form or as mixed numbers. The parentheses were used so the division would apply to the sum of 9.83E0 and 16.82E0 (and not just to 16.82E0).

17 DIV 5   Value is 3. Note that only the integer part of the quotient is given. DIV accepts only integers (not real values) and gives an integer result.

17 MOD 5   Value is 2. This is the remainder when 17 is divided by 5. MOD accepts only integers (not real values) and gives an integer result.

OUTPUT

Our main purpose in subset number one is to introduce you to Pascal and to get you to write your first program. The program is not going to do very much but it has to do something so that you can see that it is working. The most it can do is to output numbers or character strings on the CRT display. Then you can see that some action is taking place.

The statement that we will use in the program is like this

WRITELN (3, 5.1E1, 'BILL');

Output produced by the WRITELN statement is placed in successive fields across the output line. The output line has spaces for a certain number of characters. The items that are in parentheses after the WRITELN are placed one to a field going from left to right and then a new line is started. Literals are displayed, without the quotation marks, in a field the same size as the length of the literal. The size of fields reserved for integers equals the number of digits in the integer. If the integer is negative an extra position is used for the sign. Real numbers are displayed in a standard form with a minus sign or blank, as required, followed by one digit, a decimal point, and five more digits. The exponent is represented by a capital E followed by the integer which is the power of 10. If it is a negative exponent the minus sign precedes the integer. The output for the WRITELN statement we showed would be

3 5.10000E1BILL

In this form everything may be run together. A variation on this may be obtained by specifying a minimum field size for the item that is to be output. This is done by writing a colon followed by the minimum field size right after the item to be output. For example

WRITELN(3:10,5.1E1:10,'BILL':10);

will output the same items as before but in three fields of width 10 character positions each. Each item is right justified in the field size specified. If it is longer than the field size that longer size will be used. If it is shorter than the field size the output item is padded on the left with blanks. The minimum field size recommended for a real number is 13 characters since if all positions are needed this is what is required. We could use only 10 in our example because there are no minus signs here. The output for our WRITELN statement is

bbbbbbbbb3b5.10000E1bbbbbbBILL

The little b is actually a blank but we have written it this way so you could count the spaces. Mixed numbers are output in the exponent form. For example, the number -378.52 would be displayed as

-3.78520E2

You can get the mixed number form if you write

WRITELN(-378.52:8:2);

With this format specification a field size of 8 columns is used and the number is output as a mixed number with two digits to the right of the decimal point. The number of digits to the left of the decimal point depends on the size of the integer part of the number. If you do not specify a large enough field, a larger one will be used whenever necessary.

Since literals are displayed in fields whose size is the same as the length of the literal, when no field size is specified a literal should begin with a blank so that a space will separate it from other items that are displayed.

A blank line can be left by using

WRITELN(' ');

since here the literal consists only of a blank. Actually the statement

WRITELN;

will produce the same result.

Expressions other than integer and real constants and literals may also be placed in a WRITELN statement. The statement

WRITELN(2+3:10, 4/2:14);

will result in a 5 being displayed in the first field of width 10 and 2.00000 in the second of width 14. An interesting statement might be

WRITELN('2+3=',2+3);

it would print

2+3=5

Note that the quotes around the literal are not displayed. We do not specify field sizes because it is perfectly readable without them.

In all the examples of a WRITELN statement we have shown a semicolon at the end. This is necessary to separate it from the next statement in the program but is not used if the statement happens to be the last of a list of statements.

If you do not want to finish a displayed line in an output statement you use WRITE instead of WRITELN. The list of statements

WRITE(3:10);
WRITE(5.1E1:14);
WRITELN('BILL':10);

accomplishes exactly the same result as the single statement

      WRITELN(3:10,5.1E1:14,'BILL':10);

The WRITE statement is like WRITELN except it does not cause a new line to be started after its items are displayed.

To save thought it is common to choose standard field sizes such as 10 for integers and 14 for real numbers but more attractive output can be obtained by choosing field sizes more carefully. Suppose you bought 13 fattening chocolates, weighing together 0.6 kilograms at 6.87 dollars per kilogram. You could calculate and output the cost by

WRITE('I BOUGHT', 13, 'GOODIES FOR', 0.6*6.87, 'DOLLARS')

This outputs the following

 I BOUGHT13GOODIES FOR 4.12200DOLLARS

The spacing is very poor. And the form of the REAL number unfortunately has too many figures.

We can fix these problems this way

WRITE('I BOUGHT', 13:3, 'GOODIES FOR':12, 0.6*6.87:5:2,' DOLLARS')

Now the spacing and form of the REAL number is better:

 I BOUGHT 13 GOODIES FOR 4.12 DOLLARS

In the WRITE statement, the 3 after the colon following the 13 means output the 13 in a field of 3 characters. The 12 following 'GOODIES FOR' means to use a field width of 12. Since 'GOODIES FOR' has only 11 characters, there is one more blank added on the left, which separates it from the displayed 13. Following 0.6*6.87 is 5:2 which means output the answer in the form without an exponent in five columns, using 2 digits to the right of the decimal point. The blank before DOLLARS was inserted by inserting a blank in 'DOLLARS' to make ' DOLLARS', but we could just have well used 'DOLLARS':8.

The following methods of formatting can be used. Blanks are used to pad on the left to the given width.

literal:width   Output the literal string in width columns

integer value:width Output the integer value in width columns

real value:width:fractional digits
                    Output the real value in width columns with
                    "fractional digits" to the right of the decimal
                    point *without* the exponent part

real value:width   Output the real value in width columns *with*
the exponent part.

A new page of output can be started (i.e. the screen can be cleared and the next output placed on the top line of the screen) by placing the statement

PAGE (OUTPUT);

in the program.

THE PROGRAM

Now that you know two statements that will give some action, you must learn what is necessary to make a complete program. Then you can try the computer for yourself. All programs begin with a line like this

PROGRAM OPUS1;

The name OPUS1 is one we made up to describe the very first complete program. (OPUS is Latin for "work".) You must make up an identifier you like yourself. It must start with a letter and have no special characters. The first line of a program begins with the keyword PROGRAM and is terminated by a semicolon.

Now comes the big moment for a complete program.

```
PROGRAM OPUS1;
    BEGIN
        WRITELN(' 2+3=',2+3)
    END.
```

There it is, our opus number one, a complete Pascal program. The body of the program starts with the keyword BEGIN and finishes with the keyword END followed by a period. In between the BEGIN and END is a list of statements separated by semicolons. Since our list consists of only one statement, the WRITELN statement, it does not have a semicolon after it. In the next chapter we will tell you how to try out this program on your computer.

AN EXAMPLE PROGRAM

This program illustrates the use of several WRITELN statements.

```
PROGRAM ZIGZAG;
    BEGIN
        WRITELN(' Z    G','Z    G');
        WRITELN('  I   A ','I   A':5);
        WRITELN('   GZ  ','GZ':4)
    END.
```

The program causes the following pattern to be displayed.

```
 Z    GZ    G
  I   A  I   A
  GZ    GZ
```

As you can see, the top line of the pattern is displayed by the first WRITELN statement. This statement causes its first literal, ' Z   G', to be displayed in the first field of the output line and its second literal, again 'Z   G', to be displayed in the second field of the output line. Note that the first character to be displayed in the line is a blank. The next two statements cause the output of the second and third lines of the pattern. The last WRITELN statement could be replaced by the following two statements without changing the displayed pattern:

```
        WRITE('   GZ  ');
        WRITELN('GZ':4)
```

The first one does not end the line.

CHAPTER 3 SUMMARY

In this chapter, we explained how to write very simple computer programs. These programs are written in a small subset of the Pascal language which is called PS/1. The following important terms were presented.

Character - is a letter (ABC...Z), digit (012...9) or special character $+*/.;:$, etc.

Integer constant - is an integer (whole number) such as 78 and 2931. There may be a minus sign in front of the integer. A integer constant should not be preceded by a dollar sign and must not contain commas or a decimal point. The following should *not* be used: 25. 25,311.

Real constant - is a number such as 3.14159E0 (equal to 3.14159×10^0 or simply 3.14159). A real constant in the exponent form consists of a fraction (3.14159) and an exponent part (E0). A real constant in the mixed number form consists of a decimal point and must have at least one digit to the left of it and at least one on the right.

Literal (or character string constant) - is a sequence of characters enclosed in quotes, such as 'WHY NOT?'.

Arithmetic expression - composed of either a single number or a collection of numbers combined using addition, subtraction, multiplication, division, and modulo (+, -, *, /, DIV and MOD). Parentheses may enclose parts of the expression.

Rules of precedence - specify the order for applying +,-, * and / to compute the value of an arithmetic expression. Parenthesized expressions are evaluated first. Proceeding from left to right, * and / are applied first and then + and -.

WRITE - means "output". The WRITE statement prepares expressions (literals or arithmetic expressions) for output. A line is not actually completed until a WRITELN is executed.

WRITE - integers, real values and string literals such as -24, 2.7E3 and 'HELLO' are displayed using a statement of the form

WRITE(list of expressions separated by commas)

The line is not actually output until a WRITELN is executed. The values are displayed on a cathode ray tube screen.

WRITELN - this is similar to WRITE but also completes the current line so the next line can be started. The parenthesized list of values is optional for WRITELN.

Field - WRITE and WRITELN cause values to be written (displayed) in fields across a line. The size of the field can be specified by placing a colon followed by an integer after the item to be output. As a practice that requires little thought we will assign field sizes so that an integer is given a field of 10 output columns and a real value is given 14 columns. If no field size is specified integers and literals are given a field size just large enough to hold them. Real number are output in standard form with five decimal places and given just enough room to specify them. For example, if the exponent is negative an extra position is allowed for the minus sign.

Formatted writing - choosing the size of the field in a WRITE or WRITELN statement so that the output line is well spaced. For example

-15:5	produces	bb-15
'FRED':7	produces	bbbFRED
4E1:5:1	produces	b40.0

where b stands for blank.

Carriage control characters - in some computer systems the first character of each line is used for controlling the printer's carriage, for example, to make it double-space or skip to a new page. You will have to see how your printer works, if you have one, and possibly put a blank character at the start of each output line unless special printer action is required.

Output - display on a cathode ray tube screen, which the computer does at your request. The WRITELN statement produces output from the computer.

CHAPTER 3 EXERCISES

1.   What will the following program cause the computer to output?

```
PROGRAM LETTER;
    BEGIN
        WRITELN(' *    *');
        WRITELN(' ** **');
        WRITELN(' * * *');
        WRITELN(' *    *')
    END.
```

Can you rearrange the lines in this program to output a different letter?

2.   What do the following cause the computer to output?

(a) WRITELN(2,' PLUS ',3,' IS ',2+3);

(b) WRITELN('234+198+362=',
        234+198+362);

(c) WRITELN('2 FORMULAS:',2+3*5:10,(2+3)*5:10);

(d) WRITELN('SUBTRACTION',20-10-5:10,20-(10-5):10);

3.   Write statements to calculate and output the following:

(a) The sum of 52181 and 10032.

(b) 9213 take away 7918.

(c) The sum of 9213, 487, 921, 2013 and 514.

(d) The product of 21 times the sum of 816, 5 and 203.

(c) 343 plus 916 all multiplied by 82.

(f) 3.14159 (π) times 8.94 divided by 2.

(g) 3.14159 times the square of 8.94 (Note: X^2
    can be written as X*X).

Chapter 4

PUTTING THE PROGRAM ON A COMPUTER

BEGINNING A SESSION AT THE COMPUTER

After your program has been composed on a piece of paper, you are ready to enter it into the computer to see how it works. You will be typing each line on the computer's keyboard just as you would on an ordinary typewriter. As you type, the letters, digits, and special characters appear on the screen.

Before you can begin entering your program you must get the computer going and make contact with the UCSD operating system. This part of the procedure varies from one microcomputer system to another. For the Apple computer, you must place the first of the two diskettes that contain the UCSD Pascal systems programs in the disk drive and then turn the power on. If you are using an ordinary TV set as the output screen it must be turned on also. After the power is turned on, the disk drive will spin and a part of the systems program for the UCSD Pascal system will be read into the memory of the computer from the diskette. When the disk drive stops spinning, the second diskette is placed in the drive and the RESET key pressed. In a moment an announcement appears on the screen that UCSD Pascal is in operation. This means that the computer is ready for a *system command.*

At the top of the screen there will be displayed a line which reminds you of the different commands that you might give. This is called the *prompt line* and it consists of the word COMMAND followed by a list of the various commands. Here it is:

COMMAND:E(DIT),R(UN),F(ILE),C(OMPILE),X(ECUTE)...

The three dots indicate that there is more to the prompt line than we show. If the complete prompt line does not appear on your screen you can see the rest by pressing a key (or keys). For the Apple press CTRL-A to see the right side of the prompt line, then CTRL-A to return to the left side. (CTRL-A means to press the control key and, while holding it down, press A.)

Commands can be issued by just pressing the first letter of the command word. That is why the prompt line shows the other letters of each command in parentheses. In some cases the closing parentheses or the commas in the prompt line may be omitted.

When you are working on a program it is kept in a special place in the memory called the *workfile*. When you first begin to work on a program you must start a new workfile so you press the F(ILE) key to enter the *file mode*. When you do this, the prompt line changes to:

FILER: G(ET, S(AVE, W(HAT, N(EW, L(DIR...

What has happened is that you have left the highest level where the prompt line started with the word COMMAND and, by pressing the F key you have gone down to a lower level where the prompt line starts with the word FILER. At each level the list of commands available at that level can be seen in the prompt line. We say we have left the *command mode* and gone to the file mode. There is a slight problem in that at *each* level there is a choice of system commands not just at the command level. We will thus use the word "command" in capital letters to refer to the level and speak of the *COMMAND level* or *mode*. In order to enter a program we must have what is called a *workfile*. To start a new workfile press N(EW. If there is an old workfile in the memory (either yours or someone else's) the computer displays the line:

THROW AWAY CURRENT WORKFILE?

If you really want to start a new file, you respond Y(ES. (If it is all a mistake reply N(O.) Now you must return to the COMMAND level so press Q(UIT, which is one of the file mode commands not shown in our FILER prompt line. The prompt line should now be:

COMMAND: E(DIT),R(UN),F(ILE),C(OMPILE),X(ECUTE)...

To start entering your program press E(DIT). At this stage a new prompt line appears, beginning with the word EDIT. It is

>EDIT: A(DJST C(PY D(LETE F(IND I(NSRT ...

As we mentioned the system commands for UCSD are arranged in a hierarchy. When you give the E(DIT) command you leave the COMMAND mode and enter the *edit mode*. In edit mode you can give a number of different commands and these are listed in the EDIT prompt line. The particular ones that we will use for the moment are I(NSRT and D(LETE. If we want to leave the edit mode and return to the level where the prompt line begins with the word COMMAND, we would have to press Q(UIT which allows us to escape from the edit mode to the next level up in the hierarchy. The command to leave a level and go back up one level is not always Q(UIT although it has been in these first two cases.

ENTERING A PROGRAM

To input the program you have written, press the I(NSRT key and enter the *insert mode.* Now you are in the second level of the hierarchy below the COMMAND level. You pressed E to enter the edit mode then I to enter the insert mode. You know that you are in the insert mode because the prompt line begins with the word INSERT. For the moment we will ignore the INSERT prompt line and start typing in the program. On the screen below the prompt line is a bright rectangle. This is called the *cursor.* If you type a letter, the letter appears on the screen where the cursor was and the cursor moves one position along the horizontal to the right. The cursor tells you where the character you type next will appear on the screen. When you press the *return key*, the cursor jumps to the beginning fo the next line down on the screen. It is like pressing the carriage return on a typewriter. So now you can type your program. If you make a mistake in typing a character you can press the *backspace* (left arrow ←) and this will back up the cursor one space and you can type the correct character. You could wipe out a whole line by backspacing repeatedly until the cursor is at the start of the line. If you examine the prompt line you will see that there is another way to erase a line.

>INSERT: TEXT[<BS> A CHAR, <DEL> A LINE]...

This tells you that you can delete a line by pressing the DEL(ETE) key rather than pressing the backspace many times. The symbol <BS> means press the backspace key to delete a character (CHAR). The prompt <DEL> A LINE means press the delete key (on the Apple CTRL-X which remember means: hold down the control key and also press the X key) to delete a line.

So your job is to type in your program, trying to make as few mistakes as possible and correcting them as soon as you detect them. When you are finished, you are ready to return to the edit mode. The remaining part of the insert prompt line tells you how to do it. It says (if you can see it on your screen)

[<ETX> ACCEPTS,<ESC> ESCAPES]

If you are satisfied and want to continue with the program you have typed in, you must press what corresponds to <ETX>. (On the Apple this is CTRL-C.) The other way of leaving the insert mode is by pressing the escape key (<ESC>). This takes you back to the edit mode and wipes out all your efforts in the insert mode. It is only used if you have changed your mind about what you typed in the insert mode, or if you got there by mistake.

When you are entering programs on the Apple and reach the place on the line when the charaters no longer appear on the screen you may still continue on the line as there is another half of the line not visible on the screen. A special feature moves the display sideways (scrolls sideways) as the cursor moves. To invoke this scrolling, press CTRL-Z. To return to normal press CTRL-A.

RUNNING THE PROGRAM

You have now entered your program and are back in the edit mode. To run the program you must return to the COMMAND mode. To do this press Q(UIT). This enters the *quit insert mode* which has four different commands shown by the prompt lines:

>QUIT:
   U(PDATE THE WORKFILE AND LEAVE
   E(XIT WITHOUT UPDATING
   R(ETURN TO THE EDITOR WITHOUT UPDATING
   W(RITE TO A FILE AND RETURN

U(PDATE copies the workfile you have in memory onto the diskette as a file named SYSTEM.WRK.TEXT. This is the option you should use since we will be running the program now at the COMMAND level.

E(XIT is used to return to COMMAND level without saving anything you have entered at the edit level. This is used when you enter the edit mode by mistake. R(ETURN puts you back exactly where you where before you pressed Q. This is used when you press Q by mistake.

After U(PDATE is pressed, you will hear the disk whirring as your program is being copied onto the diskette. When it stops you will be back in the quit mode with these prompt lines

>QUIT:
   WRITING...
   YOUR FILE IS 480 BYTES LONG
   DO YOU WANT TO E(XIT OR R(ETURN ...

The number given as the length of the workfile in bytes varies with the length of your program. To get to the COMMAND level so that you can run, press E(XIT and the prompt line is then back to:

COMMAND: E(DIT), R(UN), F(ILE), C(OMPILE) ...

Now comes the big moment. Press R(UN. First the compiler is called, the screen is cleared, and on the top you see

COMPILING...

Below that are a number of lines describing the compilation. Ignore these unless it says you have a syntax error. If it does indicate an error you must correct it. We will suppose for now that there are no syntax errors in the program. If so the screen is again cleared, the disk whirs indicating that the translated program is being stored as SYSTEM.WRK.CODE, and at the top of the screen is displayed

RUNNING...

Below this, is any output that is produced by your own program. If the output is what you expected, you have been successful. You may want to start a new program but before you do you must save the present program if you ever intend to use it again. If you want to execute the program again immediately give the command U(SER RESTART). To return to the COMMAND level just press the return key.

SAVING THE PROGRAM

To save the contents of the workfile so that you can use your program again you must go back to the COMMAND mode and from there to the file mode. Type F(ILE and the prompt line appears:

FILER: G(ET, S(AVE, W(HAT, N(EW, L(DIR...

To save your workfile, press S and this prompt line appears:

SAVE AS WHAT FILE?

You must now type in a name for your file. It must be 7 or fewer characters with none of the characters = DOLLAR SIGN - ? . If you use the same name as your program you will be safe. We would type

OPUS1

Whenever you are typing a number of characters and you want the computer to know you are finished and respond, you must follow them immediately with <RET> (the return key). Do *not* leave a space between the last character and the return. After you have typed OPUS1 followed by <RET> the workfile SYSTEM.WRK will be stored under the name OPUS1; this means that SYSTEM.WRK.TEXT will be OPUS1.TEXT and SYSTEM.WRK.CODE will be OPUS1.CODE. You must *not* specify the TEXT or CODE part of the name as the computer does that for you automatically. TEXT is the program as written in Pascal and CODE is the program as compiled into the language that can be interpreted by the computer. After saving a file you are automatically returned to the file level. From there Q(UIT) takes you to the COMMAND level.

If you want to run the OPUS1 program again, you get into COMMAND mode, press X(ECUTE) and when the computer prompts:

EXECUTE WHAT FILE?

you type OPUS1 followed by a return. The OPUS1 program will then be executed. It will not be compiled again as the translated program is now on file.

If you G(ET instead of X(ECUTE the filed program is brought into the workfile but not executed. This is useful if you want to modify it before running it.

CORRECTING SYNTAX ERRORS

If there is a syntax error in your program the computer will stop during compilation and the line where the error was found will be displayed. A marker ($<<<<$) will be pointing at the position in the program where the error was found. As well, there will be an error message telling you the *error number* of the error. If you want to make a note of the error and continue compiling, press the space bar. If you want to return to the editor to correct the error press E. On return to the editor, a more explicit error message is given at the top of the screen with your program below. The cursor is automatically placed near the location of the error so that you can correct it.

To correct errors you must know how to insert characters, delete characters, and move the cursor around anywhere in your program. The cursor can be moved right, left, up, or down by pressing the corresponding arrow keys. On some computers, there are no up and down keys and other keys produce the results. For example, on the Apple computer, up is CTRL-0; down is CTRL-L. To insert characters, place the cursor on the character to the right of the place where the inserted character or characters are to go. Then enter the insert mode by typing I(NSRT. As you type, the additional characters are inserted and the text that began at the cursor and is to the right of the inserted characters is moved over to make room. When you are finished inserting, press CTRL-C to get the insertion accepted as official. This puts you back into edit mode and your program will have the inserted characters in it.

To delete characters, place the cursor on the first character to be deleted, then press the D(LETE key. Now press the right arrow key for each character you want deleted. If you go too far, pressing the left arrow key will restore the characters. When you have performed the deletion, press CTRL-C to return to the editor with the deletion accepted.

If you prefer, you can delete characters to the left of where the cursor was at the time you entered the delete mode, by pressing the left arrow. The first character deleted in this direction is *not* the one under the cursor on entry but the one to the left of it. We will discuss fancy moves you can make with the editor later but, for now, insert and delete will let you make all the changes you need.

CORRECTING SEMANTIC ERRORS

When the output from your program does not agree with what you expected there are two possibilities. Either your program has an error, or your expected results are improperly calculated.

If it is the program which has an error we say that it is a *semantic error.* It does not have the meaning that we intended it to have. There is no way that the compiler can detect this kind of error so that you are on your own in finding it. We will make some suggestions later about how to find semantic errors but for now just reread the program and try to see where you are going wrong. When you find the error it is corrected in the same way as you correct a syntax error. Just go into edit mode and make the necessary changes.

CHAPTER 4 SUMMARY

In this chapter we explained how to enter your program into the computer, how to run it, and how to correct errors. As well, we described how you could save your program for future use. In order to do all this it was necessary to become familiar with the command language that is part of the UCSD Pascal system. System commands are given by typing the first letter of the command. The command system is arranged in a hierarchy so that at each level of the hierarchy there are a number of possible commands. The list of the possible commands is given in a line at the top of the screen called a prompt line. Except at the top level, which is called the COMMAND level, there is always a command that causes you to return to the level above the one you are in. The following terms were presented.

Start up - the procedure that you must go through to begin a session at the computer. It consists of placing a particular diskette in the disk drive and then turning on the power. A second diskette may also be required. When the system is ready an announcement appears on the screen and at the top a prompt line will be displayed.

Prompt line - a line displayed on the screen to remind you of what level in the command hierarchy you are at and what commands are available at that level. For example at the edit level the prompt line is:

>EDIT: A(DJST C(PY D(LETE F(IND I(NSRT ...

The commands are listed with a left parenthesis after the first letter to show that only that letter is required to initiate the command. Sometimes in the prompt line there are right parentheses and commas separating the different commands. (There is little consistency in style.)

Command - an instruction given to the system by typing certain characters, often single letters, to achieve certain results such as editing, running, or saving programs.

Level or mode - a stage in the hierarchy of the command language. The top level is called the COMMAND level. Other levels are the edit level or mode, the insert mode, or the file mode. The edit mode and the file mode are at the second level, one below the COMMAND level. The insert mode is at the third level below the edit mode. If you return from the third level to the second level you go back to the particular second level mode that you left from to go to the third level.

COMMAND mode - the top level of the command hierarchy which is entered automatically when you start up your computer. Whenever you leave a second level to return to a higher level you are back in the COMMAND level. (We use capital letters for this one level to prevent confusion with the general term "command".)

Edit mode - a second level in the command hierarchy used when you want to enter or change a program. To return to the COMMAND level press Q(UIT).

Insert mode - a third level, below the edit mode, in the command hierarchy. Before entering the insert mode, the cursor is placed on the first character to the right of where the insertion is to occur. After pressing I, the characters to be inserted are typed. The characters to the right of the inserted material are moved to make room. When the insertion has been typed the <ETX> key (on the Apple CTRL-C) is pressed to accept the insertion. This returns you to the edit mode with the inserted material in place.

Typing errors - when entering a character in the insert mode, if a mistake is made, you can erase the character by pressing the <BS> or backspace key. You can delete an entire line by pressing <DEL> (on the Apple CTRL-X).

Quit insert mode - when you press Q(UIT) from the edit mode you enter an intermediate level mode called the quit insert mode. In order to return to the COMMAND level and still have the material you prepared at the edit level saved in your workfile you must press U(PDATE) followed later by E(XIT).

Workfile - the part of the memory used to store a program that you are editing or running. The U(PDATE command stores your workfile on the disk as a file named SYSTEM.WRK. This has two parts: SYSTEM.WRK.TEXT has your Pascal program and, if the program has been run, SYSTEM.WRK.CODE has the translated program. A workfile may be stored more permanently as a file on the disk under another name. This is done by entering the file mode.

Run mode - is at the second level. By pressing R(UN) at the COMMAND level the program is first compiled and, provided there are no syntax errors, is executed. After execution you may return to the COMMAND level by pressing a key such as <RET>. If instead you want to repeat the execution phase press U(SER RESTART).

Save mode - is at the third level under the file mode. You will be asked to give the name under which the workfile is to be saved on a more permanent basis. After you type the name followed by return the file is created under the new name and you are returned to the file mode. Press Q(UIT) to get back from there to the *command mode*.

Execute mode - by typing X(ECUTE) at the COMMAND level you may execute any previously saved program. You will be asked what file you want to execute. Type its name followed by return.

G(ET - is used to bring a program from the file into the workfile without executing it.

Syntax error correction - as a program is being compiled, whenever there is a syntax error, the compilation will stop and there will be a marker (< < < <) pointing to the area in the program where the error occurs. (To continue without correcting the error press the space bar.) To correct the error press E(DIT). This takes you directly to the edit mode with a description of the error at the top of the screen and the cursor located near the error. You can then correct the program by inserting and/or deleting characters.

Delete mode - a third level mode, below edit mode. Before entering delete, place the cursor on the first character to be deleted then press D(LETE). Press the right arrow key for each character to be deleted. (You can backspace if you go too far.) Then press CTRL-C to return to the edit mode with the deletion accepted.

Semantic error correction - errors in meaning of a program must be discovered by yourself, without the aid of the computer, by rereading your program or examining the output. Correction is handled by entering the edit mode and inserting or deleting.

CHAPTER 4 EXERCISES

1. Start up your computer and see that you are in the COMMAND mode. Begin a new workfile. Insert into your file the OPUS1 program from the previous chapter. When you have finished entering it, run it. If it is correct, store it in a file called OPUS1. See that it is correctly stored by trying to X(ECUTE your OPUS1 program.

2. See what program is in your workfile and, if it is not OPUS1, bring OPUS1 to the workfile by using G(ET from the file mode. You will be prompted to type in the name of the program you want to G(ET. Now modify the program to add 8 and 9 instead of 2 and 3. Run it.

3. Save your modified program from question 2 as OPUS2 in the disk file. How many bytes of memory does OPUS2 take? Try to X(ECUTE OPUS2. Is OPUS1 still there in the disk file?

4. Write a new program to output five lines listing your favorite TV stars in order of preference. Run the program then try to modify it so that your number two choice is moved into number one position.

5. Try writing a program to output a pattern like the ZIGZAG program of the previous chapter. Test it.

6. Write and test a program to output the integers 1, 2, 3, etc., five to a line. Go up as high as 25. Try to make the format as agreeable as possible. Put a title at the top of your table of integers.

Chapter 5

PS/2: VARIABLES, CONSTANTS, AND ASSIGNMENTS

In this subset you will learn how to read numerical information into the computer, how to perform arithmetic calculations on the numbers you read in, and how to output the answers. You will learn, as well, how to make your programs understandable to others (as well as to yourself) by careful choice of words that you can make up and by comments that you can add to your program. The principal concept to learn in this subset is the idea of a *variable*.

VARIABLES

We have said that a computer has a memory and that in the memory there are locations where information can be stored. Each location has its own unique address. In a high-level language like Pascal we do not ever refer to an actual machine address. Instead we use a name to identify a particular location. It is like referring to a house by the name of the owner rather than by its street address. We use the word *variable* to stand for the memory location. It is named by an *identifier*.

The identifier for a variable must begin with a letter and contain no blanks or special characters. If you think of the variable as the memory location and its name as the identifier then you will realize that the *value* of the variable will be the actual information that is stored in the memory location. Locations are arranged to hold only one type of information or data. We speak of the *data type* of a variable. A variable may hold integers, in which case we say it is an *integer variable*. It could also be a *real variable* or a *character variable*. If a variable is an integer variable its value can be any integer up to a certain maximum size. The value may be changed from time to time in the program but its *type* can never change; once an integer variable, always an integer variable.

Examples of variable identifiers are

ACCTNO, TAX, TOTAL, MARK

They are similar to the identifier we used to name a program.

It is *very* important to choose identifiers that relate to the kind of information that is stored in the corresponding locations. Well-chosen identifiers make a program easier to understand. Although identifiers may be of any length only the first 8 characters are used by the UCSD compiler.

DECLARATIONS

We must make the names we want to use as variable identifiers known to the compiler and associate them with memory locations suitable for the particular data type they will hold. This is accomplished by means of "declarations" that are placed in the program immediately following the PROGRAM heading.

We will not, at the moment, show how character variables can be declared but look only at integer and real variables. To declare that SUM is to be an integer variable we write

VAR SUM: INTEGER;

The identifier is after the *keyword* VAR and followed by a colon and the keyword INTEGER, then a semicolon. This establishes SUM as having the type INTEGER. To declare DISTANCE to be a real variable use

VAR DISTANCE: REAL;

If several integer variables are required they are all listed after the VAR, separated by commas, for example

VAR SUM,MARK,NUMBER: INTEGER;

Both integer and real variables are put into a single declaration as in the following

VAR SUM: INTEGER;
    DISTANCE,SPEED: REAL;

The keyword VAR can appear only once. Putting declarations in a program is like phoning ahead for hotel reservations; when you need it, the space is there with the right name on it. Also the compiler can substitute the actual machine address whenever it encounters a variable in the program. It does this by keeping a directory showing variable identifiers and corresponding memory locations. This directory is set up as the declarations are read by the compiler. In UCSD Pascal compilers only the first eight characters of a variable identifier are recorded in the directory so no two variables should have identifiers which are identical in the first eight characters.

You should not use as variable identifiers any of the words that are

Pascal keywords. These are PROGRAM, VAR, BEGIN, END, and others we have not yet encountered.

ASSIGNMENT STATEMENTS

In addition to declarations, in this chapter you will be learning two types of Pascal statements that cause things to happen as the program is executed. We say that they are *executable statements*. The WRITELN statement is an executable statement; it causes output to take place. One of the two new executable types we will have is the statement that *reads* input, the READ statement, but first we will look at the *assignment statement*.

There are no keywords in an assignment statement but it has a very definite form. The form is

identifier := expression;

There is a colon followed by an equal sign and on the left of this is a single word, a variable identifier. This identifier must have been declared to be either integer or real. On the right hand of the colon and equal signs there is an expression. We have looked at expressions that contained integer or real constants; now expressions can also contain integer or real variable identifiers. We have expressions like

5+10/3E0   (8+9)*7

but now we can have expressions like

SUM+1   TOTAL/1.00E2   SUM-MARK

We will not use variable identifiers in the expression of an assignment statement to begin with but instead use a simple expression, an integer constant. For example,

AGE:=5;

is an assignment statement. It causes the number 5 to be stored in the memory location called AGE. If AGE appeared in the declaration

VAR AGE: INTEGER;

then the number is stored as an integer and would be output by

WRITELN(AGE);

as 5. If, on the other hand, it were declared REAL it would be stored and displayed as 5.00000.

So far the expression on the right-hand side of the assignment has just been an integer constant, but we can have more complicated expressions:

AGE:=1982-1966;

Here we are subtracting the year of birth, 1966, from the year 1982 to get the age in 1982. This instruction would assign the value 16 to the variable AGE. We could get the same result as follows

```
BIRTHYEAR:=1966;
THISYEAR:=1982;
AGE:=THISYEAR - BIRTHYEAR;
```

Here we have two additional variables BIRTHYEAR and THISYEAR which are given values in assignment statements and then used in an expression on the right-hand side of another assignment statement. We could have another statement

```
NEXTAGE:=AGE+1;
```

which would give the age the following year to the variable NEXTAGE. Remember, if we use identifiers in a program they must *all* appear in declarations. We would need the declaration

```
VAR AGE,BIRTHYEAR,THISYEAR,NEXTAGE: INTEGER;
```

A variable may be assigned values over and over during a program. For example, we might have

```
SUM:=2+3;
WRITELN(SUM);
SUM:=3+4;
WRITELN(SUM);
```

and so on. Now we come to perhaps the most confusing type of assignment statement. Suppose in a program you were making calculations year by year and needed to keep a variable AGE that held the value of the current age for the calculation. We might change the value at the end of the year by the assignment:

```
AGE:=AGE+1;
```

Now you can see that the assignment statement is certainly *not* an equation, or this would be nonsense. What happens when this statement is executed is that the value stored in the variable AGE is added to the integer 1 and the result of the addition stored back in the same location.

In machine language, if the memory location of AGE is 336 and if there is a constant 1 stored in location 512, then the Pascal assignment statement

```
AGE:=AGE+1;
```

could be translated as

> LOAD 336
> ADD 512
> STORE 336

TRACING EXECUTION

We have seen that variables are associated with locations in the memory of the computer. We can assign values to variables and, during a program, we can change the values as often as we want. The values can *vary* and that is why the locations are called variables. The location stays the same but the value can change.

Sometimes it is helpful, when getting used to writing programs, to keep track of values stored in the memory locations corresponding to each variable. This can help us to understand the effect of each statement. Some statements change a value; others do not. We call this *tracing the execution* of instructions.

We do not need to know the numerical, or machine address of the locations. As far as we are concerned the identifier is the address of the variable. For example, if before execution of

> AGE:=AGE+1;

the value stored in the variable AGE was 13 then, after execution, the value stored in the variable AGE would be 14.

We will trace now a slightly more complicated program by writing the values of all the variables involved after each instruction is executed. Here we will use some meaningless names like X,Y, and Z because the program has no particular meaning. We just want to learn to trace execution. We will write the tracing on the right-hand side of the page and the program on the left. The labels over the right-hand side give the names of the locations; their values are listed under the names, opposite each instruction. When the value of a particular variable has not yet been assigned we will write a dash.

LINE		X	Y	Z
1	PROGRAM TRACE;			
2	VAR X,Y,Z: INTEGER;	-	-	-
3	BEGIN	-	-	-
4	X:=5;	5	-	-
5	Y:=7;	5	7	-
6	Z:=X+Y;	5	7	12

7	X:=X+5;	10	7	12
8	X:=Z;	12	7	12
9	Y:=Z;	12	12	12
10	X:=X+Y+Z;	36	12	12
11	Y:=Y*Z;	36	144	12
12	Z:=(X+Y)DIV 12;	36	144	15
13	X:=X MOD 5;	1	144	15
14	WRITELN(X:10,Y:10,Z:10)	1	144	15
15	END.	1	144	15

The lines of the program are numbered so that we can make reference to them.

First notice that the locations X,Y, and Z do not get established until the declaration VAR. They have no values assigned at this point. All is straightforward until line 7 when X appears on both sides of the assignment statement. The values shown at the right of the program are, remember, the values after execution of the statement on that line. In line 12 note that since a division between two integers is to take place and the result assigned to an integer variable that the operator DIV must be used. When the division yields an integer the answer is exact but if there is a remainder on division the fractional part of the division is dropped. We say it is *truncated*. To get the fractional part of the result in a division we must use the operator / and store the answer in a REAL variable location. If the remainder in an integer division is desired the MOD operator can be used.

The output statement in line 14 is different from the output statements in PS/1 because now we can include the names of variables in the list. We have

WRITELN(X:10,Y:10,Z:10)

The machine can tell the difference between variable identifiers and literals because identifiers have no quotes. There is no possible confusion between numbers and identifiers because an identifier may not begin with a digit. You can see now why Pascal has this rule.

In this example we showed a division with truncation. Sometimes we want to round off the results of a division, say in determining costs to the nearest cent. If COST is the value in cents of a 2-kilogram package of soap flakes then the cost of one kilogram to the nearest cent COSTKG is produced by using the function ROUND

COSTKG:=ROUND(COST/2);

The variable COSTKG has been declared to be integer so it will accept only whole number values. If you do not want to round off a REAL value but would rather truncate the fractional part, you should use the function TRUNC as in

COSTKG:=TRUNC(COST/2);

Since COST is an INTEGER variable, for this example we can get truncation more easily using COST DIV 2 instead of TRUNC(COST/2).

INPUT OF DATA

Now we will learn how to read data into the computer. We did not learn this at the same time as we learned to output data because the idea of a variable is essential to input. It is not essential to output because we can have numbers and literals, that is, integer and real constants and constant character strings. If we use

READ(X,Y,Z);

we will read three numbers that are entered on the keyboard and store them in the three variables X, Y, and Z. The numbers must be separated from each other by at least one blank. As you type, the data is displayed on the screen. Here is a sample program that reads numbers in and outputs their sum.

```
PROGRAM TOTAL;
    VAR X,Y,Z: INTEGER;
    BEGIN
        WRITELN('INPUT VALUES FOR X AND Y');
        READLN(X,Y);
        Z:=X+Y;
        WRITELN('SUM OF ',X,' AND ',Y,' IS ',Z)
    END.
```

The appearance of a sample display for this program would be:

INPUT VALUES FOR X AND Y
5 7
SUM OF 5 AND 7 IS 12

The first line of the display appears on the screen and the cursor is positioned at the beginning of the second line. The computer then waits for you to enter the data. On input, the first number entered, namely 5, is associated with the first variable X and stored in that location. The number 7 is stored in location Y. After you have entered the 7 you must press the return key so that the numbers can be accepted by the READLN statement of the program and the sum computed. When this happens the last line of the display appears. READ does not expect a return whereas READLN does. If you used READ and followed the 7 by a space the last line of output would appear on the same line with the 5 and 7. If you had used READ and typed a return after the 7, the display would be exactly as shown. So you see there is some flexibility here. It is safer to use READLN and then you will be forced to press return to get the last line of the display to appear. When a program reaches the END in execution the display will remain on the screen until you press a key to initiate something else. If wou want to execute your program again press U(SER RESTART. If you want to return to the COMMAND level press the return key.

When inputting real numbers you do not have to put any more significant figures than necessary in either the fraction or exponent; you need not type

2.00000E0

You can have only 2.0E0 or 2E0. If the exponent is zero, you may omit it completely. Thus numbers like

35.8   3.14159   0.025

are all acceptable as real numbers. Remember that there must be at least one digit on each side of the decimal point.

CONVERSION BETWEEN INTEGER AND REAL

Conversions from integer to real form will occur automatically whenever the variable that is to hold the number is of type real. If a data item is input as an integer and is read into a location defined by a variable that has been declared as REAL, then it will be converted to real. However it is not permitted to assign a real value, either in an assignment statement or by a read, to an integer variable. The real value must first be transformed into an integer using either the ROUND or TRUNC function.

```
PROGRAM CONVERT;
    VAR X,Y: INTEGER;
        Z: REAL;
    BEGIN
        WRITELN('INPUT VALUES FOR X,Y, AND Z');
        READLN(X,Y,Z);
        WRITELN(X:10,Y:10,Z:14);
        WRITELN('INPUT VALUES FOR X,Y, AND Z');
        READLN(X,Y,Z);
        WRITELN(X:10,Y:10,Z:14)
    END.
```

The display for the program might be:

INPUT VALUES FOR X,Y, AND Z
22 36 25
    22   36   2.50000E1
INPUT VALUES FOR X,Y, AND Z
2 181 50E4
     2   181   5.00000E5

Within a program it is often necessary to convert from a real value to an integer. For example, suppose that AVERAGEMARK is a real variable holding the average mark in a term examination. You would like the average to the nearest mark. Declare another variable AVERAGE as integer and write in the program

       AVERAGE := ROUND(AVERAGEMARK);

AVERAGE will then be an integer, the rounded average mark.

COMMENTS

One of the main aims of structured programming is that your programs be easily understood by yourself and by others. When you create useful programs you may store them on your diskette for future use or share them with other users. Choosing variable names that suggest what is being stored is an excellent way to make programs readable. We have shown several programs with just X,Y, and Z as variable names. This is because these are meant to show you what happens in assignment statements and READ and WRITE statements and are not about real applications. It is not advisable to use such meaningless names. We want your programs to look more like English than like algebra when you are finished.

One other thing that you can do to make a program understandable is to include comments in English along with the program. We have been providing comments to some of our examples in the accompanying text but you can write comments right into the program. To accomplish this, simply enclose the comments inside a pair of symbols that will act like brackets; in that way the comment is not mistaken for a program statement. The symbols you use are (* to begin and *) to end the comment. For example,

      (* THIS IS A COMMENT *)

could be placed *anywhere* in the program where blanks can occur. To be sensible it is best to have comments occur at the ends of lines or on separate lines.

When the special characters { and } are available, they are used to enclose comments rather than (* and *). For example,

{ THIS IS A COMMENT }

Comments must not have *) or }, as the case may be, in them, or be put in the data. From now on we will be including comments in our examples.

AN EXAMPLE PROGRAM

We now give a program which illustrates the use of variables, assignment statements, READ and WRITE statements, and comments. The program reads in the length, width, and height of a box (as given in inches) and then outputs the area of the base of the box (in square centimeters) and the volume of the box (in cubic centimeters).

```
1       PROGRAM CONVERT;
2           (* READ BOX LENGTH, WIDTH, HEIGHT IN INCHES *)
3           (* CONVERT TO CENTIMETERS AND CALCULATE *)
4           (* THE BOX'S BASE AREA AND VOLUME. *)
5           CONST CMPERINCH=2.54;
6           VAR LENGTH,WIDTH,HEIGHT,AREA,VOLUME: REAL;
7           BEGIN
8               WRITE('LENGTH=');
9               READLN(LENGTH);
10              WRITE('WIDTH=');
11              READLN(WIDTH);
12              WRITE('HEIGHT=');
13              READLN(HEIGHT);
14              LENGTH:=CMPERINCH*LENGTH;
15              WIDTH:=CMPERINCH*WIDTH;
16              HEIGHT:=CMPERINCH*HEIGHT;
17              AREA:=LENGTH*WIDTH;
18              WRITELN('AREA=',AREA);
19              VOLUME:=HEIGHT*AREA;
20              WRITELN('VOLUME=',VOLUME)
21          END.
```

This program will output the following:

LENGTH=2.6
WIDTH=1.2
HEIGHT=6.92
AREA= 2.01290E1
VOLUME= 3.53803E2

where the area is in square centimeters and the volume is in cubic centimeters. The area and volume displayed depend on the three values 2.6, 1.2, and 6.92 that you enter from the keyboard for the length, width, and height. Try this program using different values for the size of the box. The data values 2.6, 1.2 and 6.92 could be replaced by the dimensions of a different box.

Line 1 marks the beginning of the program; it causes no action on the part of the computer. Lines 2, 3 and 4 are comments intended for you, the reader of the program, and are ignored by the computer.

Line 5 of the program is a definition of a constant. The constant identified by the name CMPERINCH is given the value 2.54. (There are 2.54 centimeters in an inch.) Constants differ from variables in that they maintain the same value throughout the program's execution. Definitions of constants (CONST) must precede the declaration (VAR) of variables. Line 6 sets up memory locations for variables called LENGTH, WIDTH, HEIGHT, AREA, and VOLUME. These variables have the REAL type, instead of the INTEGER type, because they have non-integer values (such as 2.6). Lines 8 to 13 cause the data values 2.6 and 1.2 and 6.92 to be read into variables LENGTH, WIDTH and HEIGHT. Notice how the program prompts you to enter these values by displaying LENGTH= and so on.

Line 14 takes the value 2.6E0 from the LENGTH variable, multiplies it by the constant CMPERINCH and then returns the result to LENGTH. The value of LENGTH will now be the length of the box in centimeters.

Line 17 takes the values in LENGTH and WIDTH, multiplies them together, and places the result in AREA. Line 18 then outputs:

AREA= 2.01290E1

As of line 18, the variable VOLUME has not been used. An attempt to output VOLUME in line 18 would be an error because this variable has not yet been given a value.

Line 19 computes the volume and line 20 outputs the volume. Notice that this statement has no semicolon after it since it is the last in a list of statements before END. As a matter of fact no real problem is created if you do put a semicolon here since a null statement (that is, no statement at all) is a legitimate statement in Pascal. You can just assume that there is an invisible null statement after the semicolon before END. We will not take advantage of this rather weird situation because there will be places where a semicolon too many would cause an error condition. Line 21 is the end of the program and tells the computer to stop working on this program. Notice that END has a period after it.

This job would output the same thing if we made the following change.

Replace lines 8 to 13 by the three assignment statements:

    LENGTH:=2.6;
    WIDTH:=1.2;
    HEIGHT=6.92;

Now you do not need to enter the size of the box.

These changes result in a program which is given the dimensions of the box by assignment statements rather than by input statements (READ statements). The advantage of the original program, which uses READ statements, is that the program will work for a new box simply by entering different values from the keyboard.

LABELING OF OUTPUT

Just as comments help to make a program more understandable, output that is properly identified by labeling is self-explanatory. What you are trying to do is to prepare a display that need no further explanation from you when you let others see your computer output. The output data should be labeled so that there is no doubt about what the numbers are, without reading the program. Prompting words serve to label the input data.

There are two basic ways to label input or output values. If different values of the same set of variables are to be entered and displayed in columns on the screen, then a label can be placed at the top of each column. For example, the display for comparing costs of boxes of soap flakes might be

COST	WEIGHT(KG)	COST/KG
125	1	125
200	2	100
260	3	87

Here the values in the COST and WEIGHT(KG) columns are input values. You can include as many blanks as you like between input values on a line so that you can line up the entries with the column headings. You must press the blank, or space key, after you enter a number in the WEIGHT(KG) column so that the computer will know that you have finished. Do not press the return key because the output data corresponding to the two input values is to be on the same line. This is why we use READ instead of READLN. The output values are displayed in a field of size 10 so that they line up with the COST/KG column heading.

There is no reason to use exactly the same labels as the variable names, since the literals displayed at the top of the columns can be longer and contain blanks. They are displayed independently. The program that produces this table might be

```
PROGRAM SOAP;
    (*COMPUTE AND TABULATE COST PER KG*)
    VAR COST,WEIGHT,COSTKG: INTEGER;
    BEGIN

        (* PRINT HEADINGS OF TABLE *)
        WRITELN('     COST ','WEIGHT(KG)',
            ' COST/KG');

        (* PROCESS DATA FOR FIRST BOX *)
        READ(COST,WEIGHT);
        COSTKG:=ROUND(COST/WEIGHT);
        WRITELN(COSTKG:10);

        (* PROCESS DATA FOR SECOND BOX *)
        READ(COST,WEIGHT);
        COSTKG:=ROUND(COST/WEIGHT);
        WRITELN(COSTKG:10);

        (* PROCESS DATA FOR THIRD BOX *)
        READ(COST,WEIGHT);
        COSTKG:=ROUND(COST/WEIGHT);
        WRITELN(COSTKG:10)
    END.
```

You can see how comments can be inserted, how the column headings are displayed, and how each line of the table is formed. As soon as the heading of the table is displayed the program is ready to accept values for the cost and weight of the first box. Remember: after you have entered the weight, press the space bar so that the computer will know that you have finished entering the data. After the cost per kilogram is displayed the cursor will be placed at the beginning of the next line and then you are ready to enter the data for a new box. Each output statement is WRITELN (not WRITE) so each one causes a new line to be started after displaying the cost per kilogram. In the program we have repeated three statements, without change, one set of three for each box. If we had 100 boxes, this would have been a little monotonous. When we want to repeat statements we do *not* do it this way; a more convenient way is possible with a new Pascal statement that will cause this kind of repetition. But that comes in the next subset, PS/3.

A second kind of output labeling was already used in the previous example but can be illustrated by a program segment

```
COST:=5;
WRITELN('COST=',COST);
```

This would result in the output

COST=5

This method is easier when just a few numbers are being displayed.

PROGRAM TESTING

It is easy to make mistakes in programming. Always use a pencil when writing programs so you can erase your mistakes. Things that are crossed out are messy. The first thing you should do to test a program is to read over your program carefully to spot errors. It is valuable to trace the execution yourself before you enter it into the computer. Your goal should always be to produce programs that you *know* are correct without testing, but this is not always possible. You could ask someone else to read it too. If another person cannot understand your program it may show that your program is poorly written or has errors. Next you enter your program and proofread it to see that it is the same as what you wrote on the piece of paper.

If you have made errors in your program that involve the form of statements, the compiler spots these during compilation and reports them on the output. It refers to an error of a certain type and places a marker ($<<<<$) near the spot in the program where the error occurred. Errors in form are called *syntax errors*. Examples of common syntax errors are

1. leaving out the semicolon between statements
2. forgetting the END with its period
3. misspelling a keyword

In a way, a syntax error is a good error since it is detected for you by the computer. But it is frustrating to have to correct it and recompile the job. It wastes time. Some people say that having syntax errors is a symptom of sloppy programming and a sure indication that there are other errors.

If there are no syntax errors, execution can take place right after compilation. The computer tells you that the program is running. This does not, however, mean that all is well.

If answers are displayed, they should be checked against hand calculated answers. If they agree, it is possible that your program is correct. If they disagree it is possible that your hand calculations are incorrect or that your program has errors. The errors now are usually of a kind called *semantic errors.* You are asking for a calculation that you did not mean to ask for. It has a different *meaning* from your intentions. For instance, you are adding two numbers and you meant to subtract them.

To find semantic errors you must look at the program again and try to trace what it must be doing rather than what you thought it would do. To help in the tracing it is sometimes necessary to insert additional WRITELN instructions between other statements and print out the current value of variables that are changing. In this way you can follow the machine's activity. These extra WRITELN instructions can be removed after the errors have been found.

Care must be taken about the INTEGER and REAL distinction between numbers as the computer converts from integer to real automatically and will not warn you if things are going wrong.

COMMON ERRORS IN PROGRAMS

When you try running a program on a computer, the computer may detect *errors* in your program. As a result, *error messages* will be displayed. Since the computer does not understand the purpose of your program, its error messages are limited to describing the specific illegalities which it detects. Unfortunately, the computer's error messages usually do not tell you how to correct your program so that it will solve the problem you have in mind.

In order to help you avoid such errors, we list some of the errors which commonly occur in a beginner's programs.

Missing semicolons - Do not forget to put semicolons between statements and no semicolon after the last statement of a list. No semicolon follows a list containing a single statement.

Missing parentheses - Do not forget the parentheses required around the list of items in a READ or WRITE statement.

Missing first line of program - Every Pascal program must have a line of the form

        PROGRAM identifier;

Missing END. at the end of the program.

Missing quotes, especially the last quote. Consider the following erroneous statement:

> WRITELN('INVOICE);

This statement is missing a quote between the E and the right parenthesis.

Uninitialized variables - When a variable is declared, a memory location, or cell, is set aside, but no special value is placed in the cell. That is, the cell is not yet initialized. A variable must be given a value, via an assignment statement or a READ statement, before an attempt is made to use the value of the variable in a WRITE statement or in an expression.

Undeclared variables - Before a variable is used in a statement (assignment, READ or WRITE) the variable must be declared. The declaration of variables must precede all statements. Definition of constants precedes the declaration of variables.

Mistaking I for 1 - The characters I and 1 look similar, but are entirely different to the computer.

Mistaking O for 0 - The characters O(oh) and 0(zero) look similar, but are entirely different to the computer. The digit zero is sometimes displayed with a slash through it so that it is distinctly different from the oh.

CHAPTER 5 SUMMARY

This chapter introduced *variables*, as they are used in programming languages. Essentially, a variable is a memory location, or cell, which can hold a *value*. Suppose X is the name of a variable; then X denotes a cell. If X is a variable having the INTEGER type, then the cell for X can hold an integer value such as 9, 291, 0 or -11.

The following important terms were discussed in this chapter.

Identifier - can be used as the name of a variable or constant. An identifier must begin with a letter; this letter can be followed by additional letters or digits. The following are examples of identifiers: X, I, WIDTH, INCOMETAX and A1. In UCSD Pascal compilers only the first 8 characters of an identifier are used, so that no two identifiers in a program should have the same first 8 characters.

Type - Each variable has a type; in this chapter we introduced the INTEGER and REAL types. The type of a variable is determined by its declaration.

Variable declaration - establishes variables for use in a program. For example, the declaration

> VAR I: INTEGER;

creates a variable called I which can be given integer values.

Constant definition - establishes named constants for use in a program. For example, the definition

> CONST PI=3.14159;
> CONVERT=2.54;

creates named constants PI and CONVERT. Definition of constants occurs immediately after the PROGRAM heading; this is followed by the declaration of variables before the BEGIN that precedes any WRITE, READ or assignment statements.

VAR - the keyword instructing the computer to create variables. A declaration can be of the form:

VAR list of identifiers separated by commas: type;

The type must be INTEGER or REAL for the PS/2 subset. The declaration can be extended for further variables, for example:

> VAR I: INTEGER;
> X,Y: REAL;
> J,K: INTEGER;

We sometimes express the form of the declaration of variables by writing

> VAR variable{,variable}:type;
> {variable{,variable}:type;}

where the curly brackets indicate that what is contained in them can appear zero or more times.

Assignment - means a value is assigned to a variable. For example, the following is an assignment statement which gives the value 52 to the variable I:

> I:=52;

Truncation - throwing away the fractional part of a number. When a real number is to be assigned to a variable with the INTEGER type, the variable can be given the truncated value by using the TRUNC function. If X is real and Y integer

> Y:=TRUNC(X);

will assign the integral part of the value of the real variable X to the integer variable Y.

Rounding - changing a real number to the nearest integer. If X is real and Y integer

$$Y:=ROUND(X);$$

assigns the value of X, rounded off, to the integer variable Y.

Number conversion - changing an integer number to a real number or vice versa. Conversion from real to integer requires either truncation or rounding of the result. Integer values are converted automatically to real when assigned to (or read into) a real variable location.

Data (or input data) - values which a program can read are typed in on the keyboard during the execution of the program.

READ - means "Read data." The READ statement reads data values into a list of variables. As the data is read in it is displayed on the screen in the same format as it is typed.

READ statement - this statement is of the form:

READ(list of variable names separated by commas);

Reading will automatically proceed to the next line when the values of one line have all been read.

READLN statement - same as READ except that after the value for the last variable in the list to be read in has been entered the READLN statement expects a return. The computer will skip over anything else you enter until a return is given. This means that any other data either read in or output appears on the next line of the screen.

Comments - information in a program which is intended to assist a person reading the program. The following is a comment which could appear in a Pascal program:

(* THIS PROGRAM COMPUTES GAS BILLS *)

Comments do not affect the execution of a program.

Documentation - written explanation of a program. Comments are used in a program to document its actions.

Keyword - a word, such as PROGRAM or BEGIN, which is part of the programming language. Keywords must not be used as identifiers.

Syntax Errors - improper parts of a program. For example, the statement

WRITELN('HELLO';

has a syntax error in that a right parenthesis is missing. If the computer detects an error in your program, it will output an "error message".

CHAPTER 5 EXERCISES

1. Suppose that I, J and K are variables with the integer type and they presently have the values 5, 7 and 10. What will be displayed as a result of the following statements?

    ```
    WRITELN(I:3,I+1:3,I+J:3,I+J*K:3);
    K:=I+J;
    WRITELN(K);
    J:=J+1;
    WRITELN(J);
    I:=3*I+J;
    WRITELN(I);
    ```

2. RADIUS, DIAMETER, CIRCUMFERENCE and AREA are REAL variables. A value has been read into RADIUS via a READ statement. Write statements which do each of the following.

    (a) Give to DIAMETER the product of 2 and RADIUS.

    (b) Give to CIRCUMFERENCE the product of pi (3.14159) and DIAMETER.

    (c) Give to AREA the product of pi and RADIUS squared. (RADIUS squared can be written as RADIUS*RADIUS.)

    (d) Output the values of RADIUS, DIAMETER, CIRCUMFERENCE and AREA.

3. Suppose I is a variable with the INTEGER type. I has already been given a value via an assignment statement. Write statements to do the following.

    (a) Without changing I, output out twice the value of I.

    (b) Increase I by 1.

    (c) Double the value of I.

    (d) Decrease I by 5.

4. M, N and P are variables with the integer type. What will the following statements cause the computer to output?

    ```
    M:=43;
    N:=211;
    P:=M;
    M:=N;
    N:=P;
    WRITELN(M:4,N:4);
    ```

5.   (a) What will be displayed by the following program if 22 and 247 are input? How about -16 and 538?

```
PROGRAM PAIRS;
    VAR FIRST,SECOND: INTEGER;
    BEGIN
        WRITELN('INPUT TWO INTEGERS');
        READ(FIRST,SECOND);
        WRITELN(FIRST+SECOND);
        READ(FIRST,SECOND);
        WRITELN(FIRST+SECOND)
    END.
```

6.   (a) What will be displayed by the following program if the grades are 81.7 and 85.9?

```
(* CALCULATE TERM MARK *)
PROGRAM COMBINE;
    VAR GRADE1,GRADE2: REAL;
        MARK: INTEGER;
    BEGIN
        WRITELN('INPUT TWO GRADES');
        READ(GRADE1,GRADE2);
        MARK:=ROUND((GRADE1+GRADE2)/2);
        WRITELN(MARK)
    END.
```

7.   Trace the execution of the following program. That is, give the values of the variables LENGTH, WIDTH, and ABOUT and give any output after each line of the program. Use as the two input values 9.60 and 15.9.

```
PROGRAM AREA;
    VAR SIZE,LENGTH,WIDTH: REAL;
        ABOUT: INTEGER;
    (* READ SIZES CONVERT FEET TO YARDS *)
    BEGIN
        WRITE('SIZE=');
        READLN(SIZE);
        WIDTH:=SIZE/3;
        WRITE('SIZE=');
        READLN(SIZE);
        LENGTH:=SIZE/3;
        ABOUT:=ROUND(WIDTH*LENGTH);
        WRITELN('LENGTH AND WIDTH ARE',
            LENGTH:14,WIDTH:14);
```

```
     WRITELN('AREA IS:',LENGTH*WIDTH:14,
        ' THIS IS ABOUT',ABOUT:10,' (SQ YARDS)')
   END.
```

8.   Write a program which reads three values and outputs their average, rounded to the nearest whole number. For example, if 20, 16 and 25 are entered then your program should output 20. Make up your own data for your program.

9.   Write a program which reads a weight given in pounds and then outputs the weight in (1) pounds, (2) ounces, (3) kilograms and (4) grams. Note: 16 ounces equal one pound, 2.2046 pounds equal one kilogram and 1000 grams equal one kilogram. Use named constants in your program.

Chapter 6

PS/3: CONTROL FLOW

In the first two subsets of Pascal we have learned to write programs with statements that cause the computer to read data and assign values to variables, evaluate arithmetic expressions and assign the values to variables, and output results with labels. In all programs the statements were executed in sequence until the END was reached, at which time the program was terminated. In this subset we will learn two ways in which the order of executing statements may be altered. One involves the repetitious use of statements; the other involves a selection between alternate paths in the flow of statements. The first is called a *loop*, the second a *branch*. We speak of the *flow of control* since it is the control unit of the computer that determines which statement is to be executed next by the computer.

COUNTED LOOPS

The normal flow of control in a program is in a straight line. So far, in the statements that are bracketed in the list between the BEGIN and the END, one statement is executed after another. We can, however, give a statement that will cause the statement that follows it to be repeated. In the last chapter, in the example where we were computing information about boxes of soap flakes, we had to write the statements over and over to get repetitions. A statement that will produce repetition is the *counted FOR loop*. For our example we could have written

```
FOR I:=1 TO 3 DO
    BEGIN
        READ(COST,WEIGHT);
        COSTKG:=ROUND(COST/WEIGHT);
        WRITELN(COSTKG:10)
    END;
```

The three statements that we had to repeat three times are prefaced by

```
FOR I:=1 TO 3 DO
        BEGIN
```

and followed by END;

The three statements bracketed by BEGIN and END act as a single *compound statement*. The variable I is an index, which must be declared as an integer variable, and which counts the number of repetitions. First the index I is set to 1, then the compound statement is executed. After the execution, control is sent back to the FOR. At this time the index I is increased by 1, making it 2. The compound statement is again executed and, then, back we go to the FOR. This time I becomes 3 and a third execution of the compound statement in the *FOR loop* takes place. When control returns to the FOR this time, I is found be equal to the final value 3 so control goes out of the loop to the next statement after the compound statement.

A counted or *indexed* FOR loop is used whenever we know exactly how many repetitions we want to take place. We do not need to start the count at 1.

FOR COUNT:=12 TO 24 DO

Here we have called the index COUNT and are starting at 12 and going up to, and to include, 24. In these statements we have counted forward by 1. We can also count backwards by -1. If we write

FOR COUNT:=10 DOWNTO 1 DO
    statement

it will cause the "statement" to be executed with COUNT taking the values 10, 9, 8, ..., 1.

The other kinds of loop statements are the WHILE...DO statement and the REPEAT...UNTIL statement but we cannot introduce them until we look at *conditions*. The WHILE...DO is a loop statement that causes repetition as long as a certain condition is true. The condition concerned is written at the beginning of the loop after the word WHILE. The REPEAT...UNTIL is a loop statement that causes repetition until a certain condition is true. The condition is written at the end of the loop after the word UNTIL.

CONDITIONS

There are expressions in Pascal that are called *relational expressions* and these have values that are either *true* or *false*. The following is a list of relational expressions with their value written on the same line. The symbol > means is greater than, < means is less than, the equal sign means is equal to, and the sign < > means is not equal to.

relational expression	value
5＝2＋3	true
7＞5	true
2＜6	true
5＋3＜2＋1	false
6＜＞10	true
5＞5	false
5＞＝5	true

You can see how these work. These are sometimes called Boolean expressions after the logician George Boole.

There are also compound conditions formed by taking two single conditions and putting either the *Boolean (logical) operator* AND or the Boolean operator OR between them. When conditions are compounded in this way, each simple condition should have parentheses around it. This is because Boolean operators have higher precedence than relational operators.

With AND *both* conditions must be true or else the compound condition is false. For example,

$$(8＞7) \text{ AND } (6＜3)$$

is false since (6＜3) is false. With OR, if *either* or both of the single conditions is true, the compound condition is true. For example, (8＞7) OR (6＜3) is true since (8＞7) is true. It is possible to have multiple compoundings. For example,

$$((8＞7) \text{ AND } (2＝1＋1)) \text{ AND } ((6＞7) \text{ OR } (5＞1))$$

is true. The parentheses here show the sequence of the operations. There is a rule of precedence if there are no parentheses, namely, the AND operator has higher precedence than the OR operator. This means that AND operations are done before OR operations.

A Boolean operator that requires only one condition is the NOT operator. The condition

$$\text{NOT}(5＞6)$$

is true since 5 is *not* greater than 6.

BOOLEAN VARIABLES

If you want to assign a Boolean value to a variable, it must be typed by a declaration as BOOLEAN. BOOLEAN is a variable type just like REAL and INTEGER. But a Boolean variable can only have one of two values, namely TRUE or FALSE. Boolean variables can not be read or output but can be assigned Boolean values. They cannot be used in numeric expressions. For example, if you want a Boolean variable SWITCH assigned the value true you must include the declaration and the assignment.

```
VAR SWITCH: BOOLEAN;
SWITCH:=TRUE;
```

The variable SWITCH may be used in a condition.

CONDITIONAL LOOPS

We have introduced the notion of a condition; now we will actually use it. One of the major uses of conditions is in the conditional loop. There are two of these: the REPEAT...UNTIL condition loop, and the WHILE condition DO loop. We will look first at the WHILE...DO loop. The form of this loop is

```
WHILE condition DO
    statement
```

The repetition of "statement" which is called the body of the loop is to take place as long as the condition stated after the word WHILE is true. Once it is false, the control goes to the next statement after the loop. If you want to have a number of statements in the body of a loop you must make them into a compound statement using BEGIN and END.

So far we have discussed only conditions involving integer constants. These are always true or false. The condition in the WHILE loop cannot be like this, because if it were always true we would loop forever and if always false we would not loop at all. The condition must involve a variable whose value changes during the looping.

In the following program segment a WHILE...DO loop is used to accomplish what the counted FOR loop did for the soap flakes boxes.

```
1   I:=1;
2   WHILE I<=3 DO
3      BEGIN
4         READ(COST,WEIGHT);
5         COSTKG:=ROUND(COST/WEIGHT);
6         WRITELN(COSTKG:10);
7         I:=I+1
8      END;
9   WRITELN(I);
```

In statement 1 the value of the variable I appearing in the condition is set initially to 1, then we enter the loop. This stage is called *initialization*.

In line 2 we begin the loop. The condition after the WHILE is true since I is 1, which is less than 3. Thus the compound statement starting with BEGIN and going down to END is executed. This compound statement constitutes the *body* of the loop. In the body, statement 7 *alters* the value of the variable appearing in the condition. This means that it is changing each time around the loop. At the end of the first execution of the loop it becomes $1+1=2$. After the compound statement has been executed, control returns to the start of the loop. The condition is then examined and since it is true $(2<=3)$, the body is executed a second time. It will be true also on the third time but on the fourth round, I will be 4 and $(4<=3)$ is false. When I is displayed by statement 9 it is 4. This output is not part of the original example, but was included here to show you what happens to the index I.

The various phases of a WHILE...DO loop are

Phase 1. Initialization, especially of the variable in the condition

Phase 2. Test condition and if true then go to the next statement which is the body of the loop, if false go to the statement following the body

Phase 3. Execute the statement that constitutes the body of the loop which includes altering the variable in the condition

Phase 4. Return to phase 2.

Phase 1 is necessary to give the variable appearing in the condition an initial value. Since the body of the loop must alter the variable in the condition in addition to taking some other action, it almost always is a compound statement.

Before we introduce the REPEAT...UNTIL loop we will compare the use of the WHILE...DO conditional loop and the FOR...DO counted loop.

READING INPUT

As an example of looping we will look at reading data for student marks and computing an average mark for the class. The number of students in the class is not known at the time the program is prepared. The only real problem will be to stop reading marks after the last mark is entered and compute the average. There are two distinct ways of doing this. One is to count the number of students and enter the count before you begin entering the marks. Then we use a counted FOR loop to read them. The second method is to enter at the end of the data a piece of data that is impossible as a real entry. We call it a *dummy entry*. Sometimes it is called an *end-of-file marker*. In a later subset, PS/5, we will see how the EOF end of file predeclared function can be used to detect the last entry.

We will now examine the two methods in turn. Suppose, to talk specifically, that each data entry consists of a student number and a grade received in an examination. To illustrate we will have only three data entries, but you can see how it will work with more.

Method 1. Counting the number of entries

```
PROGRAM MARKS1;
    VAR STUDENTNUMBER,MARK,COUNT,I,SUM: INTEGER;
    BEGIN
        WRITE('COUNT=');
        READLN(COUNT);
        SUM:=0;
        WRITELN(' STUDENT', 'MARK':6);
        FOR I:=1 TO COUNT DO
            BEGIN
                READLN(STUDENTNUMBER,MARK);
                SUM:=SUM+MARK
            END;
        WRITELN(' AVERAGE=',ROUND(SUM/COUNT));
        WRITELN(' COUNT=',COUNT)
    END.
```

The screen will display

```
COUNT=3
 STUDENT  MARK
    1026      86
    2051      90
    3163      71
 AVERAGE=82
 COUNT=3
```

Notice that we took the trouble to label the output. Perhaps the two ENDs in the program seem strange. The first belongs to the compound statement in the FOR loop, the second to the BEGIN prefacing all statements. The machine can keep track of these just as you can tell which right parenthesis goes with which left one in this example:

$$(2+5*(2+6))$$

In the second method we will place a dummy entry with two zeros in it after we have finished all the valid entries. This will then trigger the calculation of the average mark.

Method 2. Testing for the dummy entry

```
PROGRAM MARKS2;
    VAR STUDENTNUMBER,MARK,COUNT,SUM: INTEGER;
    BEGIN
        COUNT:=0;
        SUM:=0;
        WRITELN(' STUDENT', 'MARK':6);
        READLN(STUDENTNUMBER,MARK);
        WHILE STUDENTNUMBER < > 0 DO
            BEGIN
                SUM:=SUM+MARK;
                COUNT:=COUNT+1;
                READLN(STUDENTNUMBER,MARK)
            END;
        WRITELN(' AVERAGE=',ROUND(SUM/COUNT));
        WRITELN(' COUNT=',COUNT)
    END.
```

Here the display on the screen is

```
STUDENT  MARK
    1026      86
    2951      90
    3163      71
       0       0
AVERAGE=82
COUNT=3
```

In this example you will notice that the initialization involves reading the first input line outside the loop, in order to get a value for the variable STUDENTNUMBER appearing in the condition of the WHILE...DO. In the WHILE...DO line the symbol < > means "not equal to". Since the first line has already been read, its mark must be added to the sum before a new line is read. This means that the sequence is SUM:=SUM+MARK then READLN, rather than the way it is in method 1. As soon as the new line has been read, we return to the WHILE where the condition is tested.

Methods 1 and 2 for dealing with a variable number of items are used again and again in programming. The WHILE is more difficult to program but probably more useful, since if there are many items, it is better for the user to stick in an end-of-file item than to count items.

EXAMPLES OF LOOPS

We will now give example programs to illustrate details about loops. The examples each draw a zigzag. Here is the first example:

```
1  PROGRAM WIGGLE;
2      VAR J: INTEGER;
3      BEGIN
4        FOR J:=1 TO 3 DO
5          BEGIN
6              WRITELN('      *');
7              WRITELN('      *');
8              WRITELN('       *');
9              WRITELN('      *')
10            END
11     END.
```

This program, appropriately called WIGGLE, outputs the following pattern:

```
    *
     *
      *
     *
    *
    *
     *
    *
    *
     *
      *
     *
    *
```

The WIGGLE program causes the body of the loop, lines 5 through 10, to be executed three times. The variable J is 1 during the time the first four stars are displayed. J is 2 during the time the next four stars are displayed, and J is 3 while the last four stars are displayed. After the last star is displayed, J is set to 4 and since J then exceeds the limiting value, 3, of the loop, the loop is terminated.

Notice that in this program the variable J is used for only one purpose: to see that the loop is repeated the desired number of times. Line 4 means, essentially, "Repeat this loop three times." If we replaced line 4 by the following line

     FOR J:=9 TO 11 DO

then the program would still output the same pattern. The only difference is that J would have the values 9,10, and 11 during the output of the stars and would end up with the value of 12. Although this replacement for line 4 does not change the pattern displayed, it should not be used because it makes the program more confusing for people to understand. This is because people more naturally think of "repeat this loop three times" as running through the loop with values 1, 2, and 3, rather than values 9, 10, and 11.

Here is one more possible replacement for line 4 which does not change the displayed pattern:

FOR J:=3 DOWNTO 1 DO

In this case, J will be 3 while the first four stars are displayed, then J will be 2 while the next four stars are displayed, and then J will be 1 while the last four stars are displayed. Finally, J will end up with the value of zero. This illustrates the fact that if the step size, which is -1 here, is negative, then the loop will count backwards to smaller values. Again, for this example program, the original version of line 4 is preferable because it is easier to understand its meaning at a glance.

Once a FOR loop finishes, there is some confusion about the final value of the counting variable. For example, in the WIGGLE program, does J end up as 3 (the final value) or does it end up as 4 (getting ready for the next time through but finding that 4 exceeds the limit 3). The Pascal language side steps this question by leaving the value of J "undefined" after the loop, meaning that the final value may be different depending on what compiler you are using. You should avoid this confusion by following this advice:

> When a FOR loop has finished, do not use the final value of the counting variable.

There is another possible source of confusion in FOR loops. For example, what happens in WIGGLE if we set the counting variable J to 15 by an assignment statement in the loop body? The result is that J is not in the range 1 to 3. The FOR loop no longer means: repeat for J equal to 1 then 2 then 3. To avoid this confusion, Pascal has this rule:

> Inside a counted FOR loop, the program must not alter the value of the counting variable.

We will now rewrite our WIGGLE program using WHILE...DO instead of a counted FOR. We will call our new program WAGGLE. (Did you know that in German "wiggle waggle" means "waddle" like a duck? Well it does.)

```
1   PROGRAM WAGGLE;
2      VAR J: INTEGER;
3      BEGIN
```

```
4          J:=1;
5          WHILE J<=3 DO
6             BEGIN
7                WRITELN('         *');
8                WRITELN('         *');
9                WRITELN('          *');
10               WRITELN('         *');
11               J:=J+1
12            END
13    END.
```

This WAGGLE program works like our previous WIGGLE program. Lines 4, 5, and 11 of WAGGLE are equivalent to line 4 of WIGGLE. Since it is easier to see that line 4 of WIGGLE means, "Repeat this loop three times," the WIGGLE version is preferable. We will, however, use WAGGLE to illustrate a few more points about loops.

In the WAGGLE program, consider moving line 11, which is

$$J:=J+1$$

up to between lines 6 and 7. This change does not alter the displayed pattern. It simply changes the point at which J has its value increased. J will have the value 2 while the first four stars are displayed, then 3 while the next four stars are displayed and finally 4 while the last four stars are displayed. J ends up with the value of 4. Even though J is set to 4 before the last four stars are displayed, the loop is not stopped. This is because J is not compared to the limit value 3 until control returns to line 5. This illustrates the fact that in a WHILE...DO loop, the condition is tested only once - at the top - each time through the loop.

Now let us look back at the WAGGLE program. Suppose that you prepared this program for the computer and mistakenly made line 11 into

$$J:=J-1$$

The mistake is that the plus sign was changed to a minus sign. Such a small mistake! Surely the computer will understand that a plus was wanted! But it will not do so. The computer has a habit of doing what we *tell* it to do rather than what we *want* it to do. Given the WAGGLE program, with the mistake, the computer will do the following. With J set to 1 it will output the first four stars. Then, as a result of the erroneous line 11, it will set J to 0 and will output another four stars. Then it will set J to -1 and output four more stars. Then it will set J to -2 and output four more stars and so on and so on. In theory, it will *never stop* outputting stars because the condition J< =3 will always be true. This is called an *infinite loop*. You will have to stop the computer from executing your program by pressing the reset key.

AN ALTERNATIVE CONDITIONAL LOOP

There is another conditional loop in Pascal besides the WHILE...DO loop. We can use REPEAT...UNTIL instead of WHILE...DO when we know that the loop is always executed at least once. Remember that WHILE...DO allows zero repetitions, when the condition is false when first tested. The REPEAT...UNTIL loop has this form.

        REPEAT
            list of statements separated by semicolons
        UNTIL condition

In this loop no BEGIN...END is necessary if the body of the loop contains more than one statement. The test of the condition does not occur until the end of the loop so that all REPEAT...UNTIL loops are executed at least once. We will use WHILE...DO loops for most examples but here is a program that shows how a list of marks could be averaged using REPEAT...UNTIL.

Method 3. Testing dummy entry, at least one non-dummy

```
PROGRAM MARKS3;
    VAR STUDENTNUMBER,MARK,COUNT,SUM:INTEGER;
    BEGIN
        SUM:=0;
        COUNT:=0;
        WRITELN(' STUDENT', 'MARK':6);
        READLN(STUDENTNUMBER,MARK);
        REPEAT
            SUM:=SUM+MARK;
            COUNT:=COUNT+1;
            READLN(STUDENTNUMBER,MARK)
        UNTIL STUDENTNUMBER=0;
        WRITELN(' AVERAGE=',ROUND(SUM/COUNT));
        WRITELN(' COUNT=',COUNT)
    END.
```

The display will be identical to that of method 2. This program would not work if there were no student marks at all.

BRANCHES IN CONTROL FLOW

We have learned how to change from a flow of control in a straight line, or *sequential* control, to flow in a loop, either counted or conditional. Now we must look at a different kind of structure in the sequence of control. This structure is called selection or branching. It is a little like a fork in the road where there are two paths that can be followed. The road branches into two roads. When you come to a fork in a road you must *decide* which of the two branches you will take. Your decision is based on where you are heading. Suppose one sign at the fork gives the name of your destination and the other road sign gives some other name. Suppose your destination is Toronto; an instruction for deciding which branch to take might be

        IF LEFTBRANCHSIGN='TORONTO' THEN
            take the left branch
        ELSE
            take the right branch

We have written this decision in exactly the form you use in Pascal for branching in the sequence of control. The main difference is that the part we have written as "take the left branch" must be replaced by a Pascal statement to do something. The same is true of the other part which follows the keyword ELSE.

Suppose that there is a variable called CLASSA which contains the number of students in a class called A. Students are to be assigned to Class A if their mark in computer science (CSMARK) is over 80; otherwise they are to be assigned to Class B (CLASSB). The Pascal statement which decides which class to place the student in, and counts the number going into each class, is

        IF CSMARK>80 THEN
            CLASSA:=CLASSA+1
        ELSE
            CLASSB:=CLASSB+1;

The IF...THEN...ELSE statement causes control to split into two paths but, unlike forks in roads, you will notice that it immediately comes back together again. This means that we are never in any doubt about what happens; after the execution of one or the other of the two branches, the control returns to the normal sequence. One way of looking at the IF...THEN...ELSE statement is that it provides two possibilities, only one of which is to be *selected*, depending on whether the condition following the IF is true or false. After one or the other path is executed the normal control sequence is resumed.

If you want to execute two or more statements in either the THEN branch or the ELSE branch, you must enclose them with BEGIN in front and END afterwards. For example, consider the program segment

```
IF X>Y THEN
    BEGIN
        X:=Y+1;
        Y:=5
    END
ELSE
    BEGIN
        Y:=X+1;
        X:=3
    END;
```

We will not try to give any meaning to this example. It just shows how the BEGIN and END must be used when more than one statement follows either the THEN or the ELSE.

You must always have one statement, or a compound statement bracketed by BEGIN...END, after the THEN. If there is nothing that you want to do in the ELSE branch you must leave out the word ELSE entirely. For instance, you may have the statement which would eliminate the balance in a bank account if it were less than 10 cents.

```
IF BALANCE<10 THEN
    BALANCE:=0;
```

Here there is no ELSE statement, but this just means that if the balance is larger than 10 cents we do *not* make it zero.

A program error will occur if a semicolon is placed preceding the keyword ELSE. Sometimes a superfluous semicolon will not do any harm but here it will.

THREE-WAY BRANCHES

We have seen how a sequential control structure can be split up into two branches and then brought together again. What do we write if we have a situation where more than two branches are required? We will do a three-way branch and then you will see how any number of branches can be achieved. This can also be viewed as selecting one of three alternatives.

As an example, we will write a program that counts votes in an election. Suppose that there are three political parties called Conservative (right), Radicals (left), and Mugwumps (middle-roaders) and that to vote for one of these parties you enter a 1, or a 2, or a 3 respectively. Here is the program that reads the vote entries and counts each party and the total. The last vote entry is the dummy value -1.

```
PROGRAM VOTING;
    CONST CONSERVATIVE=1;
        RADICAL=2;
        MUGWUMP=3;
    VAR VOTE,RIGHT,LEFT,MIDDLE,COUNT: INTEGER;
    BEGIN
        RIGHT:=0;
        LEFT:=0;
        MIDDLE:=0;
        WRITELN('ENTER VOTES');
        READLN(VOTE);
        WHILE VOTE<>-1 DO
            BEGIN
                IF VOTE=CONSERVATIVE THEN
                    RIGHT:=RIGHT+1
                ELSE
                    IF VOTE=RADICAL THEN
                        LEFT:=LEFT+1
                    ELSE
                        IF VOTE=MUGWUMP THEN
                            MIDDLE:=MIDDLE+1;
                READLN(VOTE)
            END;
        COUNT:=RIGHT+LEFT+MIDDLE;
        WRITELN('CONSERV.':10,'RADICAL':10,
                        'MUGWUMP':10,'TOTAL':10);
        WRITELN(RIGHT:10,LEFT:10,MIDDLE:10,COUNT:10)
    END.
```

In this program we have two different things happening. One is a three-way branch, which is accomplished by a series of three IF...THEN statements, one for each value of VOTE. This means that an invalid vote does not get counted anywhere. If we wanted notification that there was an invalid vote we could have inserted the following in the program right before READLN(VOTE) at the end of the loop body. (You must remove the semicolon after MIDDLE:=MIDDLE+1).

```
        ELSE
                WRITELN('INVALID VOTE ',VOTE);
```

This then makes it a four-way branch.

The minimum program needed for a three-way branch would be one IF...THEN...ELSE statement nested inside another:

```
IF VOTE=CONSERVATIVE THEN
    RIGHT:=RIGHT+1
ELSE
    IF VOTE=RADICAL THEN
        LEFT:=LEFT+1
    ELSE
        MIDDLE:=MIDDLE+1;
```

If there are any invalid votes, they are given to the MUGWUMP party.

There is no fixed way of doing the job. Here is another try at it.

```
IF VOTE<MUGWUMP THEN
    IF VOTE<RADICAL THEN
        RIGHT:=RIGHT+1
    ELSE
        LEFT:=LEFT+1
ELSE
    MIDDLE:=MIDDLE+1;
```

Again we have nesting of two IF...THEN...ELSE statements, but in a different sequence. It is good practice not to have a second IF...THEN...ELSE nested after the THEN; it is preferable to have it in the ELSE branch. Notice that we put the ELSE that goes with an IF vertically beneath it so that the nesting of the statements is clear. In the next section we will show how three-way and higher branches can be handled using a CASE statement.

CASE STATEMENTS

If there are more than two alternatives in a selection process it is easier to use a CASE statement. The form of this statement is

```
CASE expression OF
    case-label1: statement1;
    case-label2: statement2;
        ...
    case-labelN: statementN
END;
```

Instead of the nested IF statement in the VOTING program we could have this CASE statement

```
CASE VOTE OF
    CONSERVATIVE: RIGHT:=RIGHT+1;
    RADICAL: LEFT:=LEFT+1;
    MUGWUMP: MIDDLE:=MIDDLE+1
END;
```

The value of the variable VOTE can be the same as one of the three named constants: CONSERVATIVE, RADICAL, or MUGWUMP, and depending on its value the correspondingly labeled statement is executed. For example, if VOTE=2 (RADICAL) then we execute LEFT:=LEFT+1. The label of a statement is separated from the statement itself by a colon. Each label must be an integer constant, for example 3 or MUGWUMP. Notice that there is an END terminating the CASE statement and that there is no semicolon just preceding END.

The CASE statement expects to select exactly one of the statements, so the selecting value, VOTE in this example, must have one of the values of the case labels. If we are not sure that VOTE is 1,2 or 3, we can expand the program to

```
IF VOTE has the value 1, 2 or 3 THEN
    CASE VOTE OF
        (Same as in previous CASE statement)
    END
ELSE
    WRITELN(' INVALID VOTE ',VOTE);
```

The only thing missing is that we have not written "VOTE has the value of 1,2 or 3" in Pascal. We will see how this can be done using AND and OR in the next chapter.

Each alternative in the CASE must be a single statement. If we want a list of statements, we must enclose them in BEGIN...END, as is done in IF statements.

A particular alternative in a CASE statement can have more than one label. Suppose the Conservative and Mugwump parties form a coalition and we wish to count their votes together in the variable COALITION. We could use this CASE statement.

```
CASE VOTE OF
    CONSERVATIVE,MUGWUMP: COALITION:=COALITION+1;
    RADICAL: LEFT:=LEFT+1
END
```

Of course we would need to declare COALITION as an integer variable.

EXAMPLE IF STATEMENTS

We will now give a series of examples of IF statements which might be used in a government program for handling income tax. Let us suppose that the program is to write notices to people telling them whether they owe tax or they are to receive a tax refund. The amount of tax is calculated and then the following is executed.

```
IF TAX > 0 THEN
    WRITELN(' TAX DUE IS ',TAX,' DOLLARS')
ELSE
    WRITELN(' REFUND IS ',-TAX,' DOLLARS');
```

Notice that it was necessary to change the sign of "tax" when we output the refund. (Note: There is a space after the word IS.)

Unfortunately, our program, like too many programs, is not quite right. If the calculated tax is exactly zero, then the program will output REFUND IS 0 DOLLARS. We could fix this problem by the following.

```
IF TAX > 0 THEN
    WRITELN(' TAX DUE IS ',TAX,' DOLLARS')
ELSE
    IF TAX = 0 THEN
        WRITELN(' YOU OWE NOTHING')
    ELSE
        WRITELN(' REFUND IS ',-TAX,' DOLLARS');
```

We have used a *nested* IF statement to solve the problem, that is, an IF statement which is inside an IF statement. In general, we can nest any kind of statement inside an IF statement including assignment statements, READ and WRITELN statements, FOR statements, and IF statements.

Now suppose that when the tax is due we wish to tell the taxpayer where to send his check. We can expand the program as follows:

```
IF TAX > 0 THEN
    BEGIN
        WRITELN(' TAX DUE IS ',TAX,' DOLLARS');
        WRITELN(' SEND CHECK TO DISTRICT OFFICE')
    END
ELSE
    IF TAX =0 THEN
        WRITELN(' YOU OWE NOTHING')
    ELSE
        WRITELN(' REFUND IS ',-TAX,' DOLLARS');
```

Since we wanted more than one statement to be executed when TAX > 0 we had to group them together using the construct:

BEGIN...END

This construct acts like a set of parentheses and makes our two statements appear as one compound statement. Notice that no BEGIN...END is necessary after the ELSE because what follows is a single IF...THEN...ELSE statement.

PARAGRAPHING THE PROGRAM

In order to follow the *structure* of the nesting of IF...THEN...ELSE statements we have indented the program so that the IF and ELSE that belong to each other are lined up vertically. The statements following the THEN and the ELSE are indented. This is called *paragraphing* the program, and is analogous to the way we indent paragraphs of prose to indicate grouping of thoughts. Paragraphing makes a valuable contribution to understandability and is a *must* in structured programming.

Also, if you examine the programs with FOR loops you will see that the loop body has been indented starting right after the FOR. In the next chapter we will be examining the situation where FOR loops are nested, and then we will use two levels of indentation. We indent the statement bracketed by BEGIN and END to show the scope of the compound statement.

There are no set rules about how much indentation you should use, or exactly how, for instance, an IF...THEN...ELSE statement should be indented; but it is clear that being systematic is an enormous help.

CHAPTER 6 SUMMARY

In this chapter we introduced statements which allow for (a) repetition of statements and (b) selection between different possibilities. We introduced *conditions* which are used to terminate the repetition of statements and to choose between different possibilities. Comparisons and Boolean operators are used in specifying conditions. The following important terms were discussed in this chapter.

Loop - a programming language construct which causes repeated execution of statements. In PS/k, loops are either counted FOR loops or conditional loops.

Counted FOR loop - has the following form:

> FOR variable := start TO limit DO
>> statement

The variable, called the counting variable or index, must have the INTEGER type. Each of "start," and "limit" can be expressions; these expressions are evaluated before the repetition starts and are not affected by the statement of the loop body. Counting proceeds by 1s from the start up to and including the limit. If start is not less than or equal to limit no execution of the loop body will take place. Counting backwards by -1 is accomplished by using the form

> FOR variable:=start DOWNTO limit DO
>> statement

Limit must be less than or equal to start or else the loop will not be executed at all.

WHILE loop - has the following form:

> WHILE condition DO
>> statement

The condition is tested at the beginning of each pass through the loop. If it is found to be true, the statement of the loop body is executed and then the condition is again tested. When the condition finally is found to be false, control is passed to the statement which follows the loop body statement. Any variables which appear in the condition must be given values before the loop begins. The loop body is executed zero or more times.

REPEAT loop - has the following form

> REPEAT
>> statements separated by semicolons
> UNTIL condition

Similar to WHILE loop except that the condition is tested after the execution of the statements; repetition continues until the condition is found to be true. The loop body is executed one or more times.

Loop body - the statement that appears inside a loop. If you want to have several statements in the body of a FOR...DO loop or a WHILE...DO loop they must be made into a compound statement. To do this the statements are bracketed by BEGIN and END and separated from each other by semicolons.

Comparisons - used in conditions. For example, comparisons can be used in a condition to determine how many times to execute a loop body. The following are used to specify comparisons.

$$<\qquad \text{less than}$$
$$>\qquad \text{greater than}$$
$$<=\qquad \text{less than or equal}$$
$$>=\qquad \text{greater than or equal}$$
$$=\qquad \text{equal}$$
$$<>\qquad \text{not equal}$$

Conditions - are either true or false. Conditions can be made up of comparisons and the following three Boolean operators.

AND
OR
NOT

End-of-file (or end-of-data) detection - When a loop is reading a series of data items, it must determine when the last data item has been read. This can be accomplished by first reading in the number of items to be read and then counting the items in the series as they are read. It can also be accomplished by following the last data item by a special dummy entry which contains special, or dummy data. The program knows to stop when it reads the dummy data.

IF statement - has the following form:

IF condition THEN
    statement
[ELSE
    statement]

The square brackets are shown around the ELSE clause to show that it can be omitted. If the condition is true, the first statement is executed. If the condition is false, the second statement, if present, is executed. In either case, control then goes to next statement after the ELSE clause - or if the ELSE clause is omitted, to the next statement after the THEN clause. Any statement, including another IF statement, can appear as a part of an IF statement. If more than one statement is required after the THEN or ELSE they must be bracketed by BEGIN...END into a compound statement. Note that there can be no semicolon preceding the ELSE.

CASE statement - when there are more than two alternatives in a selection statement, a CASE statement can be more direct than a set of nested IF...THEN...ELSE statements. It has the form

```
CASE expression OF
    case-label1: statement1;
    case-label2: statement2;
        ...
    case-labelN: statementN
END
```

When the CASE statement is encountered in a program the expression is evaluated and the statement executed whose case-label matches that value. The expression must match one of the labels or the meaning of the CASE statement is undefined in standard Pascal. (In UCSD Pascal, if there is no match, the statement after the CASE statement is executed. The effect of the CASE statement is then the same as a null statement.) Each case label is an integer constant. Several case labels separated by commas can label a single choice.

Paragraphing - indenting a program so that its structure is easily seen by people. The statements inside loops and inside IF statements are indented to make the overall program organization obvious. The computer ignores paragraphing when translating and executing programs.

CHAPTER 6 EXERCISES

1. Suppose I and J are variables with values 6 and 12. Which of the following conditions are true?

    (a) $2*I <= J$
    (b) $2*I-1 < J$

(c)   (I< =6) AND (J< =6)

(d)   (I< =6) OR (J< =6)

(e)   (I>0) AND (I< =10)

(f)   (I< =12) OR (J< =12)

(g)   (I>25) OR ((I<50) AND (J<50))

(h)   (I<>4) AND (I<>5)

(i)   (I<4) OR (I>5)

(j)   NOT(I>6)

2.   The following program predicts the population of a family of wallalumps over a 2-year period, based on the assumption of an initial population of 2 and a doubling of population each 2 months. What does the program output?

```
PROGRAM EXPLODE;
    VAR MONTH,POPULATION: INTEGER;
    BEGIN
        POPULATION:=2;
        WRITELN('    MONTH',' POPULATION');
        FOR MONTH:=0 TO 24 DO
            BEGIN
                WRITELN(MONTH:10,POPULATION:10);
                POPULATION:=2*POPULATION
            END
    END.
```

3.   Suppose you have hidden away 50 dollars to be used for some future emergency. Assuming an inflation rate of 12 per cent per year, write a program to compute how much money, to the nearest dollar, you would need at the end of each of the next 15 years to be equivalent to the buying power of 50 dollars at the time you hid it.

4.   Trace the following program. That is, give the values of the variables together with any output after the execution of each statement. Use as data entries 95 110 85 -1.

```
1  PROGRAM CLASS;
2      VAR NUMBER,GRADE,SUM: INTEGER;
3      BEGIN
4          SUM:=0;
5          WRITELN('ENTER GRADES,-1 AT END');
6          READLN(GRADE);
```

```
7          NUMBER:=0;
8          WHILE GRADE<>-1 DO
9             BEGIN
10               IF(GRADE>0) AND (GRADE<=100) THEN
11                  BEGIN
12                     SUM:=SUM+GRADE;
13                     NUMBER:=NUMBER+1
14                  END
15               ELSE
16                  WRITELN(' **ERROR:GRADE=',GRADE);
17               READLN(GRADE)
18            END;
19         WRITELN(' AVERAGE IS ',SUM/NUMBER)
20      END.
```

5. Write a program that reads the following data cards and calcu-lates the average of (a) each of the two columns of data, and (b) each row of the data. You should either precede the data with a number giving the count of the following data items or add a dummy entry following these data items.

92	88
75	62
81	75
80	80
55	60
64	60
81	80

6. Write a program which reads in a sequence of grades (0 to 100) and outputs the average grade (rounded to the nearest whole number), the number of grades and the number of fail-ing grades (failing is less than 50). Assume that a "dummy" grade of 999 will follow the last grade. See that your output is clearly labeled. Answer the following questions:

(a) What will happen if the grade 74 is misentered as 7 4?

(b) What will happen if the dummy grade 999 is left off? (You can try this.)

(c) What will your program do if there are no grades, i.e. if 999 is the only data item?

(d)   What will happen if the two grades 62 and 93 are misentered as 6293?

Test your program using the following data:

85	74	44	62	93
41	69	73	999	

7.   Write a program which determines the unit price (cents per ounce) of different boxes of laundry soap. Round the unit price to the nearest penny. Each box will be described by an entry of the form:

pounds	ounces	price
5	0	125

This box of soap has a rounded unit price of 2 cents per ounce. Make up about 10 data entries describing soap boxes; if you like, use real examples from a supermarket. You are to precede these entries with one data entry containing a single integer giving the number of soap box entries. Do not use a dummy entry to mark the end of the data. Output a nicely labeled table giving weights, prices in cents, and unit costs. Answer the following questions:

(a)   What would your program do if the above example data entry were mistyped as

50   125

(b)   Would it be possible to make your program "smart enough" to detect some kinds of improper data? How or why not?

Chapter 7

STRUCTURING CONTROL FLOW

In the last chapter we introduced the two kinds of statements that cause an alteration from the linear flow of control in a program. One kind caused looping, the counted FOR, the WHILE...DO and the REPEAT...UNTIL; the other caused branching, or selective execution, the IF...THEN...ELSE and the CASE statement. Learning to handle these two kinds of instructions is absolutely essential to programming. And learning to handle them in a systematic way is essential to structured programming.

BASIC STRUCTURE OF LOOPS

It is hard to appreciate, when you first learn a concept like loops, that all loops are basically the same. They consist of a sequence of statements in the program that:

1. Initialize the values of certain variables that are to be used in the loop. These consist of assigning values to

    (a) variables that appear in the condition of a WHILE condition DO or a REPEAT...UNTIL condition.

    (b) variables that appear in the body of the loop on the right-hand side of assignment statements.

2. Indicate that a loop is to commence. If it is a WHILE...DO give the condition that is to control the number of repetitions. If it is a counted FOR loop give the number of repetitions. If it is a REPEAT...UNTIL loop the control on the number of repetitions is not given until the end of the loop body. Each of the three types of loops has a control phrase that determines the number of repetitions.

(a) A counted loop's repetition is controlled by the control phrase after the FOR, for example

FOR I:=1 TO 20 DO

(b) In the conditional WHILE...DO loop, the control phrase is, for example

WHILE I <= 20 DO

The condition should contain at least one variable.

(c) In the conditional REPEAT...UNTIL loop the control phrase is at the end of the loop, for example

UNTIL J>5

3.   Give the list of statements, called the body of the loop, that are to be executed each time the loop is repeated. Both the FOR and WHILE loops must have a single statement which may be BEGIN...END as the body. If the loop is a conditional loop, then within the body of the loop there must be some statements that assign new values to the variables appearing in the condition. Usually there is only one variable and its value may be changed by either

   (a)   an assignment statement or

   (b)   a READ statement.

4.   At the end of the loop, control is returned to the beginning.

5.   Give the next statement to be executed once the looping has been carried out the required numbers of times. Control goes from the beginning of the loop to this statement when

   (a)   the condition of the WHILE is false or

   (b)   the value of the index controlling the counted FOR loop has already reached the value indicated after the word TO.

Control passes directly from the end of a REPEAT...UNTIL loop to the next statement when the condition after the UNTIL is true.

It is to be noted very carefully that there is no *exit* from the loop, except from one fixed location (either the beginning or the end depending on the kind of loop it is), and this exit *always* goes to the statement immediately after the end of the loop. It is never possible to go somewhere else in a program. In this way we keep track of control flow and never have the possibility of getting confused about its path. The complete language Pascal offers a statement for altering the path of control called the GOTO statement. It permits you to send control to statements with "labels" in your program. Since computer scientists came to recognize the importance of proper structuring in a program, the freedom offered by the GOTO statement has been recognized as not in keeping with the idea of structures in control flow. For this reason we will *never* use it. It is *not* a member of any subset of PS/k. You will find that a Standard Pascal compiler will not prevent you from using a GOTO. Even so, you should not use it.

For many good programmers it has long become a habit to restrict the use of the GOTO to that of leaving the body of a loop somewhere in the middle and exiting to the statement following the end of the loop. An exit inside the body is usually related to a second condition. This second condition can be incorporated in the condition following the WHILE or UNTIL by having a compound condition. We will look at examples of this later in the chapter.

FLOW CHARTS

A flow chart is a diagram made up of boxes of various shapes, rectangular, circular, diamond, and so on, connected by lines with directional arrows on the lines. The boxes contain a description of the statements of a program and the directed lines indicate the flow of control among the statements. The main purpose of drawing a flow chart is to exhibit the flow of control clearly, so that it is evident both to the programmer and to a reader who might want to alter the program.

A method of programming that preceded the present method of structured programming found that drawing a flow chart helped in the programming process. It was suggested that a first step in writing any program was to draw a flow chart. It was a way of controlling complexity.

When we limit ourselves to the two standard forms of altering control flow, the loop and the selection constructs, there is little need to draw these flow charts. In a sense, especially if it is properly paragraphed, the program is its own flow chart; it is built of completely standard building blocks.

Perhaps it would be helpful to show what the flow charts of our two basic building blocks would be like in case you wanted to draw a flow chart for your whole program.

Here is the flow chart for an IF...THEN...ELSE statement.

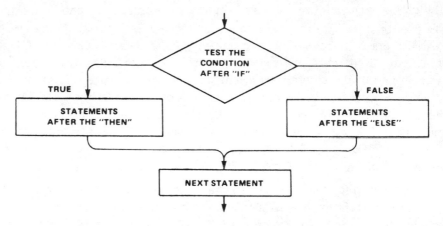

FLOW CHART FOR IF...THEN...ELSE

The flow chart for a CASE statement would be similar except that there are more than two alternative paths. For the WHILE loop that we described, the flow chart would be as shown. The various phases are numbered.

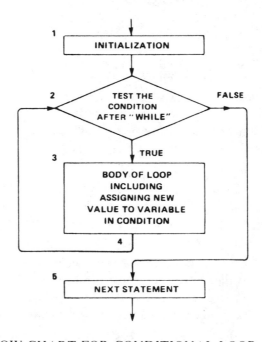

FLOW CHART FOR CONDITIONAL LOOP

The flow chart for the counted FOR would be similar except that box 2 would initialize the index to its first value, increment it by the required amount and then test to see if the loop has been executed the specified number of times. A REPEAT...UNTIL loop is similar also.

With these basic diagrams and the ordinary straight line sequence representing the compound statement, flow charts for all PS/k programs can be built. In a way, because they are so obviously related to the program, they do not really need to be drawn. Any one of the rectangular boxes in these diagrams may be replaced by a sequence of rectangular boxes, or either one of the two basic diagrams themselves. An important thing to notice is that into each of these elementary blocks there is a single entrance and, from each, a single exit. This is critical to maintaining good structure.

PROBLEMS WITH LOOPS

Certain errors are very common with loops. With counted loops the likelihood of errors is much smaller, since the initialization and alteration of the index are done by the FOR itself. You can, however, forget to initialize a variable that is used in the body of the loop. Another problem comes if by chance the index that is used to count the loop is altered in the loop body. This is strictly illegal in Pascal. The letters I, J, and K are often used as indexes, and you must be careful not to use them again before a previous use is finished. This can happen when one FOR loop is nested inside another and the index I is used by mistake for both loops. You might write

FOR I:=1 TO N DO

and forget to initialize N. You should trace the execution of all loops by hand to see if the first iteration is working correctly. Then you should also check the last one.

NESTED LOOPS

We will now look at the more complicated loops. In the following example, subsidiary output has been inserted for testing purposes. The program sums the marks of students in 4 subjects and outputs these with the average, to the nearest mark. There are a number of lines of entries, one for each student. An entry with the total number of students precedes the mark entries. We will test the program first using only three students to see if it is working.

```
PROGRAM CLASS;
    (* A SAMPLE PROGRAM WITH NESTED LOOPS *)
    VAR NUMBEROFSTUDENTS,I,J,SUM,AVERAGE,
        MARK,STUDENTNUMBER: INTEGER;
    BEGIN
        WRITE('NUMBER OF STUDENTS=');
        READLN(NUMBEROFSTUDENTS);
        WRITELN('STUDENT',' MARK1',' MARK2',' MARK3',
            ' MARK4',' AVERAGE');
        FOR I:=1 TO NUMBEROFSTUDENTS DO
            BEGIN
                SUM:=0;
                READ(STUDENTNUMBER);
                FOR J:=1 TO 4 DO
                    BEGIN
                        READ(MARK);
                        SUM:=SUM+MARK
                    END;
                AVERAGE:=ROUND(SUM/4);
                WRITELN(AVERAGE:6)
            END
    END.
```

Here is the display:

NUMBER OF STUDENTS=3

STUDENT	MARK1	MARK2	MARK3	MARK4	AVERAGE
205	55	60	65	70	63
208	83	81	96	90	88
209	72	68	78	81	75

You will notice that when we have one FOR loop nested inside another we use two levels of indentation to indicate the control structure.

AN EXAMPLE PROGRAM

We will illustrate some details about loops with another program. Like some of our previous examples, this program outputs a zigzag. However, our new program is smarter than the old ones in that it can output different sizes of and numbers of zigs and zags, depending on the input data.

```
PROGRAM PICKZIG;
    VAR MAJOR,MINOR,
          HOWMANY,HOWBIG: INTEGER;
    BEGIN
        WRITELN('HOW MANY,HOW BIG');
        READLN(HOWMANY,HOWBIG);
        FOR MAJOR:=1 TO HOWMANY DO
            BEGIN
                WRITELN(' ****');
                FOR MINOR:=1 TO HOWBIG DO
                    WRITELN(' *');
                WRITELN(' ****');
                FOR MINOR:=1 TO HOWBIG DO
                    WRITELN('    *')
            END
    END.
```

This program, given the data values 3 and 2 for HOWMANY and HOWBIG, outputs the following pattern. We have shown in parentheses values of MAJOR and MINOR during the output of each of the single-star lines.

	(MAJOR,MINOR)
`****`	
`*`	(1,1)
`*`	(1,2)
`****`	
`*`	(1,1)
`*`	(1,2)
`****`	
`*`	(2,1)
`*`	(2,2)
`****`	
`*`	(2,1)
`*`	(2,2)
`****`	
`*`	(3,1)
`*`	(3,2)
`****`	
`*`	(3,1)
`*`	(3,2)

The first data value, 3, caused the sub-pattern

```
****
*
*
****
 *
 *
```

to be displayed three times. The second data value, 2, was used in determining the height of this sub-pattern.

As you can see in the program, there are two separate loops inside the
main FOR loop. Both of these loops use the variable MINOR as a counting
variable. There is no difficulty using MINOR in this way. Each time one
of these two loops is entered, MINOR is set back to have the value 1.

We can change the pattern displayed by changing the data entries.
For example, the following pattern is displayed for data values 1 and 1.

(MAJOR,MINOR)

```
****
*
****
 *
```

(1,1)

(1,1)

In this case, the loops are each executed only once.

We can shrink the pattern down to nothing at all by using the data
values 0 and 1. When the first data value is zero, then the limit value
HOWMANY is also zero and is less than MAJOR's starting value 1. As a
result, the main loop is executed zero times. Since the main loop is not
executed, the second data value, 1, has no effect. We could supply data
values 0 and 2 instead of 0 and 1 and would still get the same pattern,
namely, no pattern at all.

Now let us switch things around so the second data value is zero, but
the first is not. For data values 2 and 0, the pattern becomes

```
****
****
****
****
```

In this case the main loop is executed twice, but the two inside loops were
each executed zero times.

The data values were used by this program to determine the pattern
to output. You could write other programs which output different pictures
for different data.

LOOPS WITH MULTIPLE CONDITIONS

Sometimes we must terminate a loop if something happens that is unusual. One of the conditions controlling the loop is the standard one; the other is the unusual one. All loops with double-headed conditions must be WHILE...DO or REPEAT...UNTIL loops, since the counted loop does not allow for the possibility of a second condition. We have seen that compound conditions can be formed from two or more simple conditions using the AND and OR Boolean operators.

As an example, we will write a program to look for a certain number in a list of numbers that you enter. If you find it in the list, immediately output the position it occupies in the list; if it is not in the list, output NOT IN LIST. The list will be positive integers terminated by an end-of-file marker -1.

```
PROGRAM HUNT;
    VAR NUMBER,LISTNO,I: INTEGER;
    BEGIN
        WRITE('NUMBER YOU ARE LOOKING FOR=');
        READLN(NUMBER);
        WRITELN('START TYPING IN LIST;FINISH WITH -1');
        READ(LISTNO);
        I:=1;
        WHILE (LISTNO<>NUMBER) AND (LISTNO <> -1) DO
            BEGIN
                I:=I+1;
                READ(LISTNO)
            END;
        WRITELN;
        IF LISTNO=NUMBER THEN
            WRITELN('I=',I)
        ELSE
            WRITELN('NOT IN LIST')
    END.
```

Here is a sample display:

```
NUMBER YOU ARE LOOKING FOR=35
START TYPING IN LIST; FINISH WITH -1
12   16   25   35
I=4
```

Notice that in the body of the loop the variable LISTNO in the condition can be changed by the READ(LISTNO) statement; it is initialized outside the loop. Since an index I is required to give the position of the number in the list, it must be incremented in the statement I:=I+1 and initialized to 1 outside the loop.

IF STATEMENTS WITH MULTIPLE CONDITIONS

Just as the conditional loop can have multiple conditions, so also can IF statements. These can be used very effectively to avoid nesting of IF statements. Suppose you want to count people in a list who fall into a particular age group, say 18-65, as ADULTS. The following program will count the number in the category ADULT in the list. The list of ages is terminated by a -1.

```
PROGRAM WORKERS;
    CONST DUMMY=-1;
    VAR ADULT,AGE: INTEGER;
    BEGIN
        WRITELN('START TYPING LIST OF AGES; FINISH WITH -1');
        READ(AGE);
        ADULT:=0;
        WHILE AGE<>DUMMY DO
            BEGIN
                IF (AGE>=18) AND (AGE<=65) THEN
                    ADULT:=ADULT+1;
                READ(AGE)
            END;
        WRITELN;
        WRITELN('NUMBER OF ADULTS=',ADULT)
    END.
```

Here is a sample display:

```
START TYPING LIST OF AGES; FINISH WITH -1
16  25  31  12  28  29  69  -1
NUMBER OF ADULTS=4
```

The IF with the compound condition could have been replaced by the more awkward construction with a nested IF statement:

```
        IF AGE>=18 THEN
            IF AGE<=65 THEN
                ADULT:=ADULT+1;
```

but this is not advisable.

CHAPTER 7 SUMMARY

In this chapter we have taken a closer look at the loop and selection constructs. We discussed flow charts and the GOTO statement as they relate to the PS/k subset of Pascal. We presented more complex examples of loops and conditions. The following important terms were discussed.

Flow chart - a graphic representation of a program. A flow chart consists of boxes of various shapes interconnected by arrows indicating flow of control. PS/k programs can be represented by flow charts.

Exit from a loop - means stopping the execution of a loop. Exit from a WHILE...DO loop occurs at the beginning of the loop when the loop's condition is found to be false. Exit from a REPEAT...UNTIL loop occurs at the end of the loop when the condition is found to be true.

GOTO statement (not in PS/k) - transfers control to another part of a program. The GOTO statement is available in full Pascal and is sometimes used to exit from a loop by transferring control to the statement following the loop. Careless use of GOTO statements leads to complex program structures which are difficult to understand and to make correct.

Nested statements - means statements inside statements. For example, FOR loops can be nested inside FOR loops.

Multiple conditions - conditions which use the AND and OR Boolean operators.

CHAPTER 7 EXERCISES

We will base all the exercises for this chapter on the same problem, which we now describe. A meteorologist keeps records of the weather for each month as a table. The first line of the table gives the number of days of the month.

The following lines give the rainfall, low temperature, high temperature, and pollution count for each day of the month. For example, the data for a month could be as follows:

```
31
0    33   37   3
1.2  34   39   3
0    35   40   0.5
0    34   38   2
etc.
```

Each of the following exercises requires writing a program which reads one month's weather and answers some questions about the month's weather. To make things easier for you, answers for the first two exercises are given.

1. Find the first rainy day of the month. (The following program finds the required day and is a solution for this exercise.)

```
PROGRAM WETDAY;
    VAR RAIN,LOW,HIGH,POLLUTION: REAL;
        DAY,MONTHLENGTH: INTEGER;
    BEGIN
        WRITE('LENGTH OF MONTH=');
        READLN(MONTHLENGTH);
        WRITELN('RAIN':5,'LOW':10,'HIGH':10,'POLLUTION':15);
        DAY:=0;
        RAIN:=0;
        WHILE (RAIN=0) AND (DAY<MONTHLENGTH) DO
            BEGIN
                READLN(RAIN,LOW,HIGH,POLLUTION);
                DAY:=DAY+1
            END;
        IF RAIN>0 THEN
            WRITELN(' DAY ',DAY,' WAS RAINY')
        ELSE
            WRITELN(' NO RAINY DAYS')
    END.
```

2. See if the data entries for the days of the month are reasonable. Verify that the rainfall does not exceed 100 and is not negative. Verify that the temperature lies between -100 and 200 and that the high is at least as large as the low. Verify that the pollution count is neither above 25 nor below zero. (The following program validates the month's data and is a solution for this exercise.)

```
PROGRAM VERIFY;
    VAR RAIN,LOW,HIGH,POLLUTION: REAL;
        DAY,MONTHLENGTH: INTEGER;
    BEGIN
```

```
WRITE('LENGTH OF MONTH=');
READLN(MONTHLENGTH);
WRITELN('RAIN':5,'LOW':10,'HIGH':10,'POLLUTION':15);
FOR DAY:=1 TO MONTHLENGTH DO
    BEGIN
        READLN(RAIN,LOW,HIGH,POLLUTION);
        IF(RAIN<0)OR(RAIN>100)THEN
            WRITELN(' DAY ',DAY,'  WRONG RAIN:',RAIN:6:2);
        IF(LOW< -100)OR(LOW>HIGH)OR(HIGH>200)THEN
            WRITELN(' DAY ',DAY,
                ' WRONG TEMPERATURES:',LOW:6:2,HIGH:6:2);
        IF(POLLUTION<0)OR(POLLUTION>25)THEN
            WRITELN(' DAY ',DAY,
                ' HAS WRONG POLLUTION:',POLLUTION:6:2)
    END
END.
```

3. What was the warmest day of the month, based on the high?

4. What was the first rainy day having a high temperature above 38?

5. What were the days of the month with more than a 5-degree difference between the high and low temperatures?

6. What were the two warmest days of the month?

7. Did the pollution count ever exceed 5 on a day when the temperature stayed above 35?

8. What three consecutive days had the most total rainfall?

9. Was it true that every rainless day following a rainy day had a lower pollution count than the rainy day?

10. Using the first 10 days' data, "predict" the weather for the 11th day. Compare (either by hand or within the program) the prediction with the data for the 11th day.

Chapter 8

PS/4: ARRAYS

So far in our programming, each memory location for data had its own special name; each variable had a unique identifier. In this chapter we will introduce the idea that groups of data will share a common name and be differentiated from each other by numbering each one uniquely.

DECLARATION OF ARRAYS

Suppose, for example, that we had a list of 50 integers and we wanted the sum of all the numbers. Rather than giving each one of 50 memory locations holding the list a different name, we give the list, or array, a name, say NUMBER, and distinguish the various members of the array by giving each a unique *index*. The index is most often an integer. The first element in the array is called NUMBER[1], the second NUMBER[2] and so on up to NUMBER[50]. (Some computers do not have the square bracket symbols on the keyboard. For the Apple use CTRL-K for [and SHIFT-M for].) To declare such an array of variables we use the declaration

VAR NUMBER: ARRAY[1..50] OF INTEGER;

Each element of the array NUMBER is an INTEGER type variable. In the declaration, after the keyword ARRAY we give, in square brackets, the *range* of the index, namely from 1 to 50. Here is the program that reads 50 integers into the array, adds them up, and outputs the sum:

```
PROGRAM SUMLIST;
    VAR NUMBER: ARRAY[1..50] OF INTEGER;
        SUM,I: INTEGER;
    BEGIN
        WRITELN('TYPE IN 50 INTEGERS');
        FOR I:=1 TO 50 DO
            READ(NUMBER[I]);
        (* ADD NUMBERS *)
        READLN;
        SUM:=0;
        FOR I:= 1 TO 50 DO
            SUM:=SUM+NUMBER[I];
        WRITELN(SUM)
    END.
```

The declaration of the array NUMBER indicates that the index has a range from 1 to 50 and that the elements of the array are integers. In the FOR loops, reference to NUMBER[I] refers in turn to NUMBER[1], NUMBER[2], to NUMBER[50]. This is what makes the array such a powerful programming tool; we need not refer to each element separately in the program but only to the general element NUMBER[I].

In this example, it is not necessary to read all the numbers and then add them up; we did it that way just to show what is necessary for reading or summing a list. We could have written only one loop, combining the two operations.

```
WRITELN('TYPE IN 50 INTEGERS');
SUM:=0;
FOR I:=1 TO 50 DO
    BEGIN
        READ(NUMBER[I]);
        SUM:=SUM+NUMBER[I]
    END;
READLN;
WRITELN(SUM)
```

If reading and adding the numbers is all that is required we could do it without an array at all as in this program:

```
PROGRAM ADDUP;
    VAR NUMBER,SUM,I: INTEGER;
    BEGIN
        WRITELN('TYPE IN 50 INTEGERS');
        SUM:=0;
        FOR I:=1 TO 50 DO
            BEGIN
                READ(NUMBER);
                SUM:=SUM+NUMBER
            END;
        READLN;
        WRITELN(SUM)
    END.
```

We should not use an array if we do not need one.

Usually, there is more to be done that requires having the list still present. For instance we could think of dividing each member of a list by the sum and multiplying by 100 before we wrote them out. This would express each entry as a percentage of the group. To do this we would add these statements to our original program:

```
    FOR I:=1 TO 50 DO
        BEGIN
            NUMBER[I]:=ROUND(NUMBER[I]*100/SUM);
            WRITELN(NUMBER[I])
        END;
```

In the FOR loop the statements with the index I result in each member of the list being operated on and changed to a percentage then displayed.

TWO-DIMENSIONAL ARRAYS

It is possible to have arrays that correspond to entries in a *table* rather than just a single list. For instance, a table of distances between 4 cities might be

	0	2	3	4
1	0	20	30	46
2	20	0	12	20
3	30	12	0	15
4	46	20	15	0

We could call this array DISTANCE. DISTANCE[1,4] is 46 and DIS-
TANCE[3,4] is 15. The first number in the parentheses refers to the row
in the table, the second to the column. You can see that DISTANCE[3,1]
has the same value as DISTANCE[1,3]; the table is symmetric, in this case,
about the diagonal line running from top left to bottom right. All entries
on this diagonal are zero; the distance from a city to itself is zero.

   We must learn how to declare such a two-dimensional array. All that
is necessary is to write

   VAR DISTANCE: ARRAY[1..4,1..4] OF INTEGER;

Here, in square brackets after the keyword ARRAY, we have the ranges of
two indexes separated by a comma. The first index is the number of rows,
the second the number of columns. As an example (a useless one as it
stands), we will read in this table and store it in the memory. On each
input line we will type one row of the data:

```
PROGRAM READTABLE;
    VAR DISTANCE: ARRAY[1..4,1..4] OF INTEGER;
        I,J: INTEGER;
    BEGIN
        WRITELN('TYPE IN 4 BY 4 TABLE');
        WRITELN('PLACE A ROW ON EACH LINE');
        FOR I:=1 TO 4 DO
            BEGIN
                FOR J:=1 TO 4 DO
                    READ(DISTANCE[I,J]);
                READLN
            END
    END.
```

In this program there is one FOR loop nested inside another. We have
used two indexes, I to give the row number, J to give the column number.
When I=1 the inner loop has J go from 1 to 4. This means the elements
of the array on the first line are stored in these variables:

DISTANCE[1,1] DISTANCE[1,2] DISTANCE[1,3] DISTANCE[1,4]

These are the elements in row 1 of the table. In giving the name of each
element of a two-dimensional array you write, in square brackets separated
by a comma, the values of the two indexes. It is just customary to think of
a table in such a way that the first index is the row number, the second the
column number. Since our table is symmetric it does not matter if we
interchange rows and columns, because we get exactly the same result. For

most tables it *does* matter, and you must be careful. A table like this is called a *matrix* by mathematicians.

AN EXAMPLE PROGRAM

We will illustrate the use of two-dimensional arrays in terms of a set of data collected by a consumers' group. This group has been alarmed about the recent rapid rise in price of processed wallalumps. They sampled grocery store prices of processed wallalumps on a monthly basis throughout 1978, 1979 and 1980 and observed that prices varied from 75 cents to 155 cents as the following table shows:

MONTH

	1	2	3	4	5	6	7	8	9	10	11	12
1978	87	89	89	89	85	85	85	75	90	100	100	100
1979	95	95	95	95	90	90	85	90	100	110	120	110
1980	110	110	115	115	115	100	100	110	120	140	145	155

These 36 prices were made available and a program was needed to analyze the price changes.

The following program reads in the data and determines the average price for 1979:

```
PROGRAM COST;
    VAR PRICE: ARRAY[1978..1980, 1..12] OF INTEGER;
      MONTH,YEAR,TOTAL: INTEGER;
    BEGIN
        WRITELN('TYPE IN TABLE');
        FOR YEAR:=1978 TO 1980 DO
          FOR MONTH:=1 TO 12 DO
            READ(PRICE[YEAR,MONTH]);
        (* DETERMINE THE AVERAGE PRICE IN 1979 *)
        READLN;
        TOTAL:=0;
        FOR MONTH:=1 TO 12 DO
            TOTAL:=TOTAL+PRICE[1979,MONTH];
        WRITELN(' AVERAGE 1979 PRICE: ', ROUND(TOTAL/12))
        (* ADD STATEMENTS TO CALCULATE OTHER AVERAGES *)
    END.
```

In this program, the array PRICE is declared so it can have a first index which can range from 1978 to 1980 and a second index which can range from 1 to 12. Effectively, the PRICE array is a table in which entries can be looked up by month and year. The first part of the program uses the data to fill up the PRICE array. The second part of the program sums up the prices for each month during 1979 and calculates the average 1979 price.

We could as well calculate the average price for a particular month. For example, the following calculates the average price in February:

```
TOTAL:=0;
FOR YEAR:=1978 TO 1980 DO
    TOTAL:=TOTAL+PRICE[YEAR,2];
WRITELN(' AVERAGE FEB. PRICE: ',ROUND(TOTAL/3));
```

We could calculate the average price for the entire three-year period as follows.

```
TOTAL:=0;
FOR YEAR:=1978 TO 1980 DO
    FOR MONTH:=1 TO 12 DO
        TOTAL:=TOTAL+PRICE[YEAR,MONTH];
WRITELN(' OVERALL AVERAGE: ',ROUND(TOTAL/36));
```

This example has illustrated the use of two-dimensional arrays. It is possible to use arrays with three and more dimensions. For example, our consumers' group might want to record prices for five grades of processed wallalumps (that makes one dimension), for three years (that makes two dimensions), for each month (that makes three dimensions). The array declaration

VAR PRICE: ARRAY[1..5, 1978..1980, 1..12] OF INTEGER;

would set up a table to hold all this data.

SUBRANGE TYPES

When we are programming we often find that we are using a particular limited set of values. In the wallalump example, we were interested in the values 1978, 1979 and 1980, because those are the years of the survey. The variable YEAR is declared as an INTEGER, but it only holds the values 1978 to 1980. The first index of the PRICE array is restricted to be 1978 to 1980. We say 1978 to 1980 is a *subrange* of the integers and in Pascal we write this subrange as 1978..1980. The two dots can be read as "to".

Instead of declaring YEAR to be an INTEGER, we could be more precise and declare it as a subrange. The declaration becomes

    VAR PRICE: ARRAY[1978..1980, 1..12] OF INTEGER;
        MONTH: 1..12;
        YEAR: 1978..1980;
        TOTAL: INTEGER;

As you can see MONTH has been declared to have only values 1 to 12. We call 1..12 a *subrange type*; it is a subset of the type called INTEGER.

This change in the declaration does not effect the program, it still calculates and outputs the same thing. But the new declaration is better than the old because it tells someone reading the program a lot about the MONTH and YEAR variables. Without looking beyond the declaration we know the small set of values that will be given to the two variables. This means it is easier to read and understand the program; when programs start getting long and complex, it is important to keep them as understandable as possible. Besides helping the reader, the new declaration may help the compiler to do a better job in translating the program; since it knows more about MONTH and YEAR, it may be able to produce a faster or smaller machine language program from the Pascal program. And when we use ranges the computer can help us locate errors; for example, if YEAR has a range of 1978..1980 but is accidently assigned the value 93482, the computer can warn us of the problem.

We do not declare TOTAL to be a subrange because we do not know much about its values. The prices are read from the data and do not fit neatly into subranges, like the twelve months of the year do.

For this Pascal subset, PS/4, each array index must be an integer subrange, such as 1..12. In the next subset we will see that there are subranges of other types that can be an array index, for example, 'A'..'D', means the subrange of characters that are 'A','B','C', and 'D'.

NAMED TYPES

You probably noticed that the declaration of the PRICE array contains the same subranges 1978..1980 and 1..12 used for YEAR and MONTH. Rather than repeating these subrange types, we can give them names.

    TYPE MONTHTYPE=1..12;
         YEARSPAN=1978..1980;
    VAR PRICE: ARRAY[YEARSPAN,MONTHTYPE] OF INTEGER;
        MONTH: MONTHTYPE;
        YEAR: YEARSPAN;
        TOTAL: INTEGER;

MONTHTYPE and YEARSPAN are *named types*. It is useful to name a type, such as a subrange, when it will be used in many declarations. This small example does not have very many declarations, but you can see the idea.

In general any type can be given a name and this type name can be used in following declarations. For example, we could give a name to the type ARRAY[YEARSPAN,MONTHTYPE] OF INTEGER and then declare PRICE using this type name.

In a Pascal program we give declarations in this order: the named constants, the named types and then the variables. For example, here are our declarations again, this time with names given to the beginning and ending years.

```
CONST FIRSTYEAR=1978;
      LASTYEAR=1980;
TYPE MONTHTYPE=1..12;
      YEARSPAN= FIRSTYEAR..LASTYEAR;
VAR ..(as before)..
```

Suppose we modify our program to use FIRSTYEAR where it uses 1978, LASTYEAR where it uses 1980, LASTYEAR-FIRSTYEAR+1 where it uses 3 and 12*(LASTYEAR-FIRSTYEAR+1) where it uses 36. Our program still works as before. But now it can be easily changed to handle another year's data, by simply changing the definition of LASTYEAR to

```
LASTYEAR=1981;
```

This sort of flexibility is important because it makes it easier to keep programs up to date.

ARRAYS OF ARRAYS

Pascal allows us to have arrays of any type including INTEGER and REAL. Since any array itself is a type, we can have an array whose parts are another array. This sounds confusing but an example should make it clear. If we have a year's data, say month by month prices, then we can place these in an array:

```
TYPE YEARSDATA=ARRAY[1..12] OF INTEGER;
VAR THISYEAR: YEARSDATA;
```

The twelve prices for one year can be recorded in the THISYEAR array. But if we are interested in three years, we can use

```
TYPE YEARSDATA=ARRAY[1..12] OF INTEGER;
VAR PERIOD: ARRAY[1978..1980] OF YEARSDATA;
```

PERIOD contains all the data for the three years and PERIOD[1979] contains the data just for 1979. The data for February 1979 is held in PERIOD[1979][2]. This is equivalent to our old variable called PRICE where the same data was in PRICE[1979,2]. In the case of PERIOD[1979][2] we use the first index [1979] to pick a year's array of data and the second [2] to pick a month within the year. With PRICE[1979,2] we choose the year and month at the same time with the index pair [1979,2].

The only advantage of using the PERIOD array instead of PRICE is that with PERIOD we can deal with an entire year at a time. Pascal allows arrays to be assigned, so if we want to set the prices in 1980 to be the same as those in 1979, we can change all 12 month values by writing the assignment

PERIOD[1980]:=PERIOD[1979];

With PRICE we would have to write a loop to copy the 12 values one at a time. Although arrays can be assigned, they cannot be compared, so we are *not* allowed to write PERIOD[1978]=PERIOD[1979] in a condition to test if the 1978 prices are the same month by month, as the 1979 prices.

ARRAYS AS DATA STRUCTURES

We have spoken of structured programming and shown how control flow is structured in a program. Now we can speak of the structure of data. Giving variables identifiers that are meaningful has been the only way we could systematize data so far. But with arrays we find that data can be structured or organized into one-dimensional forms called lists, or two-dimensional forms called tables. We can use even higher-dimensional arrays when we need them.

When we approach a problem and want to solve it by creating a computer program we must decide on the data structures we will use. We must decide in particular whether or not we need to establish arrays for any of the data, or whether single variables will serve us well enough.

Arrays will be useful whenever we must store groups of similar pieces of information. They are not necessary when small amounts of information come in, are processed, and then go out.

OTHER DATA STRUCTURES

Just so that you do not think that single variables and arrays are the only kind of data structures we can have, we will mention a few others.

One common structure is the *tree* structure. The easiest way to think of a tree is to imagine a family tree. At the risk of being called chauvinists we will show only the male members in the tree and talk of fathers and sons. This keeps it simple.

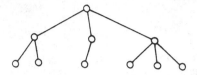

TREE STRUCTURE

The diagram shows a man with three sons. The first son has two sons, the second one son, the third three. The grandfather is the *root* of the tree. The tree is of course growing upside down. The lines joining the relatives are called *branches*; the people themselves are *nodes*.

The data we might store could be the names of the people, and the tree structure would have to be stored also. The way it is done is to have *links* or *pointers* stored with the data to give the structure. Each father entry requires a link to each of his sons.

A list can also be arranged with elements and links instead of in an array. This means that some of the information stored is used to describe the data structure and some to give the data. With arrays, the structure is given by the fact that one element follows right next to the preceding element. It does not need a link.

Later we will be investigating other data structures in detail. Often we will use the array structures to implement structures like trees or lists with links from one element to another.

CHAPTER 8 SUMMARY

This chapter has introduced array variables, which are used for manipulating quantities of similar data. An array is made up of a number of elements, each of which acts as a simple, non-array variable. The following terms are used in describing arrays and their uses.

Array declaration - sets aside memory space for an array. For example, the declaration

VAR COST: ARRAY[1..4] OF REAL;

sets aside space for the array elements COST[1], COST[2],

COST[3], and COST[4]. Each of these elements can be used like a simple, non-array REAL variable.

Array index (sometimes called array subscript) - used to designate a particular element of an array. For example, in COST[I], the variable I is an array index. An array index can be any arithmetic expression that has an integer value.

Array bounds - the range over which array indexes may vary. For example, given the declaration

   VAR PRICE:ARRAY[1978..1980, 1..12] OF INTEGER;

an array element of PRICE can be specified by PRICE[Y,M], where M can range from 1 to 12 and Y can range from 1978 to 1980.

Out-of-bounds index - an array index which is outside the bounds specified in the array's declaration. This is an error.

Subrange type - a type such as 1978..1980 that specifies a subrange of another type. 1978..1980 is a subrange of the type INTEGER.

Named type - any type, for example, 1..12, can be given a name and then used in declarations. INTEGER, REAL and BOOLEAN are predeclared named types.

Multiply-dimensioned arrays - arrays requiring more than one index, such as the PRICE array given above.

Arrays of arrays - these are similar to multidimensioned arrays. Each index is written in its own square bracket, for example PERIOD[1978][2] rather than PRICE[1978,2].

CHAPTER 8 EXERCISES

1. Write a program that will read in the length of a one-dimensional array then read the array itself. It is then to replace each element of the array by the sum of all elements up to and including that element and then output the resulting array.

2. Set the values of the elements of a two-dimensional integer array that has the same number of rows as columns so that the diagonal elements are all +1 and the off-diagonal elements -1. Read in an integer giving the size of a subset of the array and output the subset array one row to a line. You should limit the size to a maximum of 8x8.

3. In mathematics, two one-dimensional arrays of equal length may be multiplied together. The product (sometimes called the scalar product

of two vectors) is the sum of the products of corresponding elements in the two arrays. If one array is named A and the other B then the scalar product is the sum for I going from 1 to the length of the array of terms of the form

A[I]*B[I]

Write a program to find the scalar product of two one-dimensional arrays. Read in the length of the arrays as a variable.

4. In mathematics, two matrices may be multiplied together if the number of columns of the first matrix is equal to the number of rows of the second. The product is a matrix. If we have a matrix A with L rows and M columns and a matrix B with M rows and N columns the elements of the product matrix C are given by the relation

C[I,J] = sum for K going from 1 to M of A[I,K]*B[K,J]

Write a program that reads values of L,M,N then reads in matrices A and B computes matrix C and outputs it out. Limit the values of L,M, and N to be 8 or less and use two-dimensional integer arrays to represent the matrices.

Chapter 9

PS/5: ALPHABETIC INFORMATION HANDLING

We have said that computers can handle alphabetic information as well as perform numerical calculations. But most of the emphasis so far, except for labeling our tables of numerical output, has had very little to do with alphabetic data handling. It is true that we have been dealing with words, like identifiers, but these have been in the Pascal programs rather than being handled by them as data. We have, in fact, never had anything but numbers, either real or integer, entered on the keyboard during the execution of a program. In this chapter we will learn how to read in alphabetic data from the keyboard, how to move it from one place to another in the memory of the computer, how to join different pieces of information together, and how to separate out a part of a larger piece of information.

CHARACTER STRINGS

The facilities for handling alphabetic information in standard Pascal are somewhat limited. A number of extensions are included in UCSD Pascal. We will describe these extensions *after* we present the methods of standard Pascal. Then you will appreciate how they simplify your programs. The term "alphabetic information" that we used in the last section is really not general enough to describe what we will learn to handle in this subset of Pascal. We will be able to handle what you normally mean by alphabetic information, things like people's names -

SARAH MARIE WOOD

but we also want to handle things like street addresses. For example, an address like

2156 CYPRESS AVENUE

includes digits as well as letters of the alphabet. This kind of information we call *alphanumeric* or *alphameric* for short. But that is not all; we want to handle any kind of English text with words, numbers, and punctuation marks, like commas, semicolons, and question marks.

THIS TEXT CONTAINS 7 WORDS; DOESN'T IT?

We have defined a word as being a string of one or more characters preceded and followed by a blank or a punctuation mark, other than an apostrophe. This definition makes 7 a word.

The information we want to handle is any string of characters that may be letters, digits, punctuations marks or blanks. We tend to think of a blank as being not a character, but a string of blanks is quite different from a string with no characters at all. We call the special string with no characters at all a *null string*. We often write b for the blank character so that you can count how many blank characters are in a string.

HEREbISbAbCHARACTERbSTRINGbSHOWINGbTHEbBLANKS

In Chapter 3 we introduced the characters in the Pascal language. In that listing there are more than we have referred to so far in this chapter. The list of special characters includes symbols we need for arithmetic operations +, -, /, *, as well as for making comparisons in logical conditions >, <, =. Then often we used parentheses of two kinds, not to mention the characters like ; : and , .

One reason we want to be able to handle strings of any of these characters is to be able to work with Pascal programs themselves as data. This is the kind of job a compiler must do, and a programming language like Pascal should be suitable for writing a compiler program.

READING AND OUTPUTTING CHARACTERS

We can use variables that hold characters in much the same way as we have been using variables to hold integer and real numbers. If we need to store a letter, which is a character, we can make the declaration

VAR LETTER: CHAR;

CHAR is a new type. We can put the value which is letter H into the LETTER variable by the assignment statement

LETTER:='H';

We now write out the value of LETTER by

WRITE(LETTER);

This causes the 'H' to be output, without the quotation marks of course. Here is a program that outputs HI.

```
PROGRAM FRIENDLY;
   VAR LETTER: CHAR;
   BEGIN
      LETTER:='H';
      WRITE(LETTER);
      LETTER:='I';
      WRITE(LETTER)
   END.
```

This is a rather clumsy way to do the same thing that is done by the statement WRITE('HI'). But CHAR variables provide us with the ability to read and manipulate character values.

We can read in the data character by character and output it. We can use READ(LETTER) to read the next character in the data into LETTER. Reading a character is not like reading a number in that blanks are not automatically skipped. This is because a blank is a legitimate character just like other characters such as Q and *.

Here is a program that reads characters until it finds a period; then it outputs STOP TYPING.

```
PROGRAM STOP;
   VAR CHARVALUE: CHAR;
   BEGIN
      REPEAT
         READ(CHARVALUE)
      UNTIL CHARVALUE='.';
      WRITELN;
      WRITELN('STOP TYPING')
   END.
```

Here is a sample display:

HOW DO YOU DO.
STOP TYPING

Notice that the characters such as blank and period are treated the same way as letters. In the UNTIL test, CHARVALUE is compared to period. A single character, such as 'Q' or '.' can be assigned or compared to a CHAR variable. But a string with more that one character, such as 'ABC' would not be allowed.

Now if you think about it, HOW DO YOU DO is really a question and deserves a question mark at the end not a period. So we will modify our program to output the same line with a question mark instead of outputting STOP TYPING. As well, we will count the number of characters in the input line (including the spaces and the period) and output its length.

```
(* OUTPUT LINE THEN CHANGE PERIOD TO '?' *)
PROGRAM QUESTION;
    VAR LINE: ARRAY[1..80] OF CHAR;
        LENGTH,I: 0..80;
    BEGIN
        LENGTH:=0;
        REPEAT (* READ INTO LINE ARRAY *)
            LENGTH:=LENGTH+1;
            READ(LINE[LENGTH])
        UNTIL LINE[LENGTH]='.';
        WRITELN;
        LINE[LENGTH]:='?'; (* MAKE QUESTION *)
        FOR I:=1 TO LENGTH DO
            WRITE(LINE[I]);
        WRITELN; (* FINISH LINE *)
        WRITELN('THE LENGTH WAS',LENGTH:4)
    END.
```

As you can see, this program does more things than the first version did. This one displays.

HOW DO YOU DO.
HOW DO YOU DO?
THE LENGTH WAS 14

We read all the characters into an array so that we can output them with the period changed to a question mark. The program shows how an array of characters can be used to hold a line of text. We have assumed that the line is at most 80 characters long. Often we have a string of characters stored in an array with a separate variable, LENGTH in this case, to keep track of how many characters are of interest. Notice that we used WRITELN rather than READLN after the period has been read. If we had used READLN, you would have had to press the return key before any further action took place on the screen.

READING LINES

In the last example we were able to find the end of the string of characters because it ended with a period. But usually there is not a predictable character at the end of a line. If we knew the number of characters in the line of data, we could have our program count them to determine the end.

But we should avoid counting this way. Normally when the data is typed into a computer terminal, each line is ended when return is typed, and lines can be of varying lengths.

Pascal provides a way to determine if the end of the line has been reached, by EOLN, the end-of-line predeclared function. Usually EOLN is false, but becomes true when there are no more characters to be read on a line. Here we use it to read a line while counting the characters. Notice that the line has not been stored in an array so that no further processing of it can be done by the computer.

```
LENGTH:=0;
READ(CHARVALUE);
WHILE NOT EOLN DO
    BEGIN
        LENGTH:=LENGTH+1;
        READ(CHARVALUE)
    END;
WRITELN;
WRITELN('THE LENGTH WAS ',LENGTH)
```

This works even when there are zero characters on the line, which is the case when return is the first thing typed on the line. This is why we use the WHILE...DO loop more frequently than the REPEAT...UNTIL loop.

DETECTING END-OF-FILE

Now that we have Pascal statements to read a single line, we can enclose them in a loop to read a number of input data lines. This is done by pressing the end-of-file key (EOF) after the last line with no return.

```
(* READ THE DATA AND COUNT THE LINES *)
PROGRAM COPY;
    VAR LINECOUNT: INTEGER;
        CHARVALUE: CHAR;
    BEGIN
        LINECOUNT:=0;
        WHILE NOT EOF DO
            BEGIN
                LINECOUNT:=LINECOUNT+1;
                WHILE NOT EOLN DO
                    READ(CHARVALUE);
                READLN  (* GET READY TO READ NEXT LINE *)
            END;
        WRITELN;
        WRITELN(LINECOUNT,' LINES READ')
    END.
```

Here is a sample display:

MAN IS NATURALLY CREDULOUS AND INCREDULOUS,
TIMID AND RASH. (BLAISE PASCAL 1660)
2 LINES READ

We have used a new Pascal feature in this example, EOF. EOF is a prede-clared function that is much like EOLN, but tells when the end-of-file has been reached. Usually EOF is false, but becomes true when you press the EOF character on the keyboard. (On the Apple this is CTRL-C.)

READLN is used when we want to begin reading the next line of data. When EOLN becomes true, then READLN is called so the first char-acter of the next line can be read. If READLN were given when EOLN is not true, which means that there are more characters on the current data line, then READLN skips the rest of the characters on the present line and then goes to the next line.

USING EOF WHEN READING NUMBERS

Up to now, when we have read lists of numbers, we have detected the end of the list by either counting numbers or having a dummy number such as -1 at the end. Instead of using a dummy number, we can use EOF, but we have to be careful. This example is supposed to compute the sum of a list of numbers:

```
(* THIS DOES NOT WORK CORRECTLY *)
SUM:=0;
WHILE NOT EOF DO
   BEGIN
      READ(NUMBER);
      SUM:=SUM+NUMBER
   END;
```

The EOF test is not right because there may be blanks after the last number. If so, EOF remains false, because more characters (blanks) can be read, and we try to read another number. But there is no number to read.

We will assume that there is at least one number (not zero numbers); this simplifies the program. We also assume that there is a single number on each line and that you press the EOF character right after the last number. The EOF acts also as EOLN here.

```
(* READ AND SUM ONE OR MORE NUMBERS *)
SUM:=0;
REPEAT
    READLN(NUMBER);
    SUM:=SUM+NUMBER
UNTIL EOF
```

When READLN has parameters such as NUMBER, it first reads in the values, just like READ, and then skips to the beginning of the next data line. So READLN(NUMBER) is equivalent to READ(NUMBER) followed by READLN.

Since the last number is on the last data line, READLN for the last number skips any blanks following the number and causes EOF to become true.

You have to be careful when using READLN. For example, if there are three numbers on a line and READLN(NUMBER) reads the first one then the other two will be skipped. We could use READLN(N1,N2,N3) instead to correctly read the three numbers into N1, N2 and N3. Or we could equivalently use

```
READ(N1);
READ(N2);
READ(N3);
READLN
```

What all this means is that EOF can be used to detect the last number, but it is not as simple as we might hope. And when the list might contain zero numbers it is very tricky.

USING STRINGS OF CHARACTERS

We have seen how a line of data can be read a character at a time into the LINE variable declared by the type ARRAY[1..80] OF CHAR. Since arrays can be assigned, if we had another variable declared like LINE, we could assign one to the other, and move the whole string. But we cannot compare these arrays or output them except a character at a time. We can output the whole string of characters HELLO simply by using WRITE('HELLO'). But we do not yet have a way to output a whole string when it is in an array.

In standard Pascal we use *packed* arrays of characters when we want to compare or output the whole array, for example

```
PROGRAM AMICABLE;
    VAR GREETING: PACKED ARRAY[1..9] OF CHAR;
    BEGIN
        GREETING:=' GOOD-BY ';
        WRITELN(GREETING)
    END.
```

The literal string ' GOOD-BY ' is 9 characters long, including both blanks, so we can assign it to GREETING. We can use a packed array like an ordinary one. GREETING[1] holds a blank, GREETING[2] holds a G and so on. If we put the following statement before the WRITELN:

```
        GREETING[9]:='E';
```

then GOOD-BYE is output with an E on the end.

We are allowed to assign or compare a literal string such as ' GOOD-BY ' to a packed character array only if the number of characters is exactly the same, 9 in this case. Note that this literal string contains two blanks as well as a hyphen.

The range of a packed character array must begin with 1, as in 1..9, and must end with 2 or more.

COMPARISON OF STRINGS FOR RECOGNITION

To compare two strings in standard Pascal they should be of the same length and be stored as PACKED ARRAYs. We need to be able to compare one string with another for two purposes, to recognize them and to put them in order. To *recognize* a string we see if it is the same as some other string. String comparisons are made in Boolean conditions since their result is either true or false; the strings are the same or they are not. Here is a program that reads and repeats. Remember that to compare an array representing a string with a literal string the array must not only be the same length as the literal but be declared as a PACKED ARRAY since in fact literal strings are stored as packed arrays.

We will assume that each word we read has at most 10 characters and will chop any longer than that to 10.

```
(* READ AND REPEAT WORDS UNTIL 'STOP' IS FOUND *)
PROGRAM READING;
    CONST MAXLENGTH=10;
    VAR WORD: PACKED ARRAY[1..MAXLENGTH] OF CHAR;
        CH: CHAR;
        LENGTH: 0..MAXLENGTH;
        COUNT: INTEGER;
```

```
BEGIN
    COUNT:=0;
    REPEAT
        COUNT:=COUNT+1;
        LENGTH:=0;
        WHILE(NOT EOLN)AND(LENGTH<MAXLENGTH) DO
            BEGIN
                LENGTH:=LENGTH+1;
                READ(CH);
                WORD[LENGTH]:=CH
            END;
        READLN;
        WHILE LENGTH<MAXLENGTH DO
            BEGIN
                LENGTH:=LENGTH+1;
                WORD[LENGTH]:=' '
            END;
        WRITELN(WORD)
    UNTIL WORD='STOP      ';
    WRITELN(COUNT,' WORDS READ')
END.
```

The output might be:

SOUP
SOUP
SLOW
SLOW
SIP
SIP
STOP
STOP
4 WORDS READ

We had to put six blanks in the STOP to make it 10 characters long so we could compare it to WORD. Note that in UCSD Pascal we may not read a character into WORD[LENGTH] directly when WORD is a PACKED ARRAY. We can when it is not PACKED. This is why we need the intermediate variable CH. After reading each word we had to fill in the rest of the WORD array with blanks. Otherwise the WRITELN would output unpredictable characters to the right of each word, and the comparison with 'STOP   ' would not work. Notice that the word STOP itself is repeated before the word count is output.

This example shows that packed arrays of characters can be output and compared as a whole. But standard Pascal provides no way to read the whole array at once so we must do it a character at a time. We will do one more example in standard Pascal before introducing the UCSD extensions to standard Pascal that make string manipulation easier.

SEQUENCING STRINGS

String comparison can be used to sequence strings, to put them in order. Usually we speak of alphabetic order for alphabetic strings.

ABCDEFGHIJKLMNOPQRSTUVWXYZ

The alphabet and digits have the normal order among themselves: 0 comes before 9, A comes before Z. The operators > and < are used to compare the strings. In standard Pascal the two strings being compared must be of equal length. The following program reads in 10 names and outputs the one that is the last alphabetically. To do this we must be able to compare each string that is read in with the string that is presently the last alphabetically and replace the current final name if the latest one is greater alphabetically.

The names to be examined are entered one to a line starting at the beginning of the line.

```
(* OUTPUT ALPHABETICALLY LAST NAME IN DATA *)
PROGRAM LAST;
   CONST MAX=15;
      BLANKS='bbbbbbbbbbbbbbb';
      ALPHABETICFIRST='AAAAAAAAAAAAAAA';
   VAR NAME,FINAL: PACKED ARRAY[1..MAX] OF CHAR;
      CH: CHAR;
      LENGTH: 0..MAX;
   BEGIN
      FINAL:=ALPHABETICFIRST;
      WHILE NOT EOF DO
         BEGIN
            NAME:=BLANKS;
            LENGTH:=0;
            WHILE(NOT EOLN)AND(LENGTH<MAX) DO
               BEGIN
                  LENGTH:=LENGTH+1;
                  READ(CH);
                  NAME[LENGTH]:=CH
               END;
```

```
            READLN;
            IF NAME>FINAL THEN
                  FINAL:=NAME
         END;
      WRITELN('ALPHABETICALLY LAST IS: ',FINAL)
   END.
```

Here is the display (Note the EOF key is pressed after the last name in the input list):

GALLER
TSICHRITZIS
WORTMAN
GOTLIEB
ALPHABETICALLY LAST IS: WORTMAN

Notice the way that the blanks are placed in the array NAME before the characters are read in. This effectively pads the name read in, on the right with blanks, to bring it to the standard length of 15 characters.

USING UCSD PASCAL STRINGS

Because we often deal with strings of characters, standard Pascal has been extended in UCSD Pascal to make the manipulation of strings easier. A predeclared data type STRING is built into UCSD Pascal. This is similar to a user defined named data type prescribed by

TYPE STRING = PACKED ARRAY [0..80] OF CHAR

But, in addition, the string has a length that changes depending on what is stored in it. The length of the string is stored separately and can be accessed using a predeclared function LENGTH. Here is an example of the use of the STRING type. It reads a word and tells you how many letters are it.

```
PROGRAM WORDS;
   VAR WORD: STRING;
   BEGIN
      WRITELN('TYPE A WORD');
      READLN(WORD);
      WRITELN('THIS WORD HAS ',LENGTH(WORD),
         ' LETTERS')
   END.
```

Here is a display for this program:

TYPE A WORD
SICK
THIS WORD HAS 4 LETTERS

The type STRING is a PACKED ARRAY of 80 characters maximum length. This means that we can read any entire line into the variable WORD which is of type STRING. This saves a lot of problems but can only be used for input when the entire line of input is the value for a single variable.

We will rewrite the program for the alphabetically last name using the UCSD Pascal STRING type.

```
PROGRAM LAST;
    CONST ALPHABETICFIRST='AAAA';
    VAR NAME,FINAL:STRING;
    BEGIN
        FINAL:=ALPHABETICFIRST;
        WHILE NOT EOF DO
            BEGIN
                READLN(NAME);
                IF NAME>FINAL THEN
                    FINAL:=NAME
            END;
            WRITELN('ALPHABETICALLY LAST IS: ',FINAL)
    END.
```

The display is the same as before.

You will notice that the strings being compared by NAME>FINAL need not be of the same length. For the comparison the result is the same as it would be if the shorter of the two strings were padded with blanks. You can see that the predeclared STRING type in UCSD Pascal can simplify programs a lot.

Another advantage of using STRING type variables is that, as you type in the data, you can correct it provided you have not pressed return. To do this just use the backspace key and retype erroneous characters.

UCSD Pascal strings can be of any maximum length. For instance, if you wanted a maximum length of 20 characters instead of the normal 80 characters, use the data type STRING[20]. In entering data typed as STRING[20] you cannot backspace to correct once you have typed 20 characters. Also, any further characters that you may type on the same line, after the 20 but before the return, are ignored.

JOINING STRINGS TOGETHER

UCSD Pascal strings can be read in, stored, and output. But we can do more than that. We can perform certain operations on them.

The first of these operations is to join two strings together to make one longer string. The operation is called *concatenation* and to do this we use the predeclared function CONCAT. Here is an example of concatenation.

```
PROGRAM JOIN;
   VAR WORD1,WORD2:STRING;
   BEGIN
      WRITELN('TYPE IN TWO WORDS');
      READLN(WORD1);
      READLN(WORD2);
      WRITELN(CONCAT(WORD1,WORD2))
   END.
```

Here is a sample display:

```
TYPE IN TWO WORDS
UP
STAIRS
UPSTAIRS
```

Notice that each word input must be on a separate line and that the operation of concatenation joins the two strings into one string. If we had asked the program to output LENGTH(CONCAT(WORD1,WORD2)) it would have displayed 8.

Any number of strings may be concatenated at one time; just list them, separated by commas, in parentheses after the keyword CONCAT.

Here is a program using concatenation that has a loop in it:

```
PROGRAM BUILD;
   VAR STARS:STRING;
      I:INTEGER;
   BEGIN
      STARS:='';
      FOR I:=1 TO 25 DO
         BEGIN
            STARS:=CONCAT(STARS,'*');
            WRITELN(STARS)
         END
   END.
```

Here is the display:

```
*
*  *
*  *  *
*  *  *  *
```

etc. until there is a line of 25 asterisks.

In the program the string variable is initialized to the null string which is written as ''. Each time the loop is executed, an asterisk is concatenated on to the right-hand end of the string.

SELECTING PARTS OF STRINGS

It is possible using the built-in function COPY to select parts of strings. We call a part of a string a *substring*. For example, the statement:

        WRITELN(COPY('MILLION',2,3));

would result in the output

ILL

The substring ILL is copied from the string MILLION by starting at the 2nd character and going for 3 characters. The general form of the function is

        COPY(string, starting position, length of substring)

Here is another example:

        WORD:='MILLION';
        WRITELN(COPY(WORD,4,LENGTH(WORD)-3));

The output for this is LION. Any attempt to copy more characters than there are in the string beginning at the starting position will cause an execution error. In this example if you wrote

        WRITELN(COPY(WORD,4,6));

you would get an error at execution time because there are only 4 characters in WORD starting with the 4th character and this is less than 6.

INSERTING AND DELETING WITH STRINGS

In addition to joining strings together, end to end, by the CONCAT built-in function, we can also insert strings into the middle of other strings using the INSERT *procedure*. A procedure in Pascal is equivalent to a statement, such as READ or WRITE. When a statement is executed, an operation is performed. The operation that is performed is described by the keyword, such as WRITE, and the objects upon which the operation is to be performed are called the *parameters* of the procedure. These parameters are listed in parentheses after the keyword. For example, in the statement:

WRITELN(X,Y,Z);

the parameters are X, Y, and Z. They tell the computer what is to be output.

To cause the INSERT procedure to be executed in a program we would include statements such as this:

WORD:='NO LUCK';
INSERT('SUCH ',WORD,4);
WRITELN(WORD);

Provided that the variable WORD was declared as a STRING variable, the output from this would be:

NO SUCH LUCK

The first parameter of the list in parentheses after the keyword INSERT gives the string that is to be inserted; the next parameter is the string into which the insertion is to occur (the destination) and the last parameter is the position in the destination string at which the insertion is to start. After the INSERT procedure is executed the destination string will have a new form, with the material inserted. Notice that in the example the string to be inserted has one blank after the characters SUCH but none before. In our example the insertion is to begin at the position of the 4th character, the L, in the destination string. If a 3 had been used here instead, the output would have been

NOSUCH LUCK

The general form of the INSERT statement is

INSERT(string to be inserted, destination string variable, position in destination string at which insertion is to start)

Notice that the destination string must be a variable; the string to be inserted may be a variable or a string constant. The position may be any expression that has an integer value. This value must not exceed the length of the destination string.

A similar procedure exists for deleting characters from strings. Its form is:

DELETE(destination string variable, start of deletion, number of characters to be deleted)

Here is a program segment using the DELETE procedure:

```
WORD:='SPLASH';
DELETE(WORD,LENGTH(WORD),1);
WRITELN(WORD);
```

The output for this example would be

SPLAS

You can see that the deletion is to remove the last letter. If you try to delete more characters than there are in the destination string an execution error will occur. For instance the statement:

```
DELETE(WORD,5,2);
```

if given after the previous statements would result in an error. The destination string WORD (whose value is now SPLAS) would have only 5 characters and 2 cannot be deleted starting with the 5th character.

PATTERN MATCHING WITH STRINGS

The built-in function POS allows you to locate the position of any substring (called the pattern) within another string (called the source). The value of the function is the position of the first character in the source string where a match with the pattern is found. If no match is found POS is given a zero value. For example, the value of

```
POS('IS','MISSISSIPPI')
```

is 2. The general form for this function is

```
POS(pattern string, source string)
```

Here is an example that uses the POS function along with the DELETE procedure and the COPY function. The idea is to split a line of text into words. We will input a line which has no punctuation marks and where words are separated by one blank.

```
PROGRAM SPLIT;
   VAR LINE:STRING;
      POSITION:INTEGER;
   BEGIN
      WRITELN('TYPE IN LINE OF TEXT');
      READLN(LINE);
      POSITION:=POS('b',LINE);
```

```
        WHILE POSITION<>0 DO
           BEGIN
              WRITELN(COPY(LINE,1,POSITION-1));
              DELETE(LINE,1,POSITION);
              POSITION:=POS('b',LINE)
           END;
        WRITELN(LINE)
     END.
```

Here is a sample display:

TYPE IN LINE OF TEXT
HERE IS THE LINE
HERE
IS
THE
LINE

Notice that the integer variable POSITION is used to avoid the computation of the POS function twice as it is needed by both COPY and DELETE. Notice the difference in the way you use functions like POS and COPY and procedures like DELETE and WRITELN.

HANDLING ARRAYS OF STRINGS

Suppose you wanted to read in a list of names of 50 students and output them out in reverse order, that is, last first. We would need to read in the entire list before we could begin the output. This means we must have a memory location for each name. We must be able to reserve this space by a declaration. Suppose that the maximum length of a name was 20 characters. We would need an array of memory locations each one of which is of type STRING[20]. It is an array of string variables. For the list of names of students we would use the following:

        VAR STUDENT: ARRAY[1..50] OF STRING[20];

We are now ready for the program that reverses the order of a list of names. Here the array index is an integer variable I.

```
(* READ 50 NAMES AND OUTPUT IN REVERSE ORDER *)
PROGRAM REVERSE;
   CONST MAXNAMES=50;
   VAR STUDENT: ARRAY[1..MAXNAMES] OF STRING[20];
      I: 1..MAXNAMES;
```

```
BEGIN
    (* READ LIST OF NAMES *)
    FOR I:=1 TO MAXNAMES DO
        READLN(STUDENT[I]);
    (*OUTPUT REVERSED LIST *)
    FOR I:=MAXNAMES DOWNTO 1 DO
        WRITELN(STUDENT[I])
END.
```

This program requires you to enter 50 names, one to a line, then it will display these same names in reverse order, one to a line.

Again you can see what a powerful programming tool the indexed variable can be. The index I that is counting the loop is used to refer to the different members of the list. In the first FOR loop the names are read in; the first is stored in the variable STUDENT[1], the second in STUDENT[2], and so on. In contrast, the first iteration of the output loop outputs STUDENT[50], the next STUDENT[49], and so on.

AN EXAMPLE PROGRAM

Sometimes a table has different types of information in different columns of a line. We cannot use the STRING type because there is more than just the alphabetic string on the input line; there are numbers as well. We will revert to the standard Pascal method of reading the names character by character. We assume that the maximum length of names is 14. We must not start the other information until we are beyond column 14 of the line. To use a two-dimensional array we must have every element of the same type. Instead we use a number of one-dimensional arrays, one for each column of the table. We will now give an example in which the table is the timetable for teachers in a high school. The timetable has been prepared as a table. Each line has a teacher's name left-justified in columns 1 to 14, a period (1 to 6) and a room number.

The input lines look like the following:

TEACHER	PERIOD	ROOM
MS. WEBER	1	216
MRS. THOMPSON	6	214
MRS. JACOBS	1	103
MS. WEBER	4	200
MRS. REID	2	216
...		

A program is needed to output the timetable in order of periods. First, all teachers with their classrooms for the first period should be output; then all teachers with their classrooms for period 2 and so on up to period 6. The output from the program should begin this way:

```
PERIOD                    1
MS. WEBER               216
MRS. JACOBS            103
```

   ...

The following program produces this output:

```
(* OUTPUT TIMETABLE PERIOD BY PERIOD *)
PROGRAM PERIODS;
   CONST MAXLENGTH=14;
      MAXENTRIES=50;
      LASTPERIOD=6;
   TYPE NAMETYPE=PACKED ARRAY[1..MAXLENGTH] OF CHAR;
   VAR TEACHER: ARRAY[1..MAXENTRIES] OF NAMETYPE;
      PERIOD: ARRAY[1..MAXENTRIES] OF 1..LASTPERIOD;
      ROOM: ARRAY[1..MAXENTRIES] OF INTEGER;
      THISPERIOD: 1..LASTPERIOD;
      I,HOWMANY: 0..MAXENTRIES;
      N: 1..MAXLENGTH;
      CH: CHAR;
   BEGIN
      WRITELN('TEACHER','PERIOD':MAXLENGTH-1,'ROOM':5);
      (* READ TIMETABLE *)
      HOWMANY:=0;
      WHILE NOT EOF DO
         BEGIN
            HOWMANY:=HOWMANY+1;
            FOR N:=1 TO MAXLENGTH DO
               BEGIN
                  READ(CH);
                  TEACHER[HOWMANY][N]:=CH
               END;
            READLN(PERIOD[HOWMANY],ROOM[HOWMANY])
         END;
      (* OUTPUT TIMETABLE BY PERIODS *)
      FOR THISPERIOD:=1 TO LASTPERIOD DO
         BEGIN
            WRITELN('PERIOD',THISPERIOD:10);
            FOR I:=1 TO HOWMANY DO
               IF PERIOD[I]=THISPERIOD THEN
                  WRITELN(TEACHER[I],ROOM[I]:5)
         END
   END.
```

The first loop in this program reads in the lines representing the timetable. Note that because the alphabetic information of the teachers' names is followed by the integer information we do not have to be looking for the end-of-line mark as we read the character string. Nor do we need to pad the name with blanks; the blanks will be read from the input. Unfortunately we cannot correct any typing errors when we are reading one character at a time.

Our program is able to read in a timetable consisting of *at most 50 lines.* If there are more than 50 lines in the timetable, then HOWMANY will eventually set lines to 51; this value of HOWMANY will be used as an index for the TEACHER, PERIOD, and ROOM arrays. This would be an error, because the declarations specify that 50 is the largest allowed array index. The problem is that the index is *out of bounds* when I exceeds 50. You should try to take care that array indexes in your programs stay within their declared bounds.

The next three sections discuss more advanced programming ideas, namely number conversion, scalar types and enumerated types. Some readers may choose to skip these sections altogether or return to them later.

CONVERTING BETWEEN CHARACTERS AND NUMBERS

When a program outputs a number using WRITE, the number is converted to the characters that are output. And READ takes characters on an input line and converts them into a number. These conversions are automatic in that the programmer does not need to worry about how they are done. But sometimes it is desired to do these conversions explicitly, as the following example shows.

Suppose that you have written a program that requires you to enter an integer as a data item and that you are to enter many such data items. If by mistake you type a letter instead of a digit, minus sign, space or return key, then the computer will tell you that you have made an error. This means that you must start all over to input your data. Also if you type an incorrect digit there is no way to change it. What is perhaps better is to write your program to expect a string of characters (type STRING) and convert that string in the program to an integer. If you make an error you can correct it by backspacing. As you are converting the string you can test each character to be sure that it is a digit or a sign. If you find that it is something else, you can issue your own error message and ask that a corrected value for the data item be input. This gives you a chance to recover from an input error.

We will use the predeclared function ORD that changes a character value to a number value. Each character has a unique "ordinal" value, for example on most microcomputers we have

ORD('A') = 65
ORD('B') = 66
...
ORD('0') = 48
ORD('1') = 49
...

Unfortunately all computers do not use the same collating sequence. On most computers the letters 'A' to 'Z' have increasing but not necessarily contiguous ORD values, and the digits have increasing, contiguous values.

If we have a character variable C then we can read the first digit of a line and convert it to a number this way

READ(C);   (* READ CHARACTER GIVING NUMBER *)
NUMBER:=ORD(C)-ORD('0')

We assign the integer variable NUMBER the ordinal value of C as adjusted by the ordinal value of the character zero. This adjustment is necessary because for example ORD('3') does not equal 3, but ORD('3')-ORD('0') equals 3.

If the number is an integer consisting of three digits (say 216), it can be computed this way.

NUMBER:=0;
FOR I:=1 TO 3 DO
   BEGIN
      READ(C);
      NUMBER:=10*NUMBER+ORD(C)-ORD('0')
   END;

This starts with NUMBER=0 and reads the character '2'. The first time through the loop 10*NUMBER equals zero and so NUMBER takes the numeric value 2. The next digit '1' is read, and NUMBER is assigned the value 21. Finally the '6' is read and NUMBER ends as 216. The loop successively uses multiplication by 10 to slide left the previously read digits in calculating the value of NUMBER. In this example the digits were in fixed positions on the line but you can still do this kind of conversions even when the integer has blanks in front of it.

In a similar but reverse manner, number values can be converted to strings of characters. The predeclared function CHR does the opposite of ORD; it changes a number to a character. For example, if ORD(C) has the numeric value N then CHR(N) is character C. If we have a number N whose value is in the range 0 to 9, we can convert it to the corresponding character this way.

```
C:=CHR(N+ORD('0'))
```

Note that before taking the CHR we must adjust N by the ordinal of character zero.

If the number N is larger than 9, we can convert it to a character string a digit at a time.

```
VAR D: ARRAY [1..10] OF CHAR;
...
FOR PLACE:=10 DOWNTO 1 DO
    BEGIN
        D[PLACE]:=CHR((N MOD 10)+ORD('0'));
        N:=N DIV 10
    END
```

This uses the MOD operator to find the rightmost digit of N and puts this digit into the D array. The D array is successively filled up from the right while N successively loses its rightmost digit because of the division by 10.

CHAR AS A SCALAR TYPE

We have seen that integers can be used to control FOR loops, to choose alternatives within case statements, and to index arrays. For example, we can have

```
VAR I: 1..3;
    A: ARRAY[1..3] OF INTEGER;
...
FOR I:=1 TO 3 DO
    A[I]:=0;
...
CASE I OF
    1: statement1;
    2: statement2;
    3: statement3
END
```

Because of these uses we say integers are a *scalar type*.

The type CHAR is also a scalar type and we can have

```
VAR L: 'A'..'C';
    A: ARRAY['A'..'C'] OF INTEGER;
...
FOR L:='A' TO 'C' DO
    A[L]:=0;
...
CASE L OF
    'A': statement1;
    'B': statement2;
    'C': statement3
END
```

The variable L can take values 'A', 'B' or 'C'. Similarly array A and the CASE statement can be indexed by values 'A', 'B' or 'C'.

We will give an example in which each line of data gives a student's name and a grade of A, B or C. Because there are two alphabetic items on the line we must read the first character by character. The program reads the names and grades. It outputs a sentence about each student's work and reports the number of A grades, B grades and C grades.

```
(* READ AND TABULATE GRADES *)
PROGRAM GRADING;
    CONST NAMELENGTH=10;
    VAR CLASSSIZE,STUDENT: INTEGER;
        I: 1..NAMELENGTH;
        NAME: PACKED ARRAY [1..NAMELENGTH] OF CHAR;
        GRADE: 'A'..'C';
        COUNT: ARRAY['A'..'C'] OF INTEGER;
        CH: CHAR;
BEGIN
    FOR GRADE:='A' TO 'C' DO
        COUNT[GRADE]:=0;
    WRITE('CLASS SIZE=');
    READLN(CLASSSIZE);
    FOR STUDENT:=1 TO CLASSSIZE DO
        BEGIN
            FOR I:=1 TO NAMELENGTH DO
```

```
            BEGIN
               READ(CH);
               NAME[I]:=CH
            END;
         READLN(GRADE);
         WRITE(NAME);
         CASE GRADE OF
            'A': WRITELN('DID EXCELLENT WORK.');
            'B': WRITELN('DID GOOD WORK.');
            'C': WRITELN('DID FAIR WORK.')
         END;
         COUNT[GRADE]:=COUNT[GRADE]+1
      END;
   WRITELN;
   FOR GRADE:='A' TO 'C' DO
      WRITELN(COUNT[GRADE],
            ' STUDENT(S) WITH MARK ',GRADE)
END.
```

Here is a sample display:

```
CLASS SIZE=3
R. MARTY    B
R. MARTY  DID GOOD WORK.
R. SCHILD    A
R. SCHILD DID EXCELLENT WORK.
M. GREEN    B
M. GREEN  DID GOOD WORK.


1 STUDENT(S) WITH MARK A
2 STUDENT(S) WITH MARK B
0 STUDENT(S) WITH MARK C
```

We have seen that CHAR values can be used much like INTEGER values, because both CHAR and INTEGER are scalar types. But arithmetic is not allowed for CHAR values. For example, if L is of type 'A'..'Z', this is not legal:

```
      L:=L+1;
```

This statement seems to mean to set L to the next character. We can use the predeclared function SUCC to change L this way

```
      L:=SUCC(L);
```

For example, if L was '1', it becomes '2' or if L was 'A', it becomes 'B'.

Besides the successor function SUCC, there is a predecessor function PRED. For example:

L:=PRED(L);

sets L to the preceding character value. Conceptually, SUCC adds one and PRED subtracts one. If I is an INTEGER then SUCC(I) actually means I+1 and PRED(I) means I-1.

ENUMERATED TYPES

Sometimes we are interested in a particular small set of items, for example, the 12 months of the year. It is customary to represent the months as numbers, for example, January becomes 1, February becomes 2 and so on. Numbering members of a set in this way is rather artificial although sometimes convenient. Pascal provides a way of avoiding this numbering. We can define a type which has the twelve months as values.

TYPE MONTHTYPE=(JAN,FEB,MAR,APR,MAY,JUNE,
JULY,AUG,SEPT,OCT,NOV,DEC);
VAR MONTH: MONTHTYPE;

Given these declarations, we can assign any month value to MONTH, for example,

MONTH:=FEB;

We can write a FOR loop to be executed for each month, for example:

FOR MONTH:=JAN TO DEC DO ...

and we can select case alternatives using months, for example

CASE MONTH OF
    SEPT,OCT,NOV,DEC: WRITELN('FIRST TERM');
    JAN,FEB,MAR,APR: WRITELN('SECOND TERM');
    MAY,JUNE,JULY,AUG: WRITELN('SUMMER TERM')
END

We say that MONTHTYPE is an *enumerated type* because we give the names for (we enumerate) each value of the type, in this example, JAN through DEC. Enumerated types are scalar types and we can use them for array indexes as well as for CASE selection and FOR loop counters. Values of enumerated types can be compared (=, <>, >, <, >=, <=) and assigned.

In the last chapter we had an example of a two dimensional array to hold the prices of wallalumps each month for a period of three years. That example can be re-written to use our new definition of MONTHTYPE. In each FOR loop we must change "1 TO 12" to be "JAN TO DEC". Each month number must be changed to the month name, for example, 2 is changed to FEB.

We can have subranges of enumerated types, for example

VAR SUMMER: MAY..AUG;

SUMMER can take on the values MAY, JUNE, JULY and AUG. Like CHAR values, enumerated values can be used with ORD, SUCC, and PRED, for example:

ORD(JAN)=0
ORD(FEB)=1
...
SUCC(JAN)=FEB
PRED(FEB)=JAN

Essentially, CHAR is a predefined enumerated type whose values are the characters. Similarly, Boolean is a predeclared enumerated type whose values are FALSE and TRUE. Unfortunately there is no way to READ or WRITE programmer-defined enumerated types.

In principle, we never need to define new enumerated types because we can use integers instead. And we can name integer values, for example, we could define

CONST JAN=1;
    FEB=2;
    ...
    DEC=12;

But defining a new enumerated type offers the following advantages. First, it tells the reader of the program something about its purpose and so helps understandability. For example, when we see SEPT instead of 9 we immediately know that we are dealing with a month. Second, enumerated values are restricted in use, for example, if through some accident we write 3*SEPT, the compiler will tell us that this is nonsense. Similarly if we accidently write

YEAR:=SEPT

where year is an integer, the compiler will catch the error. This extra help from the compiler is possible because enumerated types provide new, distinct sets of values.

There are many uses of enumerated values; here is a list of some obvious enumerated types

```
TYPE RATING = (PRIME,ACCEPTABLE,REJECT);
     NOTES = (DOH,RE,MI,FA,SO,LA,TI);
     DAYS = (SUN,MON,TUES,WED,THURS,FRI,SAT);
     SHOEWIDTH = (AAA,AA,A,B,C,D,DD,DDD);
     SHIRTSIZE = (SMALL,MEDIUM,LARGE,XLARGE);
     STAFFCLASS = (HOURLY,SALARIED,OFFICER);
```

CHAPTER 9 SUMMARY

In this chapter we have given methods of manipulating single characters and strings of characters. The following important terms were presented.

CHAR - variables of type CHAR have characters as their values. Character values can be assigned, compared, read and written. When a CHAR variable is read, preceding blanks are not skipped, because a blank is a legitimate character.

EOLN - this is a predeclared function that becomes true when there are no more characters on the present input line. When EOLN becomes true, READLN should be called to prepare for reading the next line.

READLN - this is a predeclared procedure that reads the remaining characters, if any, on the present line and prepares for the reading of the next line. If READLN has a parameter, as in READLN(N), the parameter value is read before READLN takes effect.

EOF - this is a predeclared function that becomes true when there are no more characters that can be read. To indicate that there are no more characters press the EOF key. On the Apple this is CTRL-C.

PACKED - when an ARRAY [1..n] OF CHAR is PACKED, where n is at least 2, it can be compared, assigned or written as a unit. Literal strings, such as 'HI' are considered to be packed arrays of characters. Two packed arrays can be compared or assigned only if they have the same length.

Length of a string - The number of characters in a string. If the length of a string to be stored in an array is less than the size of the array the string can be left-justified in the array and padded on the right with blanks. Its length then becomes equal to the size of the array and it can be compared with other strings of the same length.

String comparisons - used to test character strings for equality and for ordering. Strings of equal length can be compared using the following operators:

    < comes before (less than)
    > comes after (greater than)
    <=comes before or is equal (less than or equal)
    >=comes after or is equal (greater than or equal)
    = equal
    <>not equal

STRING - a predeclared variable type in UCSD Pascal. It is similar to a packed array of character variables but its length is dynamic. An entire line of characters can be read into a variable LINE by the statement

> READLN(LINE);

The length of the actual string stored in LINE is obtained by using the built-in function LENGTH. If the line consists of the characters SCOTT then LENGTH(LINE) will have the value 5. LINE[1] will be S, LINE[2] will be C, and so on. LINE[6] is an improper reference as the string has only 5 characters.

    When two variables of type STRING are compared the shorter one is effectively padded on the right with blanks. The default length of a STRING variable is 80 characters. If other maximum lengths are required these are specified. For 20 characters use STRING[20].

In this chapter we also presented more advanced features, namely number conversion, characters as scalar types and enumerated types. These important terms were discussed:

ORD - this is a predeclared function that changes each character value to a distinct number. (ORD also accepts enumerated values and produces numbers.)

CHR - this is a predeclared function that is the inverse of ORD. If C is a character then CHR(ORD(C))=C.

Scalar type - these can have subranges and can be array indexes, CASE selector expressions, and FOR loop counters. The following are scalar types: INTEGER, CHAR, BOOLEAN, and programmer-defined enumerated types. (Technically, REAL is a scalar type but it cannot be used for these purposes.)

SUCC - this is a predeclared function that takes a value of a scalar type and produces the next value, for example, SUCC('A')='B'.

PRED - is like SUCC but produces the preceding value.

Enumerated type - a type whose values are given by listing their names (by enumerating them). Here is a type whose values are RED, WHITE and BLUE:

> TYPE FLAGCOLORS=(RED, WHITE, BLUE);

Concatenation - means putting strings together, one after the other, to form another string. This is accomplished by using the CONCAT built-in function. The statement

      WRITELN(CONCAT('PINE','APPLE'));

is to output PINEAPPLE. Any number of strings may be concatenated. The general form is

      CONCAT(string,string{,string})

where the string may be a string constant or a variable of type STRING. The curly brackets indicate that there may be any number of strings beyound two in a concatenation.

Substring - means a part of a string.

COPY - a built-in function whose value is a substring. For example,

      WRITELN(COPY('NAIL',2,3));

would result in the output AIL. In general,

      COPY(string,starting position,
          length of substring).

The length must not exceed what is possible given the string and starting position or an execution error will occur.

INSERT - a built-in procedure for inserting one string into another. To insert a string into a string variable (called the destination) starting at character position in the destination we write the statement

      INSERT(string to be inserted,
          destination string variable,
          position of insertion);

After execution the destination string has the inserted characters.

DELETE - a built-in procedure for deleting characters from a string (the destination). Its form is

      DELETE(destination string variable,
          position of first character to be deleted,
          number of characters to be deleted)

POS - a built-in function for determining the position in a string (the source) where there is the first match (from left to right) of another string (the pattern). Its form is

      POS(pattern string, source string)

This function has an integer value. If there is no match its value is zero.

Procedure - a structure in Pascal which has the effect of a Pascal statement like READ and WRITE. To call a procedure its name is placed in the program followed by a list of parameters in parentheses. The action of a procedure is to modify one or more of its parameters. For example the procedure INSERT modifies the destination string variable by inserting another string at a prescribed location.

Function - a structure in Pascal which produces a value by operating on its parameters. The function CONCAT produces a value which is a string, the result of concatenating all its parameters.

CHAPTER 9 EXERCISES

1. Which of the following comparisons of strings are true?

    (a) 'DAVID BARNARD' = 'DAVID BARNARD'
    (b) 'E. WONG   ' = 'EDMUND WONG'
    (c) 'MARK FOX ' = 'MARK FOX'
    (d) 'JOHNSTON' > 'JOHNSON '
    (e) '416 ELM ST ' < '414 ELM STREET'
    (f) 'HUME,PAT' >= 'HOLT,RIC'
    (g) 'ALLEN' <> 'ALAN '

2. Read in a phrase P from a single line, such as

    ONE SWALLOW DOES'NT MAKE A SUMMER

or

    AN OUNCE OF PREVENTION IS WORTH A POUND OF CURE

Write statements to accomplish each of the following.

    (a) Find the first blank in P and set its location into the integer variable FIRSTBLANK.

    (b) Set the integer variable LASTWORD to the location of the beginning of the last word in P.

    (c) Change P by adding a period at the end of the phrase.

    (d) Change P by replacing its first word by the character

    (e) Change P by extending it on the right by the phrase THEY SAY.

    (f) Set the integer variable COUNT to the number of words in P. You can assume that each word, except the last word, is followed by a single blank.

3. Write a program which looks up Nancy Wong's telephone number and outputs it. You are given a set of data lines, each containing a name and a phone number. For example, the first line might be

    JOHN ABEL   443-2162

4. Write a program that checks to see that the "I before E except after C" rule in spelling is followed. Your program should read some text which

appears as a series of strings. It should search for I and E appearing next to each other. If the combination is EI and is not immediately preceded by a C, then the string should be output together with an appropriate warning message. Similar action should be taken if C immediately precedes IE.

5. Write a program that will accept names of persons (first and last) in the form

LOUISA MOLYNEUX

and output

MOLYNEUX, L.

Make sure your program will work for names already abbreviated to initials. Arrange that the program will work for a number of names on each run.

6. Write a program which reads text and determines the percentage of words having three letters. For simplicity, use text without any punctuation.

7. What does the following program output?

```
PROGRAM FLOWERS;
    VAR POEM: ARRAY[1..2] OF STRING;
        PART,SAYITAGAIN: INTEGER;
    BEGIN
        POEM[1]:='A ROSE';
        POEM[2]:=' IS ';
        FOR SAYITAGAIN:=1 TO 3 DO
            FOR PART:=1 TO 2 DO
                WRITELN(POEM[PART]);
        WRITELN(POEM[1])
    END.
```

8. What else does this program output?

```
PROGRAM POLISH;
    TYPE NAMETYPE= PACKED ARRAY[1..9] OF CHAR;
    VAR NAME: ARRAY[1..20] OF NAMETYPE;
        PRICE: ARRAY[1..20] OF INTEGER;
        I,J,P,N: INTEGER;
        NAMETEMP: NAMETYPE;
        CH: CHAR;
    BEGIN
        WRITE('NUMBER OF BRANDS=');
        READLN(N);
        FOR I:=1 TO N DO
            BEGIN
                FOR J:=1 TO 9 DO
                    BEGIN
```

```
                            READ(CH);
                            NAMETEMP[J]:=CH
                      END;
                      NAME[I]:=NAMETEMP;
                      READLN(PRICE[I])
                END;
                READLN(P);
                FOR I:=1 TO N DO
                   IF PRICE[I]>P THEN
                         WRITELN(NAME[I])
          END.
```

Here is the display up to a point:

NUMBER OF BRANDS=3
JOHNSONS 518
LEMON OIL 211
DOMINO   341
    300

9. Write a program which reads yesterday's and today's stock-market selling prices and outputs lists of rapidly rising and rapidly falling stocks. A typical data entry will look like this:

GENERAL ELECTRIC 93.50 81.00

The entry gives you the company's name followed by yesterday's price, followed by today's price. Your program should output a list of companies whose stock declined by more than 10 per cent, and then a list of companies whose stock rose by more than 10 per cent.

10. Write a program that uses ORD to find the value of 10 numbers on an input line. Each number takes up a field of three columns. Each is right-justified in its field and may have a minus sign. The first and second columns of a field may be blank.

11. Write a program that reads a positive number and formats it into an array of 10 characters, in this way.

   $ZZ,ZZ9.99

Each Z means zero suppression, so the dollar sign moves right (leaving blanks to the left) until a non-zero is found. The comma is output only if it has a non-zero digit to its left. Each position given here as 9 is output as a digit even if it is zero. For example

    210732 is formatted as $2,107.32
     67150 is formatted as $671.50
         4 is formatted as $0.04

You should use the CHR function to do the number conversion.

Chapter 10

STRUCTURING YOUR ATTACK ON THE PROBLEM

STEP-BY-STEP REFINEMENT

Most of the examples of programming so far have been short examples. Nevertheless we have emphasized *some* of the aspects of good programming. These were:

1. Choosing meaningful words as identifiers.

2. Placing comments in the program to increase the understandability.

3. Paragraphing loops and selection statements to reveal the structure of control flow.

4. Choosing appropriate data structures.

5. Reading programs and tracing execution by hand, to strive for correctness before machine testing.

All of these are important even in small programs, but it is only when we attempt larger programs that our good habits will really start to pay off.

And when we work on larger programs we will find that we have something else to structure, and that is our attack on the problem. To solve a problem we must move from a statement of what the problem to be solved is, to a solution, which is a well-structured program for a computer. The language of our program will be Pascal.

The original statement of a problem will be in English, with perhaps some mathematical statements. The solution will be in Pascal. What we will look at in this chapter is the way we move from one of these to the other. We will be discussing a method whereby we go step by step from one to the other. This systematic method we will refer to as *step-by-step refinement*. Sometimes we say that we are starting at the top, the English-language statement of the problem, and moving down in steps to the bottom level, which is the Pascal program for the solution. We speak of the *top-down approach* to problem solution.

TREE STRUCTURE TO PROBLEM SOLUTION

To illustrate the technique of structuring the solution to a problem by the step-by-step refinement, or the top-down approach, we need a problem as an example. We need a problem that is large or difficult enough to show the technique, but not so large as to be too long to follow. If a program is too long and involved we will use another technique that divides the job into modules and does one module at a time. This is called *modular programming.* It is another form of structured programming. But it must wait until we have learned PS/6.

The example we choose is sorting a list of names alphabetically. We will now start the solution by trying to form a tree which represents the structure of our attack. The root of the tree is the statement of the problem. In the first move we show how this is divided into three branches:

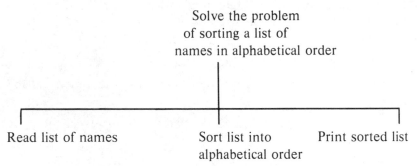

Solve the problem
of sorting a list of
names in alphabetical order

Read list of names   Sort list into   Print sorted list
                            alphabetical order

At each of the three nodes that descend from the root we have an English statement. These statements are still "what-to-do" statements, not "how-to-do-it." A statement of how to do something or other is called an *algorithm* for doing it. A set of instructions for assembling a hi-fi amplifier is an algorithm for making a hi-fi amplifier. A cake recipe in a cookbook is an algorithm for making a cake. The problem of making a cake is solved by following the recipe.

We will be moving down each branch of the solution tree replacing a statement of "what to do" by an algorithm for doing it. The algorithms will not necessarily be in the Pascal language. We will use a mixture of English and Pascal at each node until in the nodes farthest from the tree root we have a Pascal program.

CHOOSING DATA STRUCTURES

Before we try to add more branches to the solution tree, we should decide on some data structures for the problem of sorting the list of names. We need not make all the decisions at this stage, but we can make a start.

We will use an array of character strings called NAME to hold the list of names to be sorted. The length of this list we will call N and we will allow names up to 30 characters in length. What we are deciding on is really the declarations for the Pascal program, and for now we have decided that we need

```
CONST MAXLIST = 100;
VAR NAME: ARRAY[1..MAXLIST] OF STRING[30];
    TEMP: STRING[30];
    I,N: 0..MAXLIST;
```

In these declarations we are allowing a maximum size for the list of 100 names. The actual list will have N names, and we must read this number in as part of the input. We will put one name on each line left-justified in the first 30 columns. For indexing the list we will need an index I. We will assume for the moment that we will keep the sorted list in the same locations as the original list. The names will have to be rearranged, and this means some swapping will be needed. We will use the variable TEMP with type STRING[30] to do this swapping.

GROWING THE SOLUTION TREE

Having decided on at least some of the data structures, we are prepared to continue the process of structuring the solution tree. We can see how to develop the left and right branches now, even as far as transforming them into Pascal program segments. We must read in the names character by character. The middle branch can be refined a little by saying that sorting will be accomplished by element swapping. Here is the tree now:

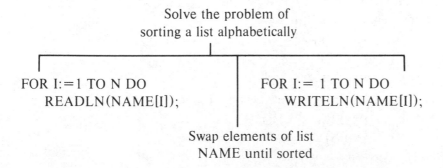

At this stage we must obviously face up to designing an algorithm for producing a sorted list by swapping.

DEVELOPING AN ALGORITHM

We want the names to be in the sorted list so that each name has a larger value than the name ahead of it in the list.

In the sorted list

    HOLT
    HORNING
    HULL
    HUME

we see that each name is alphabetically greater than the one preceding it.

In our solution tree one branch must be developed further; this is, "Swap elements of list NAME until sorted." We have seen from the example that a sorted list has the largest value in the last position. This is also true of the list if an element is removed from the end. The new last element is the largest one of the smaller list. So our next refinement in the solution is to arrange the list in this way. We write:

    Do with LAST varying from N to second,
        swap elements so largest is in LAST

In the list of four names, LAST begins with a value of 4, and the names are swapped so HUME is in position 4. Then last is set to 3 and the names are swapped so HULL is in position 3. Then last is set to 2 and HORNING is placed in position 2. The only remaining name, HOLT, is left in position 1, and the list is alphabetized.

The first part of this can be written in Pascal as

    FOR LAST:=N DOWNTO 2 DO

But we must still refine the part,

    Swap elements so largest is in LAST

We will now refine this part; it becomes

    FOR I varying from first TO (LAST-1) DO
        IF element[I] > element[I+1] THEN
            swap elements

The first two parts of this can now become Pascal; this produces

    FOR I:=1 TO LAST-1 DO
        IF NAME[I] > NAME[I+1] THEN
            swap elements;

We must now refine the statement "swap elements". It is

    TEMP:=NAME[I];
    NAME[I]:=NAME[I+1];
    NAME[I+1]:=TEMP;

Because these three statements go after a THEN, we must precede them by BEGIN and follow them by END.

Now we can assemble the complete program.

THE COMPLETE PROGRAM

```
PROGRAM SORT;
    (* SORT LIST OF N NAMES ALPHABETICALLY *)
    CONST MAXLIST=100;
    VAR NAME: ARRAY [1..MAXLIST] OF STRING[30];
        TEMP: STRING[30];
        I,N,LAST: 0..MAXLIST;
    BEGIN
        (* READ NAME LIST *)
        WRITE('LIST LENGTH=');
        READLN(N);
        WRITELN('ENTER NAMES ONE TO A LINE');
        FOR I:=1 TO N DO
            READLN(NAME[I]);
        WRITELN('HERE IS SORTED LIST');
        (* SWAP ELEMENTS OF LIST UNTIL SORTED *)
        (* LOOP WITH LAST VARYING FROM N TO SECOND *)
        (* SWAP ELEMENTS SO LARGEST VALUE IS LAST *)
        FOR LAST:=N DOWNTO 2 DO
            (* WITH I VARYING FROM FIRST TO LAST-1 *)
            (* IF ELEMENT[I] > ELEMENT[I+1] *)
            (* SWAP THESE ELEMENTS *)
            FOR I:=1 TO LAST-1 DO
                IF NAME[I] > NAME[I+1] THEN
                    BEGIN
                        TEMP:=NAME[I];
                        NAME[I]:=NAME[I+1];
                        NAME[I+1]:=TEMP
                    END;
        (* OUTPUT SORTED NAME LIST *)
        FOR I:=1 TO N DO
            WRITELN(NAME[I])
    END.
```

Here is a sample display:

LIST LENGTH=5
ENTER NAMES ONE TO A LINE
ANDREWS
CAMERON
ALLEN
BAKER
DAWSON
HERE IS SORTED LIST
ALLEN
ANDREWS
BAKER
CAMERON
DAWSON

Notice that the English parts of the solution tree remain as comments in the final program. Comments are not added after a program is written, so that it can be understood at a later date, but are an integral part of the program construction process.

ASSESSING EFFICIENCY

In this approach to problem solution we have moved step by step to refine the statement of the problem in English into a program in a language that is acceptable to a computer, namely Pascal. In the process, as we constructed the solution tree, we gradually replaced statements of what is to be done by statements of how it is to be done; we devised an algorithm for performing the process. The algorithm was expressed in English, or a mixture of English and Pascal. Then finally we had a Pascal program.

Nowhere during this process have we spoken about the efficiency of the method that we have chosen, that is, the efficiency of our algorithm. This is because the issue of efficiency complicates the solution. Since in structured programming we are trying to control complexity, we have in this first attempt eliminated efficiency from our considerations.

This means that to now add the refinement of a more efficient algorithm will require us to back up to an earlier point in the solution tree and redo certain portions. In the step-by-step refinement method of problem solution we do not always move from the top down in the solution tree. In that sense, then, the top-down approach is slightly different. In it you would move always in the one direction. In practice this would be impractical, as afterthoughts must always be allowed to improve a method of solution. The only reason to reject afterthoughts is that the work in incorporating them is not justified, considering the gain that would result.

In our particular example you can see that it is possible, at a certain stage, that the list might be sorted and that there is no need to keep on to the bitter end. What we should incorporate is a way of recognizing that the list is sorted so that the mechanical sorting process can stop.

A BETTER ALGORITHM

What we must do is to back up in the solution tree to the point where we had in the middle branch the words, "Swap elements of NAME until sorted." We have translated this essentially by the statement, "Swap elements of NAME in such a way that at the end of the swapping process the list is sure to be sorted."

We are going to change now to the statement, "Swap elements of NAME in such a way that at the end of the swapping process the list would be sorted, and stop either when the list *is* sorted or when the normal end of the swapping process is reached." You can see that we are going to have a loop now with two conditions. The condition of the swapping process's being finished is the same as what we have now. What we must add to the loop is the second condition

list is not sorted

But how do we know when the list is sorted? We must devise a method to test whether or not the list is sorted. You will notice that if the inner loop does not swap any names, the list *must* be sorted. We should have a Boolean flag called SORTED that can be set to TRUE to indicate that the list is sorted or FALSE to indicate that the list is not sorted.

The outer loop would then begin

WHILE(NOT SORTED) AND (LAST>=2)DO

We would have to initialize this loop by having these instructions precede it.

SORTED:=FALSE;
LAST:=N;

These set the flag SORTED to FALSE so that the loop will begin properly and start the count. Inside the loop we must perform the adjustment in the index LAST by -1. Since we are now using a WHILE loop instead of a counted FOR loop, we must do our own counting. This would mean we need the instruction

LAST:=LAST-1

just before the end of the loop. We want SORTED to be changed to TRUE if *no* swapping takes place in the inner FOR loop. This can be accomplished if we set it to TRUE just before we enter the inner loop and return it to FALSE if any swapping does take place. The altered part of the program is as follows. The variable SORTED must be declared as BOOLEAN.

```
(* SWAP ELEMENTS OF LIST UNTIL *)
(* EITHER SWAPPING PROCESS IS COMPLETED *)
(* OR THE LIST IS SORTED AS INDICATED *)
(* BY THE FLAG 'SORTED' BEING TRUE *)
SORTED:=FALSE;
LAST:=N;
WHILE(NOT SORTED)AND(LAST>=2)DO
    BEGIN
        SORTED:=TRUE;
        FOR I:=1 TO LAST-1 DO
            IF NAME[I] > NAME[I+1] THEN
                BEGIN
                    SORTED:=FALSE;
                    TEMP:=NAME[I];
                    NAME[I]:=NAME[I+1];
                    NAME[I+1]:=TEMP
                END;
        LAST:=LAST-1
    END;
(* OUTPUT SORTED NAME LIST *)
 (as before)
```

BETTER ALGORITHMS

In our example we could see that an improvement in the efficiency of the sorting algorithm could be achieved, and we backed up the solution tree and redid a portion to incorporate the improvement. This was an easier job than trying to think about efficiency in the first place. This is why in the step-by-step refinement method we do not consider efficiency at first. In a way we were lucky that our algorithm could be modified so readily. We might have done the swapping in an entirely different way, in which we would not be able to detect a sorted list by the absence of swapping on any iteration of the process.

To see how this might be, suppose that to sort this list each element were compared with the first element. If it were smaller, the two would be swapped. With the smallest in the first position the list would be shortened by one and the process repeated. The difficulty here is that the fact that no swapping occurs in any round only means that the smallest is already in the first position, not that the list is sorted. We have no way of seeing that the list is sorted unless we compare each list member with its next-door neighbor. And this is what we did in our sorting method.

So our method is more suited to this particular improvement than a method that involves swapping by comparison of each element with one particular element. If we had started this way we would have had to revise completely. To say that efficiency considerations are left until after a first algorithm is programmed produces disadvantages. For many standard processes like sorting, various algorithms have been explored, their efficiencies evaluated, and a best algorithm determined. The method we have developed is certainly not the best that has been devised.

This best, or optimal, algorithm often depends on the problem itself. For instance, one algorithm may be best for short lists, another for long lists. Establishing "the" best method is very difficult and depends on circumstances. Always try to pick a "good" algorithm if you are programming a standard process. At least avoid "bad" algorithms. Very often, programs are already written using good algorithms and you can use them directly in your own program. But that is something we will discuss in the subset PS/6. We can create programs from modules that are already made for us. Then one of the branches of your solution tree is filled by a *prefabricated module*. We need only learn how to hook it up to our own program. We can also create modules of our own. This technique is called *modular programming* and it is an additional way to conquer problem solving, by dividing the problem into parts.

CHAPTER 10 SUMMARY

In previous chapters we concentrated primarily on *learning* a programming language; we have covered variables, loops, character strings, arrays and so on. In this chapter, the focus has been on *using* a programming language to solve problems.

The method of problem solving which we described is based on the idea of dividing the problem into parts - the divide-and-conquer strategy. Each of these parts in turn is divided into smaller parts. This continues until eventually the solution to the problem has been broken into small parts which can be written in a programming language like Pascal. We will review this method of problem solving using the following terms:

Top-down approach to programming. When using a computer to solve a problem, you should start by understanding the problem thoroughly. You start at the "top" by figuring out what your program is supposed to do. Next you split your prospective program into parts, for example, into a reading phase, a computation phase, and a outputing phase. These phases represent the next level in the design of your program. You may continue by defining the data which these phases use for passing information among themselves, and then by writing Pascal statements for each of the phases. The Pascal statements are the bottom level of your design; they make up a program which should solve your problem. In larger programs, there may be many intermediate levels between the top - understanding the problem completely - and the bottom - a program which solves the problem. (Beware:top-down program design does *not* mean writing PROGRAM name; at the top of the page, followed by declarations, followed by statements! The top level in top-down design means gaining an understanding of the problem to be solved, rather than writing the first line of Pascal.)

Step-by-step refinement. When you are writing a program, you should start with an overall understanding of the program's purpose. You should proceed step by step toward the writing of this program. These steps should each refine the proposed program into a more detailed method of solving the problem. The last step refines the method to the level where the computer can carry out the required operations. This means that the final refinement results in a program which can be executed by the computer. As you can see, the idea behind top-down programming is step-by-step refinement leading from the problem statement to the final program.

Tree structures to problem solution. In this chapter we have illustrated top-down programming by drawing pictures of trees. The root, or base, of the tree is labelled by the statement of the problem. Once the problem has been refined into subproblems, we have our tree grow a branch for each subproblem. In turn, each subproblem can be divided, resulting in sub-branches, and so on. When you are actually solving problems, you will probably not actually draw such a tree. However, you may well use the idea behind drawing this tree, namely, step-by-step refinement leading from problem statement to problem solution.

Use of comments. One of the purposes of comments, (*...*), in a program is to remind us of the structure of the program. Comments are used to remind us that a particular sequence of Pascal statements has been written to solve one particular part of the problem.

CHAPTER 10 EXERCISES

1. You are to have the computer read a list of names and output the names in reverse order. In your top-down approach to writing your program, you first decided your program should have the overall form:

    (a) Read in all of the names;

    (b) Output the names in reverse order;

Next, you decided that the names will be passed from part (a) to part (b) via an array declared by

    VAR NAME: ARRAY[1..50] OF STRING[10];

The index of the last valid name read into this array will be passed to part (b) in a INTEGER variable called HOWMANY. Making no changes to this overall form, you must now complete the program. Include comments at the appropriate places to record the purpose of the two parts of your program. Answer the following questions about your completed program.

    - Can you think of another way to write part (a) of your program without changing part (b)? How?

    - Can you think of another way to write part (b) of your program without changing part (a)? How?

2. The school office wants a list of all A students and a list of all B students. The input line should be of the form:

DAVID TILBROOK A-

Each grade is A,B,C,D or F, which may be followed by + or -. The school's programmer has designed the following two possible structures for a program to read the input and output the two required lists.

First program structure: (a) Read names and grades and save all of them in arrays; (b) Output names having A grades; (c) Output names having B grades;

Second program structure: (a) Read names and grades and save only those with A's or B's in arrays; (b) Output names having A grades; (c) Output names having B grades;

Suppose the final program will have room in arrays to save at most 100 students' names. What advantage does the second program structure have over the first one? You do not need to write a program to answer these questions.

3. A company wants to know the percentage of its sales due to each salesman. For each salesman there is an identification number and the dollar value of his sales. The top-down design of a program to output the desired percentages has resulted in this program structure:

(a)   Read in salesmen's numbers and sales and add up total sales;

(b)   Calculate each salesman's percentage of the total sales;

(c)   Display the salesmens' numbers and percentages.

Parts (a) and (c) have been written in Pascal. You are to write part (b) in Pascal, add declarations and complete the program. Here is part (a):

```
(* READ IN SALESMEN AND SALES, TOTAL SALES *)
TOTALSALES:=0;
I:=1;
WHILE NOT EOF DO
    BEGIN
        READLN(SALESMAN[I],SALES[I]);
        TOTALSALES:=TOTALSALES+SALES[I];
        I:=I+1
    END;
N:=I-1;
```

Here is part (c) written in Pascal:

```
(* DISPLAY SALESMEN AND PERCENTAGES *)
WRITELN('   SALESMAN','   PERCENT');
FOR I:=1 TO N DO
    WRITELN(SALESMAN[I]:10,PERCENT[I]:10);
```

Chapter 11

THE COMPUTER CAN
READ ENGLISH

In the subset PS/4 you learned how to handle character strings. You learned how to compare strings, either for the purpose of recognizing particular strings or for putting various strings in order. But there are more things that you can do with strings. In this chapter we will show how to create the illusion that the computer does things that we normally associate with people; we might say that it is "intelligent". We say it has an artificial intelligence, since it is of course *not* human, and thinking is what humans do. The field of artificial intelligence in computer science concerns itself with getting the computer to perform acts that we think of as the province of humans. Of course, when we see how it is done, we realize it is just a mechanical process. It has to be mechanical or a machine could not do it. But if you do not know how the "trick" is performed, it does seem as if the machine can "think".

The field of artificial intelligence is involved with many different activities of man as imitated by machine, but one of the most interesting is the way that a machine is made to deal with statements made in *natural language*. We call a language, like English, a natural language because it evolved over a period of time through use. A language like Pascal is a *formal language*. It has been defined, it is unambiguous and it is really very limited. Trying to get computers to deal with natural language is a major task. We would like to be able to write questions in natural language and have the computer provide answers to our questions from a bank of information. This is a goal in information retrieval systems.

We have not yet got very far along the way towards question-answering systems in natural language, but it is clear there are basic "skills" the computer must have before it can cope with this. One of these skills is the ability to read.

WORD RECOGNITION

When you first learn how to read you must learn to recognize words. To do this you must recognize what a word is. You learn the basic characters, the letters, then you learn that a word is a string of characters with a blank in front and a blank after it and no blanks in between. We are now going to write a program that will input a line of text and split it up into words. To simplify the job, we will begin our problem without any punctuation marks in the text. As an example,

HEREbISbAbTEXTb

where we have used b to represent a blank. The method of dealing with problem solving by simplification is very helpful. Solve a simpler problem before you try a harder one. We will learn to cope with punctuation marks later.

Our solution tree for this problem is:

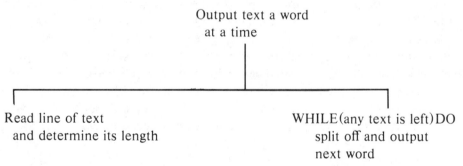

All the parts are straightforward except "Split off and output next word." We will refine it further:

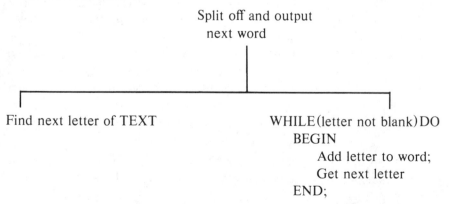

To determine the next letter of the text we use a pointer which indicates the position in the text string that you are currently working on. We will call this pointer COLUMN. The next letter will be TEXT[COLUMN]. To add a letter to WORD we use another pointer called LETTER.

WORD[LETTER]:=next letter

We are ready now for the program:

```
PROGRAM READING;
    (* READ TEXT A WORD AT A TIME *)
    CONST BLANK=' ';
        MAXCOL=40;
        MAXCOLPLUS1=41;
    VAR TEXT,WORD: STRING[MAXCOLPLUS1];
        TEMP: STRING[MAXCOL];
        LETTER,LENGTHLINE,LENGTHWORD,I: 0..MAXCOL;
        COLUMN: 1..MAXCOLPLUS1;
    BEGIN
        WHILE NOT EOF DO
            BEGIN
                WRITELN('TYPE LINE OF TEXT,MAX 40 CHAR');
                (* READ LINE AND DETERMINE LENGTH *)
                READLN(TEMP);
                TEXT:=TEMP;
                LENGTHLINE:=LENGTH(TEXT);
                (* ADD A BLANK TO END OF TEXT *)
                TEXT:=CONCAT(TEXT,BLANK);
                COLUMN:=1;
                WHILE COLUMN< =LENGTHLINE DO
                    BEGIN
                        (* SPLIT OFF AND OUTPUT NEXT WORD *)
                        WHILE(COLUMN< =LENGTHLINE)AND
                                    (TEXT[COLUMN]=BLANK) DO
                            COLUMN:=COLUMN+1;
                        LETTER:=1;
                        WHILE(COLUMN< =LENGTHLINE)AND
                                    (TEXT[COLUMN]< >BLANK) DO
                            BEGIN
                                WORD[LETTER]:=TEXT[COLUMN];
                                LETTER:=LETTER+1;
                                COLUMN:=COLUMN+1
                            END;
                        LENGTHWORD:=LETTER-1;
                        IF LENGTHWORD< >0 THEN
```

```
                          BEGIN
                            FOR I:=1 TO LENGTHWORD DO
                                WRITE(WORD[I]);
                            WRITELN
                          END
                  END
          END
    END.
```

This program has been somewhat complicated because several blanks might separate words and there might be trailing blanks after the last word on a line. These trailing blanks cause the program to determine that LENGTH-WORD=0, so we avoid any output when this is true. We made the TEXT array one column longer than the maximum allowed line width because the WHILE test to see if TEXT[COLUMN] is blank is sometimes made when COLUMN is one beyond MAXCOL. The array index must not have a value outside the declared range of the index for TEXT.

WORD STATISTICS

We have learned to read words of a text, recognize certain words such as STOP, replace words and to treat words in a list in different ways as we did with the list of names. Another important use of a computer in dealing with words involves keeping statistics about the lengths of words. Different authors have different patterns of use of words and this shows up in the frequency with which they use words of different lengths. Some authors use a lot of long words; others rarely do.

In this section we will read a text and from it prepare a frequency distribution of word lengths. To add a little extra interest to this problem, we will display the results in graphic form. For instance, we will have a display like this for output:

LENGTH OF WORD	FREQUENCY
1	***
2	******
3	********
4	*****

This display, called a histogram, represents the result of analyzing the frequency of different word lengths in a text. It shows that there were 3 one-letter words, 6 two-letter words, 8 three-letter words, and 5 four-letter words. The spacing in the display we show is not the same as what you will see on your screen because typesetting uses different widths for different characters. On your screen each character in the display occupies the same amount of space.

We will not read the entire line of text this time before breaking it into words but will read a word at a time. We will presume that there are no punctuation marks, just words with blanks between them.

```
PROGRAM DISPLAY;
    (* DETERMINE FREQUENCIES OF WORD LENGTHS *)
    CONST MAXLENGTH=20;
    VAR FREQUENCY: ARRAY[1..MAXLENGTH] OF INTEGER;
        LENGTH,I,J: INTEGER;
        CH: CHAR;
    BEGIN
        FOR I:=1 TO MAXLENGTH DO
            FREQUENCY[I]:=0;
        WRITELN('ENTER TEXT,THEN EOF');
        WHILE NOT EOF DO
            BEGIN
                CH:=' '; (* INITIALIZE TO START LOOP *)
                WHILE(NOT EOLN)AND(CH=' ')DO
                    (* SKIP LEADING BLANKS *)
                    READ(CH);
                IF CH <> ' ' THEN
                    (* IF LINE HAS A WORD THEN *)
                    BEGIN
                        LENGTH:=1;
                        WHILE (NOT EOLN) AND (CH <> ' ')DO
                            BEGIN
                                READ(CH);
                                LENGTH:=LENGTH+1
                            END;
                        IF CH=' ' THEN
                            LENGTH:=LENGTH-1;
                                (* IGNORE TRAILING BLANK *)
                        IF LENGTH<=MAXLENGTH THEN
                            FREQUENCY[LENGTH]:=FREQUENCY
                            [LENGTH]+1
                    END;
                IF EOLN THEN
                    READLN
            END;
        WRITELN('LENGTH OF WORD':16,'FREQUENCY':11);
```

```
        FOR I:=1 TO MAXLENGTH DO
            BEGIN
                WRITE(I:10,'       ');
                FOR J:=1 TO FREQUENCY[I] DO
                    WRITE('*');
                WRITELN
            END
    END.
```

Here is a sample display:

ENTER TEXT, THEN EOF
ROSES ARE RED
VIOLETS ARE BLUE
HONEY IS SWEET
AND SO ARE YOU

LENGTH OF WORD	FREQUENCY
1	
2	**
3	******
4	*
5	***
6	
7	*
...	
20	

READING PASCAL

We have been reading English text and performing operations on it, or as the result of it. All these operations, we see, are absolutely mechanical but give you the impression that the computer is capable of doing things we think of as "intelligent work". One of the fields of artificial intelligence that has been explored is the translation from one language to another. The translation of one natural language into another, such as English to French, has had only qualified success. It works, but not well when the text is ambiguous or difficult. The translations are not good literature, to say the least.

But computers are being used for language translation every day, for the translation of programming languages into machine languages. The reason this is possible is that programming languages are well defined and quite limited.

Your Pascal programs are translated by the compiler program into machine language programs before execution. A Pascal program is made up of keywords and identifiers such as FOR, READ and WHILE and special symbols such as semicolon and colon. A translator for Pascal first reads in the characters of the Pascal program and separates them into keywords, identifiers and special symbols. It can tell which keyword it has read by comparing the word it has read to the known keywords. When a statement keyword such as WHILE is recognized, the translator knows it is to produce machine language for a loop.

CHAPTER 11 SUMMARY

In this chapter we have shown how the computer can, in a sense, understand English. The computer can recognize words by scanning for their beginnings and endings. Typically, words in English are surrounded by blanks or special characters; programs can be written which separate out words by searching for these characters. Due to the great speed of computers, they sometimes have the appearance of being intelligent, in spite of the fact that their basic mode of operation is very simplistic, such as seeing if a given character is a blank. Pascal compilers have been developed to read text which looks somewhat like English; the text which they have been designed to read is Pascal programs.

CHAPTER 11 EXERCISES

1. A *palindrome* is a word or phrase which is spelled the same backwards and forwards. The following are examples of word palindromes: "I", "mom", "deed" and "level". Blanks and punctuation are ignored in phrase palindromes, for example, "Madam, in Eden I'm Adam" and "A man, a plan, a canal, Panama". Write a program which reads a string and determines if it is a palindrome.

2. You are to write a program which will help in reviewing a script to determine its suitability for television screening. Your program is to give a list of the frequency of use of the following unacceptable words:

   PHOOEY SHUCKS JEEPERS GOLLY

Make up a few lines of script to test out your program.

3. You are employed by an English teacher who insists that "and" should not be preceded by a comma. Hence, "Crosby, Stills, Nash and Young" is acceptable, but "Merril, Fynch, and Lynn" is not. Write a program which

reads lines of text, searches for unacceptable commas, removes them, and makes stern remarks such as the English teacher would make about errors. (We are somewhat ambivalent about this!)

4. Write a program which reads text and then outputs it so that its left and right margins are vertical. First the program is to read the number of characters to output per line. Whenever enough words for one line have been collected, blanks are inserted between words to expand the line to the desired width. Then the expanded line is output.

Chapter 12

PS/6: SUBPROGRAMS

In this subset we will be introducing the idea of subprograms other than the main program that has constituted all programs so far. The purpose of having subsidiary programs or subprograms is so that a larger program can be divided into parts. In this way we "divide and conquer" a complicated problem. Sometimes a part of the solution of one problem can be used in many different problems, and making it into a subprogram creates a module or building block which can be used in many programs.

PROCEDURES

There are two kinds of subprograms in Pascal: procedures and functions. Essentially, procedures allow you to invent new Pascal statements, while functions allow you to invent new operations. We will give an example of a procedure first.

Suppose we wish to determine the larger of two INTEGER numbers. We could write a procedure to find the larger one; this is done in the following *procedure declaration*:

```
PROCEDURE LARGER(FIRST,SECOND: INTEGER;
          VAR RESULT: INTEGER);
   BEGIN
      IF FIRST>SECOND THEN
         RESULT:=FIRST
      ELSE
         RESULT:=SECOND
   END;
```

The heading of the procedure declaration is the keyword PROCEDURE, followed by the name of the procedure, LARGER, followed in parentheses by a list of *formal parameters* with their types. There are two kinds of formal parameters: *value parameters* and *variable parameters*. A variable parameter is sometimes called a VAR parameter because it is declared using the keyword VAR in the formal parameter list. Variable parameters can be used to feed information into a subprogram and also to feed information back out. Value parameters can only feed information into the subprogram.

The body of the procedure is a compound statement prefaced by BEGIN and terminated by END. Note that the END of a procedure has a semicolon after it. To use this procedure in a main program its declaration is included immediately after any variable declarations of the main program. Here is an example.

```
PROGRAM BEST;
    VAR DATA1,DATA2,MAXIMUM: INTEGER;

    (* THIS IS THE DECLARATION OF THE PROCEDURE *)
    PROCEDURE LARGER(FIRST,SECOND: INTEGER;
            VAR RESULT: INTEGER);
      BEGIN
          IF FIRST>SECOND THEN
              RESULT:=FIRST
          ELSE
              RESULT:=SECOND
      END;

    (* THIS IS THE BODY OF THE MAIN PROGRAM *)
    BEGIN
        WRITELN('ENTER TWO INTEGERS');
        READ(DATA1,DATA2);
        LARGER(DATA1,DATA2,MAXIMUM);
        WRITELN('THE LARGER IS ',MAXIMUM)
    END.
```

Here is a sample display:

ENTER TWO INTEGERS
5 31 THE LARGER IS 31

We have included a blank line before and after the procedure declaration but this is not necessary.

When the LARGER procedure is called, via the *procedure statement* in the main program

LARGER(DATA1,DATA2,MAXIMUM);

the value formal parameter FIRST takes the value of the *actual parameter* DATA1, SECOND takes the value of the actual parameter DATA2 and

RESULT which is a variable formal parameter becomes another name for MAXIMUM. Inside the procedure, whenever the value of RESULT is changed, the effect is to change the value of MAXIMUM. The LARGER procedure is entered and RESULT, which is really MAXIMUM, is set to the larger of FIRST and SECOND. When the end of the LARGER procedure is reached, execution returns to the statement just beyond the procedure statement, which invoked its use. It returns to the WRITELN statement. Conceptually, our procedure provides us with a new Pascal statement which we can use whenever we want to find the larger of two numbers.

This has been a very simple example; if you were writing such a simple program as this one you would not bother to use a procedure.

FUNCTIONS

We will now show how function subprograms are declared and used. We could have found the larger number by writing a function rather than a procedure. A function named BIGGER is used in the following version of the program.

Here is the declaration for a function named BIGGER:

```
FUNCTION BIGGER(FIRST,SECOND: INTEGER): INTEGER;
    BEGIN
      IF FIRST>SECOND THEN
        BIGGER:=FIRST
      ELSE
        BIGGER:=SECOND
    END;
```

The heading for a function declaration is the keyword FUNCTION followed by the name of the function, here BIGGER, then in parentheses the formal parameters and their type. After the parentheses we have a colon and then the type of the function itself. The name of the function acts like a variable which must be assigned a value before you finish execution of the function. In this example the variable BIGGER is assigned the value of the value parameter FIRST or SECOND depending on which is bigger. Functions are not allowed to have variable (VAR) formal parameters; the single output value is assigned to the function itself.

Here is a program using this function.

```
PROGRAM BIGONE;
    VAR DATA1,DATA2,MAXIMUM: INTEGER;
```

```
(* THIS IS THE FUNCTION DECLARATION *)
FUNCTION BIGGER(FIRST,SECOND: INTEGER): INTEGER;
   BEGIN
       IF FIRST>SECOND THEN
           BIGGER:=FIRST
       ELSE
           BIGGER:=SECOND
   END;

(* THIS IS THE BODY OF THE MAIN PROGRAM *)
BEGIN
   WRITELN('ENTER TWO INTEGERS');
   READ(DATA1,DATA2);
   MAXIMUM:=BIGGER(DATA1,DATA2);
   WRITELN('THE LARGER IS ',MAXIMUM)
END.
```

The display is the same as before. The BIGGER subprogram is a function because it provides a value to its name, BIGGER in its declaration. Since it is a function, it must be given a type, the type of the value its name is to be assigned. The BIGGER function is entered as a result of the fact that its name appears in the assignment statement of the main program:

```
MAXIMUM:=BIGGER(DATA1,DATA2);
```

When the BIGGER function is entered, the value formal parameter FIRST is assigned the value of the actual paremeter DATA1 and SECOND the value of DATA2. Conceptually, our function provides us with a new arithmetic operation which we can use in arithmetic expressions. We could have replaced the assignment to MAXIMUM and the immediately following WRITELN statement by the statement

```
WRITELN(' THE LARGER IS ',BIGGER(DATA1,DATA2));
```

This change would not affect the outputed answer.

Our example subprograms LARGER and BIGGER illustrate the following differences between procedures and functions. The definition of a function must include the type of the function itself. The value assigned to BIGGER must match this type. For example, in the function called BIGGER, the value assigned to BIGGER matches the INTEGER type given in the function heading. A procedure is entered when it is invoked using its name as the first word in a statement, followed by a list of actual parameters in parentheses. A function is entered when its name appears in an expression, such as the right side of an assignment statement, followed by a list of actual parameters in parentheses.

NESTING AND SUBPROGRAMS

Once a procedure has been defined, it can be used, by name, just like any other Pascal statement. It is even possible to use statements that invoke procedures inside other procedures. We will give simple examples to show the use of nesting with procedures. The following job prints the largest of its three data values.

```
PROGRAM BIGGEST;
    VAR DATA1,DATA2,DATA3,MAXIMUM: INTEGER;
    PROCEDURE LARGER(FIRST,SECOND:INTEGER;
                        VAR RESULT: INTEGER);
        (exactly as previous LARGER procedure)
        END;
    PROCEDURE LARGEST(FIRST,SECOND,THIRD:INTEGER;
                        VAR RESULT:INTEGER);
        VAR GREATER: INTEGER;
        BEGIN
            LARGER(FIRST,SECOND,GREATER);
            LARGER(GREATER,THIRD,RESULT)
        END;

    BEGIN
        WRITELN('ENTER THREE INTEGERS');
        READ(DATA1,DATA2,DATA3);
        LARGEST(DATA1,DATA2,DATA3,MAXIMUM);
        WRITELN('THE LARGEST IS ',MAXIMUM)
    END.
```

Here is a sample display:

ENTER THREE INTEGERS
5 31 27 THE LARGEST IS 31

The procedure named LARGEST determines which of its first three value parameters is largest and assigns the largest value to its variable parameter, named RESULT. It accomplishes this by first using LARGER to assign the larger of the first two parameters to the variable GREATER, and by using LARGER again to assign the larger of GREATER and the third parameter to RESULT. The variable GREATER is declared as a variable inside the procedure LARGEST. This variable is referenced only inside the LARG-EST procedure. It is a *local variable* and is not known to either LARGER or the main program BIGGEST. To be accessible to a program (or procedure) a variable must be either declared in that procedure or in a procedure that contains it.

The procedures LARGER and LARGEST both have parameters named FIRST and SECOND. This causes no trouble because the parameters of LARGER are hidden from LARGEST and vice versa. As a rule it is good programming practice to avoid duplicate names, as they may confuse people reading a program. However, in some cases, such as this example, it seems natural to repeat names in separate procedures. Since duplicate names in separate procedures are kept separate in Pascal, this causes no difficulty.

We will now show an example of nesting with our BIGGER function. We will use it in the following job to output the largest of three numbers.

```
PROGRAM BIGONE;
    VAR DATA1,DATA2,DATA3: INTEGER;
    FUNCTION BIGGER(FIRST,SECOND:INTEGER):INTEGER;
        (Exactly as previous version of BIGGER)
        END;
BEGIN
    WRITELN('ENTER THREE INTEGERS');
    READ(DATA1,DATA2,DATA3);
    WRITELN('LARGEST IS ',
            BIGGER(BIGGER(DATA1,DATA2),DATA3))
END.
```

This job finds the larger of the first two data items using the BIGGER function, and uses the BIGGER function again to compare that value to the third data value. In the WRITELN statement, the first actual parameter to the BIGGER function is another call to the BIGGER function. This causes no trouble, because the inner call to BIGGER first returns 31, which is the larger of 5 and 31. Then the outer call to BIGGER compares 31 to 27 and returns the value of 31. Using a call to BIGGER inside a call to BIGGER is actually no more complicated than, say,

$$((5+31)+27)$$

This expression means add 5 and 31 and add 27 to the result. By comparison,

BIGGER(BIGGER(5,31),27)

means find the larger of 5 and 31 and then find the larger of this and 27.

We will now show another kind of subprogram nesting. If the procedure named LARGER is to be used only inside the procedure named LARGEST, we can give the definition of LARGER inside LARGEST. This is done in the following job:

```
PROGRAM BIGONE;
    VAR DATA1,DATA2,DATA3,MAXIMUM: INTEGER;
    (* DECLARATION OF LARGEST, LARGER NESTED IN IT *)
    PROCEDURE LARGEST(FIRST,SECOND,THIRD:INTEGER;
            VAR RESULT:INTEGER);
        VAR GREATER: INTEGER;

        PROCEDURE LARGER(FIRST,SECOND:INTEGER;
                VAR RESULT: INTEGER);
            (Exactly as previous version of LARGER)
            END;
        BEGIN
            LARGER(FIRST,SECOND,GREATER);
            LARGER(GREATER,THIRD,RESULT)
        END;

    (* BODY OF MAIN PROGRAM *)
    BEGIN
        WRITELN('ENTER THREE INTEGERS');
        READ(DATA1,DATA2,DATA3);
        LARGEST(DATA1,DATA2,DATA3,MAXIMUM);
        WRITELN('THE LARGEST IS ',MAXIMUM)
    END.
```

The job works just like the previous job which contains a procedure named LARGEST. The only difference is that since LARGER has been hidden inside LARGEST, the LARGER procedure is no longer available for use in the main program. The fact that LARGER and LARGEST have formal parameters with the same names does not cause trouble; each procedure will use its own local meanings for the names FIRST, SECOND and RESULT. This example has shown how a procedure declaration can be nested inside another procedure declaration.

ACTUAL PARAMETERS AND FORMAL PARAMETERS

We have introduced two terms in connection with procedures and functions: actual parameters and formal parameters. The formal parameters are the identifiers used in the declaration of a subprogram for information that is to be fed into a subprogram or, in the case of procedures, to be given out. Actual parameters are the expressions (often variables) in the *calling procedure* that are to be put into correspondence with the subprogram formal parameters. And there must be a one-to-one correspondence between the number and type of the actual parameters and the formal parameters.

Each formal parameter is declared to be a *variable* parameter by specifying VAR or a *value* parameter by not specifying VAR. Procedures can have both kinds of formal parameters but functions can have only value parameters.

All references to variable parameters in a procedure effectively refer to the corresponding actual parameter. This is done by means of pointers to the locations that hold the actual parameters. These pointers are set automatically at the time the procedure is called. When the procedure is executing, each time the value of a variable parameter is changed the corresponding actual parameter is effectively altered.

An actual parameter corresponding to a variable formal parameter is restricted to be a variable such as GREATER and cannot be an expression or constant such as $X+1$ or 25. This restriction is made so that changing the actual parameter makes sense, for example, it makes sense to change the value of GREATER but we cannot change the value of 25.

Value parameters are different from variable parameters and can receive expressions and constants, as well as variables, as actual parameters. The value of the actual parameter is used to give an initial value to the formal parameter. After this initialization, there is no relation between the actual and formal parameters, and the value parameter acts just like a local variable.

Here is a diagram to show the association between formal parameters and actual parameters for the program BEST given as the first example of the use of a procedure. The directions of the arrows shows the direction of flow of the data.

```
PROCEDURE LARGER        PROGRAM BEST
       FIRST     <---    DATA1
       SECOND    <---    DATA2
       RESULT    <-->    MAXIMUM
```

FIRST and SECOND are value parameters and receive data from the program. These values are stored on entering the procedure LARGE and are the values contained in DATA1 and DATA2. RESULT is a variable parameter which is assigned a value in the procedure; this value is assigned to the variable MAXIMUM of the program BEST.

The formal parameters of a subprogram are associated with actual parameters at the time the subprogram is called, so a subprogram may be used in the same program with different sets of actual parameters in other statements. Notice that local variables are ordinary variables in the subprogram. These local variables cannot be referenced outside the subprogram. Each time the subprogram is called, these variables must have values before being used, because their values from any previous calls are discarded.

ARRAY VARIABLES AND CONSTANTS AS ACTUAL PARAMETERS

We will do another simple example to show how array variables and constants can be used as actual parameters. Suppose we write a procedure that will add the elements of an integer array, LIST, of N elements and call the total SUM. Let us name the procedure TOTAL. The type of any array variable used as a parameter must be defined in the calling program. Here is the declaration for the procedure TOTAL.

```
(* ADD THE N ELEMENTS OF LIST *)
PROCEDURE TOTAL(LIST: INTARRAY;N: INTEGER;
                    VAR SUM: INTEGER);
    VAR I: INTEGER;
    BEGIN
        SUM:=0;
        FOR I:=1 TO N DO
            SUM:=SUM+LIST[I]
    END;
```

Now let us write a calling program for this:

```
PROGRAM BILL;
    TYPE INTARRAY=ARRAY[1..10] OF INTEGER;
    VAR INVOICE: INTARRAY;
        I,GROSS: INTEGER;
    (include declaration of TOTAL procedure here)
    BEGIN
        WRITELN('ENTER 5 INTEGERS');
        FOR I:=1 TO 5 DO
            READ(INVOICE[I]);
        READLN;
        TOTAL(INVOICE,5,GROSS);
        WRITELN('GROSS=',GROSS)
    END.
```

Here is a sample display:

ENTER 5 INTEGERS
25 36 21 7 2
GROSS=91

In this example, notice that the actual parameter INVOICE is in correspondence with the parameter LIST. The declaration of LIST must be of the same type as INVOICE. This type, namely INTARRAY, is defined in the main program. It is a user-defined type.

In this example, we have a constant 5 as the actual parameter in correspondence with the value parameter N. When the procedure is entered, N is assigned the actual parameter's value, which is 5. After that N can be used or changed without any effect on the actual parameter.

When the TOTAL procedure is called, the entire INVOICE array is copied into the LIST array, because LIST is a value parameter. Copying of big arrays is inefficient and can be avoided by declaring the array formal parameter using VAR. With VAR we have a variable parameter instead of a value parameter, so instead of copying all of INVOICE into LIST, a pointer to INVOICE is used instead. With this change, our TOTAL procedure still works as before. References in the procedure to LIST[1] will then point at INVOICE[1]. There is no location in the memory identified by LIST[1], but there is for INVOICE[1], and LIST[1] simply points to INVOICE[1].

Pascal requires that the type of each formal parameter be given by a type identifier. For example, the following would not be allowed

PROCEDURE TOTAL (LIST: ARRAY[1..10] OF INTEGER; etc)

We avoided this problem by using

TYPE INTARRAY=ARRAY[1..10] OF INTEGER;

in the main program and then declaring LIST to be of type INTARRAY. In a similar way, the result type of a function must be given by a type identifier and for functions this type cannot be an array or record; we will talk about records in a later chapter.

GLOBAL AND LOCAL VARIABLES

Any variable declared inside a procedure is said to be local to that procedure. It is a *local variable*. Variables declared in a main program are available by the same name to all subprograms whose declaration is nested in the main program. We say that variables declared in the surrounding program are *global* to the nested program. Notice that the same variable identifier I is used in the main program BILL and also as a local variable in the procedure TOTAL. These are treated as absolutely separate variables. These is no need to worry about accidental coincidences between names of local and global variables. Inside the procedure, the local one is used exclusively. Outside the procedure, the one local to the procedure is not visible.

The statements inside a subprogram can use variables declared in the surrounding program without passing them through the parameter list. We have not done this in any example so far, because our purpose in having subprograms was to separate the parts of the program completely; the only communication has been through the list of parameters. Sometimes, if a great deal of information is to be passed, and if the procedure is being custom-made exclusively for your own program, it is appropriate for the subprogram to reference variables that are declared *only* in the main program. Remember we call such variables *global* to the subprogram since they are declared in a surrounding program. Variables that are declared in the subprogram are said to be *local* to that subprogram. Sometimes we refer to the *scope* of a variable. The scope of a local variable in the subprogram is the subprogram itself. A global variable has a larger scope; its scope is the main program and the subprogram. Variables are considered local or global depending upon where they are declared; similarly user-defined constants, types and subprograms are also either local or global. A procedure can both change and read global variables but a function should only read them.

CHAPTER 12 SUMMARY

In this chapter we have introduced subprograms. Subprograms allow us to build up programs out of modules. The reasons for using subprograms in programs include the following:

1. Dividing the program into parts which can be written by different people.

2. Dividing a program into parts which can be written over a period of time.

3. Making a large program easier to understand by building it up out of conceptually simple parts.

4. Factoring out common parts of a program so they need not be written many times within a program.

5. Factoring out commonly-used logic so that it can be used in a number of different programs.

6.   Separating parts of a program so they can be individually tested.

There are two kinds of subprograms in Pascal: procedures and functions. Essentially, a procedure provides a new kind of Pascal statement and a function provides a new kind of operation. The following important terms were discussed in this chapter.

Subprogram declaration - means giving the meaning of a subprogram to the computer. Subprogram declarations in Pascal must come after constant definitions, type definitions, and variable declarations. Procedures can be declared using the following form:

PROCEDURE identifier[([VAR] identifier{,identifier}:type
       {;[VAR] identifier{,identifier}:type})];
   [constant declaration]
   [type declaration]
   [variable declaration]
   {subprogram declaration}
   BEGIN
      statement{;statement}
   END;

The curly brackets indicate zero or more repetitions of what is inside them. The square brackets indicate that the enclosed item is optional. Procedures may have no parameters whatsoever in which case the procedure's identifier has no list in parentheses following it.

Functions can be declared using the following form:

FUNCTION identifier[(identifier{,identifier}:type
       {;identifier{,identifier}:type})]:type;
   [constant declaration]
   [type declaration]
   [variable declaration]
   {subprogram declaration}
   BEGIN
      statement{;statement}
   END;

If a function has no parameters, the parameters and their enclosing parentheses are omitted. Functions must not have any variable parameters. The function is given a value by assigning to its name in the function's body. The type of a function is given following the list of formal parameters and must be a named type.

Procedure (or function) name - follows the rules for variable identifiers.

Calling a procedure (invoking a procedure) - causing a procedure to be executed. A procedure is called by a statement of the form

procedure name(actual parameters);

If the procedure has no formal parameters, then the actual parameters with their enclosing parentheses are omitted. A function is called by using its name, followed by a parenthesized list of actual parameters if required, in an expression. Value actual parameters may be any expressions which yield a value of the right type. VAR actual parameters must be variables.

Returning from a procedure or function - terminating the execution of a subprogram and passing control back to the calling place. When the end of a procedure is reached, there is a return to the statement just beyond the calling statement. After a function is finished it causes the returned value to be used in the expression containing the function reference.

Actual parameters - A call to a procedure or function can pass it actual parameters. These must be the same in number, sequence, and type as the formal parameters.

Formal parameters - the list of parameters that are to be used by the procedure and produced as results. Information to be used can be passed in through a value parameter; information passed out *must* go through a variable parameter. Declarations of variable parameters are prefaced by the keyword VAR. All parameters must be typed in the procedure heading. Parameters that are arrays must be given a type that is named in the calling procedure. The parameter type is given after the identifier of the parameter and separated from it by a colon.

Value parameters - those formal parameters in a procedure or function heading that are not preceded by the keyword VAR are passed to the procedure as values. The actual arguments corresponding to value parameters can be any expression that evaluates to a value of the same type as the formal parameter.

Variable parameters - those formal parameters in a procedure heading that are preceded by the keyword VAR. Assignments may be made to variable parameters in the procedure and such assignments are equivalent to assignments to the actual parameter that is in correspondence with the formal variable parameter. Functions may not have variable parameters.

Scope - of a variable is the extent of the program over which the variable is meaningful. Local variables have a meaning only within the subprogram where they are declared.

CHAPTER 12 EXERCISES

1. What does the following program output? What are the formal parameters and actual parameters in this program?

```
PROGRAM NUMBERS;
    VAR I,MAGNITUDE: INTEGER;

    PROCEDURE ABSOLUTE(K: INTEGER; VAR L: INTEGER);
        BEGIN
            IF K>=0 THEN
                L:=K
            ELSE
                L:=-K
        END;

    BEGIN
        FOR I:=-2 TO 2 DO
            BEGIN
                ABSOLUTE(I,MAGNITUDE);
                WRITELN(MAGNITUDE)
            END
    END.
```

2. What does the following program output? What are the parameters and arguments in this program?

```
PROGRAM WEATHER;
    TYPE REALARRAY=ARRAY[1..31] OF REAL;
    VAR TEMPERATURE,RAIN: REALARRAY;
        DAY,TIME: INTEGER;

    PROCEDURE AVERAGE(VAR LIST: REALARRAY;
                HOWMANY: INTEGER);
        VAR TOTAL: REAL;
            I: INTEGER;
        BEGIN
            TOTAL:=0;
```

```
        FOR I:=1 TO HOWMANY DO
            TOTAL:=TOTAL+LIST[I];
        WRITELN(TOTAL/HOWMANY)
    END;

BEGIN
    WRITE('NUMBER OF DAYS=');
    READLN(TIME);
    WRITELN('ENTER WEATHER FOR ',TIME,' DAYS');
    WRITELN('TEMPERATURE RAIN');
    FOR DAY:=1 TO TIME DO
        READ(TEMPERATURE[DAY],RAIN[DAY]);
    WRITE(' AVERAGE TEMPERATURE:');
    AVERAGE(TEMPERATURE,TIME);
    WRITE(' AVERAGE RAINFALL:');
    AVERAGE(RAIN,TIME);
    WRITELN
END.
```

3. Write a procedure that reads an array of names counting how many it gets and another which sorts the array of names into alphabetic order. For example, your procedure could be used in the following program:

```
PROGRAM ORDER;
    TYPE LISTTYPE=ARRAY[1..100] OF STRING[20];
    VAR WORKERS: LISTTYPE;
        I,NUMBER: INTEGER;
    PROCEDURE READLIST(VAR COUNT: INTEGER ;
                    VAR PEOPLE: LISTTYPE);
        (you write this part)
        END;
    PROCEDURE SORT(LENGTH: INTEGER;
                    VAR NAMES: LISTTYPE);
        (You write this part)
        END;
BEGIN
    READLIST(NUMBER,WORKERS);
    SORT(NUMBER,WORKERS);
    FOR I:=1 TO NUMBER DO
        WRITELN(WORKERS[I])
END.
```

4. What does the following procedure do? Write a small program which uses this procedure.

```
PROCEDURE METRIC( VAR LENGTH: REAL);
    BEGIN
        LENGTH:=2.54*LENGTH
    END;
```

5. What does the following procedure do? Write a small program which uses this procedure.

```
FUNCTION CONVERT(VAR INCHES: REAL): REAL;
    BEGIN
        CONVERT:=2.54*INCHES
    END;
```

Chapter 13

UCSD PASCAL GRAPHICS

One of the important extensions that the UCSD Pascal has over standard Pascal is the ability to display graphic images. When we use WRITE statements in our Pascal programs we are displaying characters on the screen. These characters are arranged in lines. There is a maximum number of lines of characters that we can see on the screen at any time and a maximum number of characters in a line. If you write a program that outputs more lines than can be held on the screen at any time, the image will *scroll*. This means that lines disappear from the top and new lines appear at the bottom. The screen is a *window* that lets us see only so much output or program at one time. In this chapter we will show how to write programs that draw lines that can be seen through the window of the screen. We call the line drawings *graphics*.

TEXT AND GRAPH MODES

The two kinds of display available in UCSD Pascal cannot be used at the same time. We can either have lines of characters, called *text mode*, or graphic images, called *graph mode*. We, in fact, will be able to display characters in graph mode, to label our drawings, but these are not produced by WRITE statements. The graphics program package for UCSD Pascal is called *Turtle Graphics*. It is based on a robot demonstration devised at the Massachusetts Institute for Technology. The robot was called a turtle and it could be programmed to move around the floor. As it moved, it dragged a pen that left a trace of where it had been thus producing graphics on the floor. The name turtle has just stuck. When you use Turtle Graphics you can think of a "turtle" located at a particular point on the screen and, on command, moving in various directions for various distances. If you want to write programs in UCSD Pascal that draw graphics, you must first initiate the graphics system. This is done by the statement

INITTURTLE;

This clears the screen, changes from the text mode to the graph mode, and places the turtle at the center of the screen facing, along the horizontal, to your right. When you are all finished with drawing a graph in a program you should switch back to the normal text mode. This is done by including the statement

TEXTMODE;

before the END of your program.

CHANGING THE PEN COLOR

We mentioned that you can think of the turtle dragging a pen and drawing lines as it moves. We can control the pen to the extent that it does or does not make a line as the turtle moves. If we use the statement

PENCOLOR(NONE);

the turtle's moves will not leave a trace. To have the turtle's pen leave a white line on the screen use the statement

PENCOLOR(WHITE);

This probably is the best for drawing but you can try, if you like,

PENCOLOR(BLACK);

If you have a color display screen you can use GREEN, VIOLET, ORANGE, or BLUE. With a color display you have other kinds of WHITE and BLACK called 1 and 2, for use with the different colors. You can also fill the screen with the same colors as you use for pen colors by

FILLSCREEN(color);

If you use the statement

FILLSCREEN(REVERSE);

the negative of what is there appears; white on black becomes black or white. The statement

CLEARSCREEN;

erases everything.

MOVING THE TURTLE

The display window that takes the whole screen has a certain size. Call it SIZEX wide and SIZEY high. We call these sizes by x and y because they are related to the way of describing any point on the screen. We say that a point has two *coordinates*. The coordinates describe a trip that you might take from the bottom left corner of the screen which is called the origin to the point in question. The trip has two legs, first from the origin along the bottom of the screen to a point directly below the point in question. The length of this leg of the trip is the *x-coordinate.* The length of the trip from directly below up to the point is the *y-coordinate.* The coordinates of a point are written in this way,

(x-coordinate, y-coordinate)

A point whose coordinates are

(50, 35)

is reached by starting at the origin and travelling 50 units along the bottom of the screen (horizontally), then travelling 35 units directly up (vertically). All the trips have to be in integral numbers of units in Turtle Graphics. The coordinates of the top right-hand corner of the screen are

(SIZEX,SIZEY)

The origin has coordinates

(0,0)

The mid-point of the screen has coordinates

(ROUND(SIZEX/2),ROUND(SIZEY/2))

The values of SIZEX and SIZEY differ from one microcomputer to another. For the Apple they are

SIZEX=279
SIZEY=191

Distances chosen for the drawings must be large enough so that the drawings are easily seen but small enough so that the lines do not disappear off the edge of the screen.

There are two kinds of statements for moving the turtle. One kind is

MOVETO(X,Y);

which causes the turtle to move from its present location (wherever that may be) to the point whose coordinates are (X,Y).

Here is a program which draws a square whose bottom left corner is at (50,50) and whose sides are 100 units long.

```
PROGRAM SQUARE;
   USES TURTLEGRAPHICS;
   BEGIN
      INITTURTLE;
      MOVETO(50,50);
      PENCOLOR(WHITE);
```

```
            MOVETO(150,50);
            MOVETO(150,150);
            MOVETO(50,150);
            MOVETO(50,50);
            PENCOLOR(NONE);
            READLN;
            TEXTMODE
        END.
```

Here is the appearance of the screen:

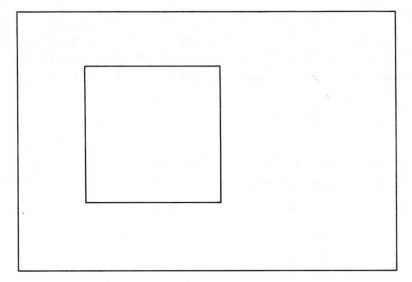

There are several points to notice about the program. If we want to use the Turtle Graphics features in our program we must include the line

USES TURTLE GRAPHICS;

right after the program heading. Remember that the INITTURTLE statement causes the system to be put in graph mode and the turtle placed at the center of the screen and the pen color set to NONE. We want the drawing to start at (50,50) so we do not set the pen color to white until after we get there. The square is drawn by the four MOVETO statements that follow. It is a good practice to put the pen color back to NONE. We must also return to text mode or else we will not be able to see any prompt line but when we do the graph will disappear. This is why we put in a READLN. The statement TEXTMODE will not be executed until we press return which READLN expects.

The other kind of move instructions do not involve x and y coordinates. Instead you can rotate the direction the turtle is pointing by the statement

TURN(ANGLE);

where ANGLE is the angle of rotation in degrees counterclockwise from its present direction of pointing. Then you can move the turtle, in the direction that it is pointing, by a given distance using

MOVE(DISTANCE);

Here is the program for drawing the same square as before using TURN and MOVE.

```
PROGRAM SQUARE2;
    USES TURTLEGRAPHICS;
    BEGIN
        INITTURTLE;
        MOVETO(50,50)
        PENCOLOR(WHITE);
        MOVE(100);
        TURN(90);
        MOVE(100);
        TURN(90);
        MOVE(100);
        TURN(90);
        MOVE(100);
        TURN(90);
        PENCOLOR(NONE);
        READLN;
        TEXTMODE
    END.
```

The program is the same as far as getting the turtle to the point (50,50) after that the sides are drawn by the MOVE and the turtle is turned by 90 ° by TURN after each side is drawn. It is a good practice to bring the turtle back to pointing in the same direction as it does initially that is why we included the final TURN statement. It is really unnecessary here but is a good habit to get into for when you create procedures.

GRAPHICS PROCEDURES

We will now program a procedure for drawing a regular polygon with N sides. A square is a regular polygon with four sides. An equilateral triangle is one with three sides. We will presume that the drawing will begin from the point where the turtle is located on entry to the procedure, and that the first side will be drawn in the direction that the turtle is pointing on entry. Here is the procedure

```
PROCEDURE POLYGON(N,SIDE:INTEGER);
   VAR I,ANGLE:INTEGER;
   BEGIN
      ANGLE:=ROUND(360/N);
      FOR I:=1 TO N DO
         BEGIN
            MOVE(SIDE);
            TURN(ANGLE)
         END
   END;
```

It is necessary to round the angle because the angle in the TURN must be an integral number of degrees just as the distance in the move must be integral. Here is a program which uses the POLYGON procedure to draw two hexagons that are different.

```
PROGRAM HEXAGONS;
   USES TURTLEGRAPHICS;
   VAR I:INTEGER;
   (copy procedure POLYGON here)
   BEGIN
      INITTURTLE;
      MOVETO(50,50);
      PENCOLOR(WHITE);
      POLYGON(6,20);
      PENCOLOR(NONE);
      MOVETO(150,100);
      PENCOLOR(WHITE);
      FOR I:=1 TO 6 DO
         BEGIN
            POLYGON(3,20);
            TURN(60)
         END;
      PENCOLOR(NONE);
      READLN;
      TEXTMODE
   END.
```

Here is the output for this program:

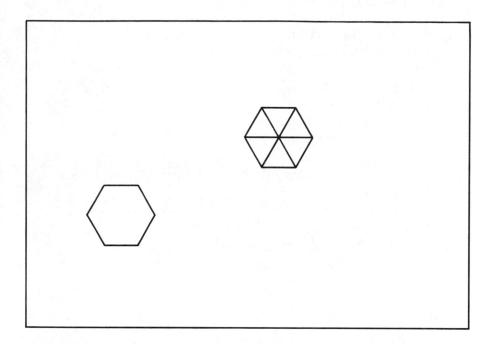

Notice that the hexagon on the upper right part of the screen is really made of six triangles.

We can use the polygon procedure to try to draw a circle. We would like to have a circle of radius 50 units that has its center at the center of the screen. We cannot really draw a smooth curve since all of the turtle moves are in a straight line so we make each move very small and then you do not notice the curve is made up of straight line segments. We will draw a regular polygon with 100 sides; then each side will be very short. If we want a circle of radius 50 units, the circumference of the circle should be 2 times PI times 50 where PI = 3.14159. If the distance around the polygon with 100 sides is approximately the same as the circumference then

100 times SIDE = 2 times PI times 50.

If we want the center of the circle to be at the center of the screen we must first move the turtle 50 units from the center and turn it into the vertical direction before starting to draw the 100-sided polygon. Here is the program to do it. We will make the program fairly general.

```
PROGRAM CIRCLE;
    USES TURTLEGRAPHICS;
    CONST PI=3.14159;
    VAR SIDE,RADIUS,NUMBEROFSIDES:INTEGER;
    (copy POLYGON procedure here)
    BEGIN
        WRITE('RADIUS=');
        READLN(RADIUS);
        WRITE('NUMBER OF SIDES=');
        READLN(NUMBEROFSIDES);
        INITTURTLE;
        SIDE:=ROUND(2*PI*RADIUS/NUMBEROFSIDES);
        MOVE(RADIUS);
        TURN(90);
        PENCOLOR(WHITE);
        POLYGON(NUMBEROFSIDES,SIDE);
        PENCOLOR(NONE);
        READLN;
        TEXTMODE
    END.
```

You can experiment with the number of sides required to make a convincing circle. It will be larger, the larger the radius of the circle is. Try it for yourself and see. Note particularly what happens when the number of sides is larger say 200. Why does this happen?

LABELING GRAPHICS

In the last example we stayed in text mode while we were reading in the radius of the circle and the number of sides in the polygon that would approximate the circle, then we gave the INITTURTLE statement which put us into graph mode. If we executed a WRITE statement in graph mode we would not see what is output. There are really two separate displays, the text display and the graph display, and we can only see one or the other. If we want to have text on our graphics, perhaps to label the graphics, we must use the built-in procedures WCHAR or WSTRING. These procedures put either a character or a string of characters on the screen starting at the position where the turtle is located at the time of executing the procedure. The characters are of a fixed size and are placed horizontally on the screen. After execution of either of these procedures, the turtle should be moved to a definite position because the procedures move it along as the characters are displayed. Here is a procedure that produces polygons and labels them:

```
PROCEDURE POLYTYPE(N,SIDE:INTEGER);
    VAR NAME:ARRAY[3..8] OF STRING;
       TURTX,TURTY,TURTANG,I,ANGLE:INTEGER;
    BEGIN
       NAME[3]:='TRIANGLE';
       NAME[4]:='SQUARE';
       NAME[5]:='PENTAGON';
       NAME[6]:='HEXAGON';
       NAME[7]:='SEPTAGON';
       NAME[8]:='OCTAGON';
       (* DRAW POLYGON *)
       ANGLE:=ROUND(360/N);
       PENCOLOR(WHITE);
       FOR I:=1 TO N DO
          BEGIN
             MOVE(SIDE);
             TURN(ANGLE)
          END;
       (*LABEL POLYGON*)
       PENCOLOR(NONE);
       TURTX:=TURTLEX;
       TURTY:=TURTLEY;
       TURTANG:=TURTLEANG;
       MOVETO(TURTX,TURTY-10);
       WSTRING(NAME[N]);
       MOVETO(TURTX,TURTY);
       TURNTO(TURTANG)
    END;
```

In this procedure we have used a number of new features of the Turtle Graphics other than the WSTRING procedure. Because we want the procedure to finish with the turtle at exactly the same point, pointing in the same direction, as it started from, we must return it to that point before the procedure's END. The polygon drawing leaves the turtle's position unchanged, but the labeling of the polygon with the string changes that position. What we do is to store the position and orientation of the turtle in the variables TURTX, TURTY, and TURTANG. This is possible because there are built-in functions in Turtle Graphics that give you these values. TURTLEX is a function whose value is the x-coordinate of the turtle; TURTLEY has a value equal to the y-coordinate; TURTLEANG's value is the direction that the turtle is pointing. To label the polygon we first move down from it using

```
MOVETO(TURTX,TURTY-10);
```

Then the appropriate name, chosen from the NAME array is displayed by WSTRING. To return the turtle to its proper position we use

    MOVETO(TURTX,TURTY);

and then we use a statement type we have not met before

    TURNTO(TURTANG);

This sets the direction to the proper angle. The TURN instruction merely turns an additional angle from whatever it happens to be.

Notice that we do not have to set the pencolor before using WSTRING. It is automatically set to white and restored to none after the procedure is executed.

Here is a program that uses POLYTYPE.

```
PROGRAM DRAW;
    USES TURTLEGRAPHICS;
    VAR X,Y,N,SIDE:INTEGER;

    (copy POLYTYPE procedure here)

    BEGIN
        INITTURTLE;
        REPEAT
            TEXTMODE;
            WRITE('X=');
            READLN(X);
            WRITE('Y=');
            READLN(Y);
            WRITE('N=');
            READLN(N);
            WRITE('SIDE=');
            READLN(SIDE);
            GRAFMODE;
            MOVETO(X,Y);
            POLYTYPE(N,SIDE);
            READLN
        UNTIL EOF
    END.
```

This program keeps drawing polygons of different types and sizes starting at different points on the screen as you prescribe. To input the specifications for each polygon you draw you must be in text mode. Then to see the drawing you go back to graph mode. This is done by the statement GRAF-

MODE. To stop the process, type EOF before you press return. If you do it the other way around you will find yourself back in the loop again.

As this program is run, whenever you draw a septagon an error becomes noticeable due to the fact that the angle of turning in the polytype procedure is rounded off to an integral number of degrees.

Here is a sample display wich has two parts.

Text mode display: (Note: Each assignment is on a separate line in actual display.)

X=30 Y=30 N=3 SIDE=50 X=100 Y=30 N=4 SIDE=50 X=150 Y=100 N=6 SIDE=25

Graph mode display:

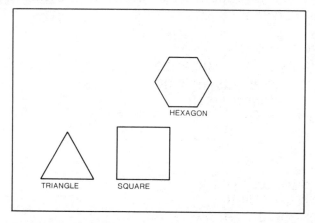

PLOTTING HISTOGRAMS

It has often been said that "a picture is worth a thousand words". A very common way of presenting statistical information to people is in terms of a picture or graph called a *histogram*. A histogram is a graph that conveys to the viewer the relative numbers of values of a quantity that fall into different classes. For instance, you could gather statistics for the throws of a pair of dice and plot a histogram showing the relative number of throws that have the values 2,3,4,...12. There are 11 possible results. Here the "distance" from one class to the next is constant; it is 1. This means the histogram can be a series of rectangles of equal width whose heights are proportional to the numbers in each class. We will write a procedure that will draw a histogram for N equal classes whose relative frequencies are stored in an array of integers called FREQ.

```
(* PROGRAM MUST DEFINE TYPE INTARRAY *)
PROCEDURE HISTOGRAM(N:INTEGER;FREQ:INTARRAY);
   VAR I,SCALEX:INTEGER;
      SCALEY:REAL;
```

```
PROCEDURE RECTANGLE(WIDTH,HEIGHT:INTEGER);
    BEGIN
        MOVE(WIDTH);
        TURN(90);
        MOVE(HEIGHT);
        TURN(90);
        MOVE(WIDTH);
        TURN(90);
        MOVE(HEIGHT);
        TURN(90)
    END;

FUNCTION MAX(NUMBER:INTEGER;LIST:INTARRAY):INTEGER;
    VAR I,TEMP:INTEGER;
    BEGIN
        TEMP:=LIST[1];
        FOR I:=2 TO NUMBER DO
            IF TEMP<LIST[I] THEN
                TEMP:=LIST[I];
        MAX:=TEMP
    END;

    BEGIN
        PENCOLOR(NONE);
        MOVETO(250,10);
        PENCOLOR(WHITE);
        MOVETO(30,10);
        SCALEX:=ROUND(200/N);
        SCALEY:=150/MAX(N,FREQ);
        FOR I:=1 TO N DO
            BEGIN
                RECTANGLE(SCALEX,ROUND(SCALEY*FREQ[I]));
                MOVE(SCALEX)
            END;
        PENCOLOR(NONE)
    END;
```

Here is the program that uses HISTOGRAM:

```
PROGRAM STATISTICS;
    USES TURTLEGRAPHICS;
    TYPE INTARRAY=ARRAY[1..20] OF INTEGER;
    VAR FACT:INTARRAY;
        I,CLASS:INTEGER;
    (copy HISTOGRAM procedure here)
```

```
BEGIN
    WRITE('NUMBER OF CLASSES=');
    READLN(CLASS);
    WRITELN('ENTER ',CLASS,' INTEGERS,ONE TO A LINE');
    FOR I:=1 TO CLASS DO
        READLN(FACT[I]);
    INITTURTLE;
    HISTOGRAM(CLASS,FACT);
    MOVETO(30,0);
    WSTRING('HISTOGRAM OF RELATIVE FREQUENCIES');
    PENCOLOR(NONE);
    READLN;
    TEXTMODE
END.
```

Notice that we entered the array of integers one to a line. This means that backspacing and correction of the integer entry is possible as long as the return has not been pressed and provided you did not enter any character but a digit. The label on the histogram is not very informative but you would have to read in the label as a string from the keyboard if a more precise label was wanted.

Here is a sample output for the program.

Text mode display:

NUMBER OF CLASSES=4
ENTER 4 INTEGERS, ONE TO A LINE
8
10
6
3

Graph mode display:

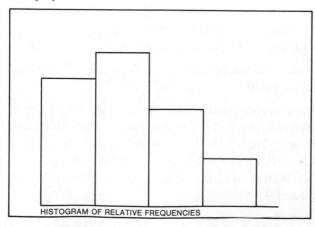

HISTOGRAM OF RELATIVE FREQUENCIES

CHAPTER 13 SUMMARY

In this chapter we introduced the UCSD extension to standard Pascal called Turtle Graphics. This extension permits you to make drawings composed of straight line segments on the screen. The normal display mode, called text mode, allows you to display a number of lines of characters. The computer can be switched to graph mode which is the mode in which the line drawings are displayed. These two display modes cannot be on the screen at the same time. In graph mode you can imagine the lines being drawn on the screen by a "turtle" dragging a pen as it moves from point to point. Each individual move is in a straight line. The following terms were discussed.

Window - the area of the screen in which a line drawing is displayed. The size of the window is measured in some arbitrary units. For the Apple the window is 279 units wide by 191 units high. When the turtle is moved outside the window no lines produced can be seen on the screen.

Scroll - the movement of lines of characters on the screen in text mode as additional lines are added to an already filled screen. The top line disappears as all lines are moved up one to make room for a new line at the bottom.

Text mode - the mode for the screen in which lines of characters can be displayed.

Graph mode - the mode for the screen in which line drawings, made up of straight line segments, can be displayed.

Turtle Graphics - a line drawing package for UCSD Pascal based on a robot, called a turtle, devised at the Massachusetts Institute for Technology.

INITTURTLE - the statement that invokes the built-in procedure in UCSD Pascal to initialize the Turtle Graphics system. The mode is set to graph mode, the screen is cleared, and the turtle is placed in the center of the screen facing along the horizontal to the right.

TEXTMODE - the procedure that is used to return the system to text mode after using Turtle Graphics.

PENCOLOR - the procedure that sets the color of the line that is drawn as the turtle moves. It has one parameter: the color to be used. The choices are: NONE, WHITE, BLACK, and, for color displays, also GREEN, VIOLET, ORANGE, or BLUE. As well, there are two kinds of WHITE and BLACK for use with color. These are numbered 1 and 2.

FILLSCREEN - the procedure that floods the screen with color. The same colors as can be used with the pen are possible. If REVERSE is used, a negative of the display is created.

CLEARSCREEN - the procedure to clear the screen to begin a new drawing.

Coordinates - the two numbers that specify the position on the screen. The x-coordinate gives the distance the point is from the left side of the screen. The y-coordinate gives the distance the point is from the bottom of the screen. The coordinates are written in this form

(x-coordinate,y-coordinate)

Origin of coordinates - the point whose coordinates are (0,0). For the Apple this point is the bottom left corner of the screen. The coordinates of the upper right corner of the Apple screen are (279,191). Other microcomputer systems have different locations for the origin (such as the center of the screen) and use different distance units.

TURTLEGRAPHICS - the name of the program package in the UCSD Pascal library that permits you to use Turtle Graphics. The declaration

USES TURTLEGRAPHICS;

must appear immediately after the program heading in any program in which you want to use the Turtle Graphics package of functions and procedures.

MOVETO(X,Y) - moves the turtle to the point whose coordinates are (X,Y).

MOVE(DISTANCE) - moves the turtle in the direction it is already pointing DISTANCE units.

TURN(ANGLE) - turns the turtle from the present direction through ANGLE degrees counterclockwise.

TURNTO(ANGLE) - sets the direction of the turtle to ANGLE degrees.

WSTRING - a procedure for displaying, in graph mode, the string of charaters that is the parameter of the procedure. The string is displayed horizontally starting at the present turtle position. After displaying a string the turtle should be moved to a known location.

WCHAR - a procedure to display a single character.

TURTLEX - a built-in function whose value is the x-coordinate of the turtle's present position.

TURTLEY - a function whose value is the turtle's present y-coordinate.

TURTLEANG - a function whose value is the turtle's direction. All these last three functions have integer values.

Histogram - a graph for displaying statistical information, composed of a series of rectangles.

CHAPTER 13 EXERCISES

1. Write a procedure to plot a rectangle whose sides are parallel to the sides of the screen and whose center is at the center of the screen. Test your procedure by writing a program that draws a number of such rectangles of different sizes. Arrange to input the size of each rectangle just before you draw it.

2. Write a procedure to draw an equilateral triangle whose center is at a given point and which has a given orientation.

Test the procedure by writing a program to draw two concentric triangles that form a six-pointed star. Can you now make a "star" procedure?

3. A graph of a mathematical equation such as $Y = X^2$ can be obtained by computing corresponding values of X and Y for a series of equally spaced values of X. These become a series of points in the graph. For example, for the equation we give these points are computed

$(0,0),(1,1),(2,4),(3,9),(4,16),...$

Write a procedure that would take N such points and draw a graph joining consecutive points. You will have to scale the values of x and y so that the graph is the right size (large enough to see well but still inside the screen's window). What adjustments would be necessary if some of the coordinates were negative?

4. Write a highly interactive graphics program which first asks you to type in a DISTANCE and an ANGLE and then produces a graph as a series of steps. The first step is to move horizontally DISTANCE units then pause waiting for you to type a "+" or a "-" followed by return. If you type "-" it turns clockwise through ANGLE degrees. Then it moves 2*DISTANCE and again waits for instructions about turning. After you type + or -, the next step is 3*DISTANCE, and so on. You will not see what you type in as the change in direction because you are in graph mode. But from the action in graph mode you can see that it is responding to your instructions. Have fun with this one. It has no practical use.

Chapter 14

MORE UCSD PASCAL SYSTEM COMMANDS

In Chapter 4 we introduced you to the UCSD Pascal operating system and showed you how to use enough of the commands to let you enter programs, edit them, run them, and file them. This introduced the UCSD Pascal command language.

LEVELS IN THE COMMAND LANGUAGE

The language is hierarchical in that there are various levels. The uppermost level is the COMMAND level. (We write COMMAND in capital letters to distinguish it from the general word command, since commands are available at all levels, not just at the COMMAND level.) At the COMMAND level you have at your disposal a number of commands which take you down one level in the hierarchy. For example, by pressing E(DIT you are placed in the edit level (or mode). At the edit level there is another set of commands that is available. For example, by pressing I(NSRT you are placed in the insert level. The insert level is at the third level. The COMMAND level is level one, the edit level is level two, and the insert level is level three.

At each level, except at level one, there is a command that will return you to the level from which you came. There may, as well, be a number of commands that will take you to higher levels. This structure of the command language is a tree structure, with the tree's root at the COMMAND level. From there, branches take you to the second levels such as the edit, file, run, or execute levels.

So far we have only introduced the basic commands that you need to get along. But there are more that are useful when you are using your computer a great deal. We will, however, not explain *all* the available commands even now.

EDIT MODE COMMANDS

We have explained how, in the edit mode, to establish a new workfile, how to type in programs, how to erase characters or lines, how to move the cursor, and how to use the insert and delete commands. As well, we learned how to leave the edit mode with the workfile updated.

We will now look at some additional features available from the edit mode.

COPY COMMAND

The command C(PY is used to copy material stored on the disk memory into the program in the workfile. Move the cursor to the place in your program where you want the copied material to be inserted, just as you would for an insert, then press C(PY. This causes this prompt line to appear:

>COPY: B(UFFER F(ROM FILE<ESC>

Type F(ROM and the prompt line changes to:

>COPY: FROM WHAT FILE[MARKER,MARKER]?

For the moment we will assume that you will copy the whole file; it may, for example, be a procedure that you want to include in your program. (It is possible to have placed markers in a file and copy only the portion between the markers.) To copy the whole file, type its name, followed by return. The file being copied is not altered in any way. If markers are being used the notation [marker,marker] after the file name copies the file between the markers; [,marker] copies the file up to the marker; the notation [marker,] copies from the marker to the end of the file. We will tell you later how to insert markers into files.

An alternative way of including a complete file in a program is to use the compiler option invoked by placing

(*$I file name *)

in the program at the place where the copy is to be located. The $ sign indicates that it is not a comment; the I stands for INCLUDE. The include option is useful when programs grow large.

USE OF COPY BUFFER

Whenever material is either copied, inserted, or deleted in the edit mode it is stored in the copy buffer. It is possble to gain access to the material in the copy buffer and copy it into your program. To do this, place the cursor at the point where the insertion is to be located, enter the copy mode and then type B(UFFER. The material from the copy buffer is placed between where the cursor sits on typing B and the character to the left of the cursor. The contents of the copy buffer itself remain unchanged.

This facility is very useful for moving material from one place to another. Simply delete the material from its original position. On deletion it is placed in the copy buffer from which, after moving the cursor, it can be copied into the new location. Also you can copy the same material several times to different places in the program since the contents of the copy buffer are not changed when it is copied into a program. But remember that any insertion or deletion changes the contents of the copy buffer.

CHANGING WORDS AND CHARACTERS

A simple way to change one character to another in a program is to type X(CHANGE from the edit mode. This prompt line appears.

>EXCHANGE: TEXT[<BS> A CHAR][<ESC>ESCAPES;
       <ETX>ACCEPTS]

Before you enter the *exchange mode* place the cursor on the character to be substituted for. On entry to the exchange mode type in the new character or characters. This is a one-for-one substitution but as many characters as you want may be exchanged. If you want to correct a typing error that you may make during the exchange, backspace <BS> will restore the original character. When you are finished, type <ETX> to have the exchange accepted. You cannot go beyond the end of a line in an exchange.

In general, the *replace mode* is more versatile since the substitution need not be character-for-character. To enter the replace mode, type R from the edit mode. The prompt line will be:

>REPLACE[1]: L(IT V(FY <TARG> <SUB> =>

The string of characters that is to be replaced is called the *target string* (<TARG>); the string that is to be substituted is <SUB>. These two strings are now entered each one surrounded by a slash (/). For example, suppose that you wanted to replace the string PROCEEDURE by the string PROCEDURE you will type

/PROCEEDURE//PROCEDURE/

The first instance of the word PROCEEDURE in your program, following the present position of the cursor and going toward the end of the program, is replaced by the word PROCEDURE. If there are several instances of this same substitution, say it occurs twice, you can change both by typing 2R as you enter the replace mode. If you want to replace all instances type /R.

An option called the verify option is available by typing V(FY before you type the target string. Each target string that is found is displayed so that you can decide whether or not to replace it. Type R to replace, space bar to skip by that occurrence without replacement.

The *find mode* is similar to the replace mode but no substitution is made. The cursor is moved to the end of the string named as the target string. If you then type FS the cursor will move to the next occurrence of the same target string. If you type 2F the cursor stops at the second occurrence of the specified string following its present location.

FORMAT COMMANDS

By typing A(DJST in the edit mode you enter the *adjust mode* where the prompt line is:

> ADJUST: L(JUST R(JUST C(ENTER <LEFT,RIGHT,UP,
DOWN-ARROWS>[<ETX>TO LEAVE]

One of the purposes of the *adjust mode* is to alter the indentation of lines. By pressing one of the left or right arrow keys the whole line in which the cursor is located can be moved in that direction one space. When you have moved it far enough, press <ETX> to have the new position accepted. If you want a number of lines moved, after you have adjusted one line the required number of character positions, left or right, and before you press <ETX>, move the cursor up or down, to each of the other lines that you want adjusted. After you have moved to each in turn, press <ETX> to have all the changes accepted.

Adjust can also be used to center text, left justify it (bring all the lines to a common left margin), or right justify it. Just type C, L, or R from the adjust mode and the line in which the cursor is located will be adjusted accordingly. By moving the cursor up or down, each line it moves to will be similarly adjusted. After you are finished press <ETX> to have all the adjustments accepted.

MARKERS

It is often convenient to have markers placed in a long program so that the cursor may be moved rapidly to a particular part or so that portions of the program may be copied from a program on file. To set a marker, move the cursor to the spot where the marker is to be placed and press S(ET. Then type M(ARKER at which point the prompt line becomes:

SET WHAT MARKER?

You must give this marker a name (up to 8 characters), then press return. A maximum of 10 markers is allowed in a file.

When editing a file you can jump to any marker by pressing J(UMP at which time the prompt line becomes:

>JUMP: B(EGINNING E(ND M(ARKER

B or E causes the cursor to jump to the beginning or end of the file but M produces this question:

JUMP TO WHAT MARKER?

At which point you type the name of the marker to which you want the cursor moved. Press return after you are finished. The use of markers for copying was explained before.

FILE MODE COMMANDS

So far we have used only two file mode commands. One of these is N(EW, which is used to create a new workfile. This file is created blank, both in the memory and on the disk, under the name SYSTEM.WRK. It is the workfile that is referred to whenever we give a R(UN command at the COMMAND level. The other file mode command we have used is S(AVE to get the workfile saved as a named file on the disk.

Another file mode command is G(ET which brings a named file into the workfile area of memory. The command E(XT-DIR causes the extended directory of what is stored on the diskette presently located in the disk drive to be displayed. This is a list of the name of the set of files followed by the names of each file stored on the diskette. The set of files is called a *volume*. All volume names end with a colon. The directory contains the date at which each file was last modified. This date is added automatically whenever a file is saved but the computer must be told the date whenever you first start it up on a particular day. To do this, use the D(ATE command in the file mode. A prompt line like this appears:

DATE SET: <1..31>-<JAN..DEC>-<00..99>
TODAY IS 17-MAR-82
NEW DATE ?

If the date displayed is correct you do not need to put a new one in just press return; but if it is not correct, type the day's date, in the same form as shown, after the NEW DATE? prompt. When return is pressed, the new date will be displayed.

ORGANIZING DISK FILES

If you want to change the name of a file or a volume (a diskette) use the file mode command C(HNG. You must supply the old name when asked:

CHANGE WHAT FILE?

and the new name when prompted:

CHANGE TO WHAT?

To remove a file from the diskette, use R(EM. You are asked:

REMOVE WHAT FILE?

So you type its name. This removes the file from the directory only and you cannot use it any more but it still remains on the diskette. You must compact the contents of the diskette using the K(RNCH command to get rid of it. But we will describe that later.

To move a file from one diskette (volume) to another use T(RANSFER. You must provide both the volume names followed by the file name. When asked:

TRANSFER WHAT FILE?

you type for example

DISK1: FILE5.TEXT

After you type return, the next prompt line is:

TO WHERE?

to which you respond the volume name followed by the file name that is the destination. If you have only one disk drive on your computer, you will have to change diskettes. Do not take out the original diskette (the source) until prompt lines like these appear:

PUT IN DISK2:
TYPE <SPACE> TO CONTINUE

Take out the source diskette, insert the destination diskette (here called DISK2:) and then press the space bar. You will be notified on the screen that the transfer is successful.

Using T(RANSFER is a method of obtaining hardcopy by naming, as the destination volume,

PRINTER:

Of course, you must have a printer on line.

COPYING DISKETTES

To copy, or transfer, the entire contents of a diskette you should reply to the T(RANSFER prompt by giving just a volume name. (This always must end with a colon.) Copying diskettes with two drives is relatively simple but it is a slower process if you have only one drive. The disk drives have volume numbers. If you have only one drive it is unit #4. (The keyboard is #2, the screen is #1, a printer is #6, and a second disk drive is #5.)

Suppose that you want to copy a diskette called DISK1:. First you must format a blank diskette in the format that is required by the UCSD Pascal system. To do this you must go to the COMMAND level and type X(ECUTE when the question:

EXECUTE WHAT FILE?

appears you reply:

volume name: FORMATTER

The volume containing the FORMATTER program must be in the disk drive. It asks:

FORMAT WHICH DISK?

You remove the FORMATTER diskette, place the blank diskette in the drive, and reply 4; then press return. The message is:

NOW FORMATTING DISKETTE IN DRIVE 4

When the computer asks if you have further disks to format, your blank disk has been formatted and given the name BLANK:. This is a standard name given to a formatted blank diskette. Press return if you are finished formatting blank disks, 4 if you have more.

Now that you have a formatted blank diskette you can copy any other diskette on to it. To copy DISK1:, from the file mode press T and this exchange takes place:

TRANSFER WHAT FILE?   (place DISK1: in drive)
DISK1:
TO WHERE?
BLANK:
TRANSFER 280 BLOCKS ?(Y/N)
Y
PUT IN BLANK: (remove DISK1:, put in BLANK:)
TYPE <SPACE> TO CONTINUE   (do so)
DESTROY BLANK:?
Y
PUT DISK1: IN UNIT #4   (do so)
TYPE <SPACE> TO CONTINUE
PUT BLANK: IN UNIT #4   (do so)
TYPE <SPACE> TO CONTINUE

   ... (about 20 times)

DISK1: ---> BLANK:

You should write DISK1: on the disk's envelope that was formerly
BLANK: as the copying is complete. It is important that diskettes be
labeled so that you can read what they are. When diskettes are reused,
relabel them.

COMPACTING DISK FILES

If you examine the directory of a disk you will see, after the file's
name, the number of blocks that the file occupies. (The total capacity of
the diskette is 280 blocks on the Apple diskette.) On the right of the date is
the starting address of the file in terms of block number. You can tell if
there are unused blocks from this list. Since new files can only be stored at
the end of the list, it is important to compress the files. whenever there is
a space shortage. To do this, type K(RNCH to crunch the files. You will
be prompted:

CRUNCH WHAT VOL?

to which you reply 4 (since it is the disk), or better the name of the
diskette. If asked

FROM END OF DISK, BLOCK 280? (Y/N)

respond Y(ES. Do not touch anything until you have been informed that
crunching is complete.

Before any compaction operation on the diskette is initiated, it is a good idea to look for *bad blocks* and mark them as bad so that they will not be used. All new diskettes should be examined after they have been formatted. To locate bad blocks type B(AD-BLKS. The prompt becomes:

BAD BLOCKS OF WHAT VOL?

you type the name of the diskette in the disk drive. Then the prompt is:

SCAN FOR 280 BLOCKS? (Y/N)

Answer Y(ES. As the checking process proceeds all bad blocks are listed in a display such as

BLOCK 5 IS BAD
BLOCK 6 IS BAD
2 BAD BLOCKS

You must now prevent these blocks from being used again. To do this type X(AMINE and the prompt is:

EXAMINE BLOCKS ON WHAT VOLUME?

Respond with the name of the diskette in the drive. The prompt appears:

BLOCK-RANGE?

Respond: 5-6. If there are files stored in these blocks you get a message

FILE(S) ENDANGERED
OPUSI.TEXT 4 6
FIX THEM?

Respond Y(ES. The reply may vary, one reply might be:

BLOCK 5 MAY BE OK BLOCK 6 IS BAD MARK THEM?

Respond Y(ES and the filer creates a special file which is listed in the directory as a *marked file*. When you crunch, this marked file prevents the bad blocks from being used.

CHAPTER 14 SUMMARY

In this chapter we presented more UCSD system commands that are available in the edit and file modes of the command structure. These commands give you additional flexibility beyond what is described in Chapter 4.

The following additional commands are available from the edit mode:

C(PY - used to copy material from a file on disk into the workfile in memory. The copying is effectively an insertion at the location of the cursor. Partial files may be copied provided markers have been placed in the file. As files are being copied they are stored in the copy buffer.

Include option - a compiler option which has the effect of copying a file into a program. To invoke it place the line

(*$I file name *)

in the program where the inclusion is to be. The file will be included when the program is run.

B(UFFER - used to copy material from the copy buffer to the workfile, the material being inserted at the location of the cursor. All material that is either deleted or inserted in edit mode gets stored in the buffer so that this command is useful for moving material from place to place in the workfile. Just delete it form one place and use B(UFFER to copy it into another.

X(CHANGE - used to replace character for character in memory.

R(EPLACE - used to replace a target string by a substitute string. Can be used for multiple substitution.

V(FY - if this is typed before you enter the target string in a replacement, each occurrence of the target string is displayed. Type R to actually replace by substitute string; type space not to replace but move to next occurrence.

F(IND - similar to R(EPLACE except that the cursor is placed at the end of the target string; no substitution occurs.

A(DJST - used to move lines of text in the workfile left or right, and to center them. Text may also be left- or right-justified to preset margins.

S(ET - must be used before you can place a marker.

M(ARKER - places a marker in the text in the workfile. This is useful in the C(PY operation.

J(UMP - used to jump the cursor to a particular marker in the text. This can speed up the cursor moving operation in editing. Another way to do this is to type an integer N before a cursor moves to cause N repetitions of the move.

The following additional commands are available from the file mode:

G(ET - brings a named file into the workfile area of memory.

E(XT-DIR - lists the contents of a named diskette (called a volume). The diskette must be in the disk drive. The directory shows the location of each file and its size in terms of blocks. (For the Apple, a diskette contains 280 blocks).

D(ATE - used to set the day's date in the computer so that this date may be stored in the directory showing when files are saved. Whatever date is in the computer is automatically placed in the directory entry of a saved file.

C(HNG - used to change the name of a file or volume. This changes the directory entry.

R(EMOVE - used to remove a file from a directory. The space that the file occupies is not recovered until a compressing operation is done on the volume by K(RNCH.

T(RANSFER - used to move a file from one diskette (volume) to another. When only one disk drive exists, diskettes must be interchanged in the drive as requested by the computer. To copy an entire volume to a new diskette requires about 20 interchanges of diskettes. Blank diskettes must be formatted before volumes can be copied onto them.

K(RNCH - used to compact files that have unused blocks scattered about (often due to a removal).

B(AD-BLKS - used to locate blocks on the diskette that are faulty. These blocks must not be used in the future. It is a good idea to test freshly formatted diskettes for bad blocks.

X(AMINE - used to doublecheck on bad blocks and to mark those that are really unusable so that they are not used in future.

Chapter 15

SEARCHING AND SORTING

When a large amount of information is stored in a computer, it must be organized so that you are able to get at the information to make use of it. This problem of *data retrieval* is at the heart of all business operations. Records are kept of employees, customers, suppliers, inventory, in-process goods, and so on. These records are usually grouped in some way into what are called *files*. We might have, for example, a file of employee records, a file of customer records, an inventory file, and so on. Each file must be kept up to date.

A file that we all have access to is printed in the telephone book. It consists of a series of *records* of names, addresses, and telephone numbers. We say that there are three *fields* in each of these records: the name field, the address field, and the phone-number field. The file is in the alphabetic order of one of the three fields, the name field. We say that the name field is the *key* to the ordering of the file. The file is in alphabetic order on this field because that is how it can be most useful to us for data retrieval. We know someone's name and we want his phone number. We might also want his address and that too is available. The telephone company also has the same set of records, ordered using the phone-number field as the key.

In this chapter we will be investigating how a computer can search for information in a file and how records can be sorted.

LINEAR SEARCH

One way to look for data in a file is to start at the beginning and examine each record until you find the one you are looking for. This is the method people use who do not have large files. But for more than about 12 records it is not a good filing system. It will serve as an example to introduce us to the idea of searching mechanically and give us a bad method to compare our better methods to. We will create a file which consists of names and telephone numbers but the file will not be ordered by either name or number.

We will keep the file in two one-dimensional arrays, one called NAME and one called NUMBER. NUMBER[I] will be the correct telephone number for NAME[I]. We will read this file, then read a list of names of people whose phone numbers are wanted. Here is the program to do this job. We are assuming that our file of names and phone numbers is entered so that the name is left-justified in the first 20 columns followed by the phone number in the next 8 columns.

```
(* LOOK UP PHONE NUMBERS IN DIRECTORY *)
PROGRAM PHONES;
   CONST NAMEWIDTH=20;
      NUMBERWIDTH=8;
      DIRECSIZE=50;
      DUMMY='*';
   TYPE NAMETYPE=PACKED ARRAY[1..NAMEWIDTH] OF CHAR;
      NUMBERTYPE=PACKED ARRAY[1..NUMBERWIDTH] OF CHAR;
      DIREC=ARRAY[1..DIRECSIZE] OF NAMETYPE;
      DIRECINDEX=0..DIRECSIZE;
   VAR NAME: DIREC;
      NUMBER:ARRAY[1..DIRECSIZE] OF NUMBERTYPE;
      FRIEND,BLANKS: NAMETYPE;
      FILESIZE,I: DIRECINDEX;
      J: 0..NAMEWIDTH;
      K: 1..NUMBERWIDTH;
      CH: CHAR;
   BEGIN
      (* READ IN FILE OF NAMES AND NUMBERS *)
      WRITELN('ENTER PHONE DIRECTORY');
      WRITELN('NAME','PHONE':21);
      I:=0;
      REPEAT
         I:=I+1;
         FOR J:=1 TO NAMEWIDTH DO
            BEGIN
               READ(CH);
               NAME[I][J]:=CH
            END;
         FOR K:=1 TO NUMBERWIDTH DO
            BEGIN
               READ(CH);
               NUMBER[I][K]:=CH
            END;
         READLN
```

```
        UNTIL NAME[I][1]=DUMMY;
        FILESIZE:=I-1;
        FOR J:=1 TO NAMEWIDTH DO
            BLANKS[J]:=' ';
        WHILE NOT EOF DO
            BEGIN (* LOOK UP FRIEND'S NUMBER *)
                WRITELN('ENTER FRIEND''S NAME');
                FRIEND:=BLANKS;
                J:=0;
                WHILE (NOT EOLN) AND (J<NAMEWIDTH) DO
                    BEGIN
                        J:=J+1;
                        READ(CH);
                        FRIEND[J]:=CH
                    END;
                READLN;
                IF EOF THEN
                    WRITELN;
                I:=1;
                WHILE(FRIEND<>NAME[I]) AND (I<=FILESIZE)DO
                    I:=I+1;
                IF FRIEND=NAME[I] THEN
                    WRITELN(FRIEND,NUMBER[I])
                ELSE
                    WRITELN(FRIEND,'UNLISTED')
            END
    END.
```

Here is a sample display:

```
ENTER PHONE DIRECTORY
NAME                    PHONE
PERRAULT,R.             483-4865
BORODIN,A.              782-8928
COOK,S.A.               763-3900
ENRIGHT,W.H.            266-1234
*                       999-9999
ENTER FRIEND'S NAME
BORODIN,A.
BORODIN,A.              782-8928
ENTER FRIEND'S NAME
DAVIES,R.
DAVIES,R.                       UNLISTED
```

We have stored the phone number as a character string because of the dash between the first three and the last four digits.

TIME TAKEN FOR SEARCH

In the last section we developed a program for a linear search. The searching process consists of comparing the friend's name, FRIEND, with each name in the file of names NAME[1], NAME[2], NAME[3], and so on until either the name is found or the end of the file is reached. For a small file, a linear search like this one may be fast enough, but it can be time-consuming if the file is lengthy.

If there are N records in the file and the name is actually in the file, then on the average there will be N/2 comparisons. The largest number of comparisons would be N if the name were last in the file, the least number would be 1 if the name were first. A file of 1000 names would require 500 comparisons on the average. This gets to look rather formidable. It is for this reason that we do something to cut down on the effort. What we do is to sort the file into alphabetic order and then use a method of searching called *binary searching*. We will look at sorting later, but first we will see how much faster binary searching can be.

BINARY SEARCH

The telephone book is sorted alphabetically and the technique most of us use for looking up numbers is similar to the technique known as binary searching. We start by opening the book near where we think we will find the name we are looking for. We look at the page that is open and compare any name on it with the name being sought. If the listed name is alphabetically greater we know we must look only between the page we are at and the beginning of the book. We have eliminated the second part of the book from the search. This process is repeated in the part that might contain the name until we narrow the search down to one page.

In binary searching, instead of looking where we think we might find the name, we begin by looking at the name in the middle of the file and discard the half in which it cannot lie. This process cuts the possible number of names to be searched in half at each comparison.

A file of 16 names would require a maximum of 4 comparisons: one to cut the list to 8, another to 4, another to 2, and another to 1. Of course, we might find it earlier, but this is the *most* work we have to do. It is the maximum number of comparisons. With a linear search of 16 records we might have to make 16 comparisons, although 8 is the average. If we have a file of 1024 records, the binary search takes a maximum of 10 comparisons. This can be calculated by seeing how many times you must divide by 2 to get down to 1 record. Put mathematically, 1024 is equal to

$$2*2*2*2*2*2*2*2*2*2$$

Just one more comparison, making 11 altogether, will let you search a list of 2048 entries. Then 4096 can be done with 12 comparisons. You can see how much more efficient binary searching can be when the file is a long one.

A PROCEDURE FOR BINARY SEARCH

We will now design a program for doing a binary search and write it so that it can be called as a procedure. When we write

SEARCH(BASICFILE,KEY,SIZE,LOCATION)

we are asking for the value of LOCATION for which BASICFILE[LOCATION]=KEY, where BASICFILE is an array of items declared as of type NAMETYPE. If the KEY is not in the file, LOCATION will be set to zero.

We will develop the algorithm for the binary search in two stages as an illustration of step-by-step refinement. We will write out our proposed solution in a form that is a mixture of English and Pascal.

```
        Set LOCATION to zero in case KEY is not in BASICFILE;
        WHILE(there is more of the file to search) DO
            BEGIN
                Find middle of file;
                IF middle value matches KEY THEN
                    BEGIN
                        Set LOCATION to middle;
                        Discard remainder of file
                    END
                ELSE
                    IF middle value comes after KEY THEN
                        Discard last half of remainder of file
                    ELSE
                        Discard first half of remainder of file
            END;
```

It will be important to know the FIRST and LAST of the remainder of the file at any time in order to establish the MIDDLE and to discard the appropriate half. We initially set FIRST to 1 and LAST to SIZE. Then to find the middle we use

MIDDLE:=TRUNC((LAST+FIRST)/2);

It will not matter that this division is truncated as the process of finding the middle is approximate when the number of entries in the file is an even number. Refining the expression, "Discard last half of remainder of file," becomes

LAST:=MIDDLE-1;

and, "Discard first half of remainder of file," becomes

FIRST:=MIDDLE+1;

Notice that we are discarding BASICFILE[MIDDLE] as well in each case. The procedure can now be written:

```
(* LOCATE KEY USING BINARY SEARCH *)
PROCEDURE SEARCH(BASICFILE:DIREC; KEY:NAMETYPE;
    SIZE:INTEGER; VAR LOCATION:DIRECINDEX);
  VAR FIRST,LAST,MIDDLE: INTEGER;
  BEGIN
    (* SET LOCATION TO ZERO IF KEY NOT IN FILE *)
    LOCATION:=0;
    (* INITIALIZE THE SEARCH LOOP *)
    FIRST:=1;
    LAST:=SIZE;
    (* SEARCH UNTIL FILE IS EXHAUSTED *)
    WHILE FIRST<=LAST DO
      BEGIN
        MIDDLE:=(FIRST+LAST) DIV 2;
        IF BASICFILE[MIDDLE]=KEY THEN
          BEGIN
            LOCATION:=MIDDLE;
            (* DISCARD ALL OF FILE *)
            FIRST:=LAST+1
          END
        ELSE
          IF BASICFILE[MIDDLE]>KEY THEN
            (* DISCARD LAST HALF *)
            LAST:=MIDDLE-1
          ELSE
            (* DISCARD FIRST HALF *)
            FIRST:=MIDDLE+1
      END
  END;
```

A program that uses this procedure can now be written. We will use it to look up telephone numbers. We will replace the following serial search in the PHONES program:

```
I=1;
WHILE(FRIEND<>NAME[I]) AND (I<=FILESIZE) DO
    I:=I+1;
IF FRIEND=NAME[I] THEN ...
```

This becomes:

```
SEARCH(NAME,FRIEND,FILESIZE,I);
IF I<>0 THEN ...
```

We are assuming that the file of names is sorted alphabetically. The procedure SEARCH should be included right after the declaration of variables in the main program.

You will notice that the binary search program has more instructions than the linear search that it is replacing. Each step is more complicated, but the process is much faster for a large file because fewer steps are executed.

SEARCHING BY ADDRESS CALCULATION

We have seen that the efficiency of the searching process is very much improved by having a file sorted. The next method of searching uses data organized in a way so there is "a place for everything, and everything in its place".

Suppose you had a file of N records numbered from 1 to N. If you knew the number of the record, you would immediately know the location. The number would be the index of the array that holds the file entries. Each entry would have a location where it belonged. The trouble usually is to find the location of a record when what you know is some other piece of information such as a person's name.

Files are sometimes arranged so that they are organized on serial numbers that can be calculated from some other information in the record. For example, we could take a person's name and, by transforming it in a certain definite way, change it into a serial number. This transformation often seems bizarre and meaningless, and we say the name is *hash-coded* into a number. When the number has been determined, the location is then definite and you can go to it without any problem.

Usually with hash coding it happens that several records have the same hash code. This means that, instead of the code providing the address of the exact record you want, what you get is the address of a location capable of containing several different records. We call such a location a *bucket* or *bin*. We then must look at the records in the bin to find the exact one we are interested in. Since the number is small they need not be sorted. A linear search is reasonable when the number of items is small.

If fixed-size bins are used to store the file, it is important to get a hash coding algorithm that will divide the original file so that roughly the same number of records is in each bin.

As an example of a hash-coding algorithm, suppose that we had 1000 bins and wanted to divide a file of 10,000 records into the bins. The file might already have associated with each record an identifying number. For example, it might be a Social Insurance number or a student number. These numbers might range from 1 to 1,000,000. One way to divide the records into bins would be to choose the last three digits of the identifying number as the hash code. Another hash code might be formed by choosing the third, fifth, and seventh digit. The purpose is to try to get a technique that gives about the same number of records in each bin. More complicated hashing algorithms may be necessary.

SORTING

We have already developed a sorting program as an example of step-by-step refinement in Chapter 10. The method we used is called a *bubble sort*. Each pair of neighboring elements in a file is compared and exchanged, to put the element with the larger key in the array location with the higher index. On each exchange pass, the element with the largest key gets moved into the last position. The next pass can then exclude the last position because it is already in order.

We have shown that the binary search technique is much more efficient for a large file than a linear search. In the same way, although a bubble sort is a reasonable method for a small file, it is not efficient for a large file. What we usually do to sort a large file is to divide it into a number of smaller files. Each small file is sorted by a technique such as the bubble sort, then the sorted smaller files are merged together into larger files.

We will look at an example in which two sorted files are merged into a single larger sorted file.

SORTING BY MERGING

We will develop a procedure called MERGE to merge FILE1, which has SIZE1 records ordered on the field KEYFILE1, with FILE2, which has

SIZE2 records ordered on the field KEYFILE2, and store it in FILE3. We
will invoke this procedure with the statement

      MERGE(KEYFILE1,SIZE1,KEYFILE2,SIZE2,KEYFILE3);

Here is the MERGE procedure:

```
(* MERGE TWO SORTED FILES *)
PROCEDURE MERGE(KEYFILE1:FILETYPE; SIZE1:INTEGER;
    KEYFILE2:FILETYPE; SIZE2:INTEGER;
                    VAR KEYFILE3:FILETYPE);
  VAR I1,I2,I3: INTEGER;
  BEGIN
      I1:=1;
      I2:=1;
      I3:=1;
      (* MERGE UNTIL ALL OF ONE FILE IS USED *)
      WHILE(I1<=SIZE1)  AND  (I2<=SIZE2)DO
        BEGIN
            IF KEYFILE1[I1]<KEYFILE2[I2]THEN
                BEGIN
                    KEYFILE3[I3]:=KEYFILE1[I1];
                    I1:=I1+1
                END
            ELSE
                BEGIN
                    KEYFILE3[I3]:=KEYFILE2[I2];
                    I2:=I2+1
                END;
            I3:=I3+1
        END;
      (* ADD REMAINING ITEMS TO END OF NEW FILE *)
      WHILE I1<=SIZE1 DO
        BEGIN
            KEYFILE3[I3]:=KEYFILE1[I1];
            I1:=I1+1;
            I3:=I3+1
        END;
      WHILE I2<=SIZE2 DO
        BEGIN
            KEYFILE3[I3]:=KEYFILE2[I2];
            I2:=I2+1;
            I3:=I3+1
        END
  END;
```

EFFICIENCY OF SORTING METHODS

The number of comparisons required to merge the two previously sorted files in our example is SIZE1+SIZE2. To sort a file of length N by the bubble sort we can count the maximum number of comparisons that are needed. It is

$$(N-1) + (N-2) + (N-3) + ... + 1$$

This series can be summed and the result is

N(N-1)/2 which is
$N^2/2 - N/2$

When N is large, the number of comparisons is about $N^2/2$, since this is very large compared to N/2. We say the execution time of the algorithm varies as N^2; sorting 100 items takes 100 times the number of comparisons that sorting 10 items does. We will now make calculations to see why sorting by merging is useful for long files. To sort a file of N items, by first using a bubble sort on two files N/2 in length then merging, requires $N^2/4$-N/2 for the bubble sort and N for the merge. This makes a combination total of

$N^2/4 + N/2$ comparisons.

Using a bubble sort on the whole file gives a result of

$N^2/2 - N/2$ comparisons.

When N is 100, the bubble sort merge method requires 2,550 comparisons, the straight bubble sort requires 4,950 comparisons. We can keep dividing files and subfiles, sorting them by merging, with further improvements. In the limit we have a *successive merge* sort that is efficient enough to be used for large files.

CHAPTER 15 SUMMARY

This chapter has presented methods of searching and sorting that are used in computer programs. These methods manipulate *files* of *records*. Each record consists of one or more *fields*.

A search is based on a *key*, such as a person's name, that appears as one field in a record of a file. A *linear search* locates the desired record by starting at the first record and inspecting one record after another until the given key is found. A linear search is slow and should not be used for large files; a faster search method, such as binary search, should be used for large files.

A *binary search* requires that the file be ordered according to the key field of the records. An unordered file can be ordered using one of the sorting methods given in this chapter. The binary search inspects the middle record to determine which half of the file contains the desired record. Then the middle record of the correct half is inspected, to determine which quarter of the file contains the desired record, and so on, until the record is located.

If the key is a number that is identical to the index of the desired record then no searching is required, because the key gives the location of the record. Sometimes the key can be manipulated to create a *hash code* that locates a small set of records, called a *bucket*, that includes the desired record.

A file of records can be ordered using the bubble sort. This method repeatedly passes through the file, interchanging adjacent out-of-order records until all records are in order. The bubble sort is slow and should not be used for large files; a faster sorting method, such as sorting by merging, should be used for large files.

A file can be sorted by merging in the following manner. First the file is divided into two sub-files and each of the sub-files is sorted by some method, such as the bubble sort. Then, starting with the first records of the two sub-files, the ordered file is created by passing through the sub-files and successively picking the appropriate (smaller key or alphabetically first key) record. If the sub-files are large, they should be sorted by a fast method, such as a merge, instead of by a bubble sort.

CHAPTER 15 EXERCISES

1. Prepare a file of names and addresses, enter the file and order it alphabetically. Now try looking up the address of a friend in your file. We will find this is all more practical once we learn about files on disk.

2. Write a program that maintains a "lost and found" service. First the program reads entries giving found objects and the finders' names and phone numbers. For example, this entry

SIAMESE CAT MISS MABEL DAVIS 714-3261

means Miss Mabel Davis, having phone number 714-3261, found a Siamese cat. These entries are to be read and ordered alphabetically and then a similar set of entries for losers of objects is to be processed. If a lost object matches a found object, then the program should display the name of the object as well as the finder, the loser and their telephone numbers. Assume the loser entries are not alphabetized. Process each loser entry as it is read, using a binary search.

Chapter 16

MAKING SURE THE PROGRAM WORKS

Throughout this book, we have emphasized structured programming techniques; these include step-by-step refinement, programming without the GO TO statement, choosing good variable names and so on. These techniques make it easier to write correct programs. We have also given techniques for testing and debugging programs. In this chapter we will collect and expand upon these techniques for making sure a program works.

SOLVING THE RIGHT PROBLEM

The *specifications* for a program tell what the program must do to solve a problem. Before starting to write a program, the programmer needs the detailed specifications for the program. Suppose the problem is to prepare pay checks for the employees of a company; there is an entry giving each employee's name and amount of payment. The programmer needs to know the format of the data entry as well as the format for the pay checks. These formats are part of the specifications for the program to prepare pay checks.

Sometimes the program specifications are not completely agreed upon and written down. If an employee's entry indicates an amount of $0.00, this may mean that the employee is on leave and is to receive no pay check. If the programmer does not know the special significance of $0.00 - because the specifications are not complete - he may write a program that prepares hundreds of worthless pay checks. Often programs fail to handle special situations such as $0.00 correctly. If the programmer is in doubt, he should check the specifications and make sure they are complete.

DEFENSIVE PROGRAMMING

Errors are sometimes made in the preparation of data for a program. Amounts may be entered incorrectly; more data may be supplied than anticipated. The method of handling data errors may be given in the program specifications, or it may be left to the discretion of the programmer. Sometimes a programmer can write his program so that it detects and reports bad data. This is called *defensive programming.* Some programs are written to accept absolutely any data; after reporting a bad data item, the program ignores the item or attempts to give it a reasonable interpretation. If a program is written assuming no data errors, bad data items may prevent the program from doing its job. It is the programmer's responsibility to make his program sufficiently defensive to solve the problem at hand.

ATTITUDE AND WORK HABITS

The quality of a computer program is determined largely by the attitudes and work habits of the programmer. Some programmers underestimate the programming task. They write programs too quickly, they do not test their programs sufficiently, and they are too willing to believe that their programs are correct.

Most programs, when first written, contain some errors. This is not surprising when you consider the vast number of possible programming errors and the fallibility of every programmer. The programmer should take the attitude that a program is not correct until it is shown to be correct.

One good method of preparing computer programs is to write them using a soft lead pencil. This allows easy corrections and improvements by erasing and replacing lines. If a major change is required, an entire page should be recopied. The program should be submitted to the computer only when the programmer feels confident that no more changes are required. This method of program preparation can save the programmer a lot of time. The savings come because it is easy to change a program when it is still on paper and fresh in the programmer's mind. Each later change requires the programmer to relearn the program before he can confidently make modifications. A few minutes of desk-checking a program can save hours of debugging time. The programmer who tries to "do it right the first time" comes out ahead, saving his own time and writing programs with fewer errors.

PROVING PROGRAM CORRECTNESS

The most effective way to make sure a program works correctly is to study the program thoroughly. It should be read again and again until the programmer is thoroughly convinced that it is right.

It helps if a second programmer reads and approves the program. Ideally, the second programmer should read the program after its author feels that it is correct, but before it is submitted to the computer. The second reader provides a new point of view and may be able to find typical errors such as incorrect loop initialization.

This process of studying programs to make sure they are correct can be called "proving program correctness". Sometimes programs are proven correct using a mathematical approach; proving that a program is correct is then similar to proving that a theorem in geometry is true. More often, programs are proven correct by a non-mathematical, common-sense approach. The program is considered to have errors until proven correct.

PROGRAMMING STYLE

A program should be easy to read and understand; otherwise the job of studying it to verify its correctness will be hopeless. The programmer should strive for a good *programming style*, remembering that other readers will be in a hurry and will be critical of sloppiness or unnecessary confusion in the program. It commonly happens that as a programmer makes a program clearer and easier to understand, he discovers ways to improve or correct the program.

It takes work to write programs that are easy to read - just as it takes work to write clear English. Good writing requires care and practice. One way of making programs readable and understandable is to give them a simple organization - so the reader can easily learn the relationship among program parts. We have previously presented step-by-step refinement and division into subprograms, often called modular programming, as techniques for designing programs. As well as aiding in the writing of programs, these techniques help make programs easier to read.

USE OF COMMENTS AND IDENTIFIERS

One of the rules of good programming style is this: comments and identifiers should be chosen to help make a program understandable. Comments should record the programmer's intentions for the parts of the program. It is a good idea to write comments as the program is being written.

Better programs require fewer comments, because the program closely reflects the intentions of the programmer. Programs become more difficult to read if they are cluttered with obvious comments such as

(* INCREASE N BY 1 *)

N:=N+1;

Comments are usually needed to record:

- *Overall purpose of a program*. What problem the program is to solve. As well, comments may be used to record the program's author and its date of writing.

- *Purpose of each module*. Similar to the comments for an overall program.

- *Purpose of a collection of statements*. Such a comment might give the purpose of a loop.

- *Assumptions and restrictions*. At certain points in a program, assumptions and restrictions may apply to variables and the data. For example, one program part may assume that another program part has set NUMBEROFACCOUNTS to a positive number less than 20 to indicate the number of customer accounts.

- *Obscure or unusual statements*. As a rule, such statements should be avoided. If they are required they should be explained.

Well-chosen identifiers make a program easier to read. Each identifier should record the function of the named object. For example, an array used to save account numbers should be named ACCOUNTNUMBER and not ARRAY. A procedure used to read accounts should be named READACCOUNTS and not P1 or MARGARET.

If a variable has a very simple purpose, such as indexing through an array, a one-letter name such as I, J or N may be appropriate. This is because these letters are commonly used for indexing in mathematics. But if the index variable has some additional meaning, such as counting input data entries, a longer name may help the reader.

Avoid abbreviations, such as TBNTR for table entry. Avoid acronyms, such as SAX for sales tax. Unless abbreviations or acronyms are well known to the reader before seeing the program, they impose an extra memorization task that interferes with understanding the program.

Avoid meaningless identifiers such as A, B, C, D and TEMP1. A single-letter identifier such as D is sometimes appropriate for a simply-used variable when the name D is relevant, for example, it stands for diameter. Adding a digit such as 1 or 2 to the end of an identifier, as in TEMP1, can be confusing unless it explains the purpose of the named object.

TESTING

After the program has been written and studied to verify its correctness, it should be tested. The purpose of testing is to run the program to demonstrate that it is working properly.

The tests must be chosen with care because only a limited number of them can be run. Consider a program designed to sort any list of 100 names into alphabetic order. Certainly we could not test it exhaustively by trying every possible list of 100 names. We would be testing for years! Rather than exhaustive testing we need to design tests which try every type of situation the program is to handle.

Well-designed tests should point out any errors in the program. Ultimately, testing demonstrates errors better than it demonstrates program correctness. When testing reveals an error, that is, a *bug*, in the program, the programmer is faced with a *debugging* task. We shall present debugging techniques later. Right now, we will give techniques for testing.

The programmer will need to study the program in order to design good tests. The tests should make each statement execute at least once - but this is not enough. Suppose the statement

AVERAGE:=TOTAL/COUNT;

is tested and computes the desired average. This does not demonstrate that all is well; it may be that in some situations COUNT can become zero. If this statement is executed with COUNT set to zero, the statement does not make sense. So, not only should every statement be executed, but it should be executed for the type of situation it is expected to handle. Care should be taken to:

- *Test end conditions.* See that each loop is executed correctly the first time and last time through. See that indexes to arrays reach their smallest and largest possible values. Pay particular attention to indexes and counters which may take on the value zero.

- *Test special conditions.* See that data which rarely occurs is handled properly. If the program displays error messages, see that each situation requiring such a message is tested.

Designing tests to exercise all end conditions and special conditions is not easy - but it is worthwhile in terms of program reliability.

The programmer should be able to tell from test results if the program is executing correctly. Sometimes this is easy because the program prints intermediate results as it progresses. Sometimes the programmer will need to add special printing statements so he can verify that the program is running correctly. These statements can:

Display messages to record the statement being executed. For example, a message might say READING ACCOUNTS PROCEDURE ENTERED.

Output values of variables. This allows the programmer to verify by hand that the values are correct. The best time to output variables is when modules start and when they finish, so the programmer can verify that variables were modified correctly.

Display warnings of violated assumptions. Suppose a procedure is used to set WHERE to the index of the smallest number in a list of 12 numbers. The assumption that WHERE receives a value from 1 to 12 can be tested by

```
IF (WHERE<1) OR (WHERE>12)THEN
    WRITELN(' ERROR:WHERE=',WHERE);
```

Care must be taken to design appropriate write statements for testing. Too much output will not be read by the programmer; too little will not give the programmer sufficient information about the execution of the program.

Ideally, tests should be designed before the program is submitted to the computer. With the program still fresh in his mind, the programmer can more easily invent tests that try out every statement. Sometimes a programmer discovers that parts of a program are difficult to test; a slight change in the program may overcome this difficulty. It is best to make these changes when the program is still on paper, before time has been invested in entering the program into the computer. Designing tests requires the programmer to read his program with a new point of view. It sometimes happens that this point of view uncovers errors in the program. The best time to fix these errors is when the program is still on paper.

As programs become larger, it becomes increasingly difficult to test them thoroughly. Large programs can be tested by first testing the modules individually. Then the modules are combined into larger modules and these are tested and so on. The process is called *bottom-up testing.* This method of testing uses specially-written test programs that call the modules with various values of parameters, shared variables and input data.

Whenever a program is modified, it should be retested. All the changed parts should be tested. In addition, it is a good idea to test the entire module containing changes, or even the entire program. The reason is that modifications often require a precise understanding of the surrounding program, and this understanding is sometimes not attained. Very commonly, program modifications introduce errors.

DEBUGGING

A program has bugs (errors) when it fails to solve the problem it is supposed to solve. When a program misbehaves we are faced with the problem of debugging - correcting the error. The program's misbehavior is a symptom of a disease and we must find a cure. Sometimes the symptom is far removed from the source of the problem; erroneous statements in one part of a program may set variables' values incorrectly and trigger a series of unpredicted actions by the program. When the symptoms appear via incorrect program output, the program may be executing in a different module. The programmer is left with a few clues: the incorrect output. He has to solve the mystery and cure the disease. Solving these debugging mysteries can take more time than writing the program.

When a program contains a bug, this means that the programmer made at least one mistake. We can categorize programmer errors as follows:

Errors in entering the program. PROCEDURE might be mistyped as PROCDEURE. These are typing errors.

Errors in using the programming language. The programmer did not understand a language construct. For example, to compare two character arrays they must be of the same length.

Errors in writing program parts. Although a particular program part was properly designed, it was not correctly written in Pascal. For example, a loop designed to read in account cards might always execute zero times because of writing the loop's terminating condition incorrectly.

Errors in program design. The program parts and their interactions might be improperly designed. The program designer might forget to provide for the initialization of variables used by some modules. He might overlook the fact that one module, say, DISPLAYACCOUNTS, should be called only after calling another module, say, READAC-COUNTS.

Solving the wrong problem. The programmer did not understand the nature of the problem to be solved. He may have misunderstood the program specifications. Perhaps the specifications were not correct or complete.

This list of possible errors has proceeded from the least serious to the most disastrous. The first kind of errors, such as typing errors, can be corrected easily once detected. The last type of error, misunderstanding the purpose of the program, may require scrapping the entire program and starting over again.

Some programmers are overly optimistic and immediately conclude that any bugs in their programs are not very serious. Such a programmer is quick to make little changes in his program to try to make the symptoms of the problem disappear. The wise programmer knows that program misbehavior is an indication of sloppiness and that sloppiness leads easily to disastrous errors. He takes program misbehavior as a sign that the program is sick - he gives it a checkup by studying it.

The overly optimistic programmer is forever saying, "I just found the last bug." When the wise programmer finds a bug, he looks for five more.

Many of the least serious errors, such as misspelled keywords, arc automatically pointed out by error messages, because the error results in an illegal Pascal program. These errors are usually easy to fix. Some errors are particularly treacherous; they seem to defy attempts to correct them. Here is some advice - some of it repeated from earlier parts of this book - to help you track down treacherous bugs.

Read all error messages. In their hurry to read their program's output, some programmers fail to notice error messages. These messages may pinpoint a bug.

The first error messages may help more than later ones. This is because the first messages are closer to the source of the problem. Later messages may simply indicate that a previous error is still causing trouble.

Beware of confusion between I and 1. Some people can consistently read X:=X+I; to mean increase X by one. Errors like this can be found by reading the program character by character - as a computer does! In general, the human tendency to read what we want to be there, rather what is actually there makes debugging difficult.

Beware of misspellings. Some words are easily misspelled. A person who is concentrating on understanding a program may overlook RECEIPT occasionally spelled as RECIEPT.

Beware of language peculiarities. Pascal was designed to minimize language peculiarities, but it still has some traps for the naive programmer. Among the worst of these are:

(a) *Putting a semicolon after THEN.* The following lines of Pascal will check to see if X is greater than 2:

```
IF X > 2 THEN;
    Y:=X;
```

Whether this is true or not, Y will be set to X. The semicolon after THEN acts as a null statement, which is executed when X is greater than 2.

(b) *Omitting VAR for parameters returning results* The following procedure is intended to change the sign of X in the statement NEGATE(X).

```
        PROCEDURE NEGATE(J: REAL);
        BEGIN
            J:=-J
        END
```

Unfortunately, the programmer forgot to put VAR before the declaration of J, so J is a value parameter rather than a variable parameter. As a result, J is given a copy of X's value and this copy is negated without affecting X. The procedure should be corrected by inserting VAR before J:REAL.

If everything else fails in the debugging effort, the programmer is forced to rerun his program to gain more information about the errors. The programmer may add statements to output variables or to trace the program's execution. These statements are designed using the same techniques used in testing to show programs work properly. If the original tests had been carefully enough designed, there is a good chance they would have pinpointed the error and eliminated later time-consuming debugging.

CHAPTER 16 SUMMARY

In this chapter we have listed techniques for making sure a program works. There are a vast number of ways a program can be wrong, so the programmer should learn to be careful at all the stages of program preparation. When a programmer is too hasty to submit his program to the computer, this results in persistent bugs and excessive time spent in debugging. The following important techniques and terminology were presented in this chapter.

Program specifications - explanation of what a program is to do. This should include the forms of the input and output data and the type of calculation or data manipulation to be performed. Essentially, program specifications explain how the computer is to be used to solve a particular problem.

Programming habits - the way a programmer goes about his work. Ideally, he should take the slow but sure approach, completing his program in pencil and thoroughly studying it before submitting it to the computer.

Program correctness - studying a program to verify that it satisfies its specifications.

Programming style - if the style is good, then the program can be easily read and understood.

Use of comments and identifiers - good programming style requires that comments and identifiers be chosen to make a program understandable. Comments should record the programmer's intentions; identifiers should record the function or use of the named object.

Testing - running a program to demonstrate that it meets its specifications. Tests should be designed to try every type of situation the program is to handle. Ultimately, testing is better at demonstrating bugs than demonstrating program correctness.

Debugging - correcting errors in a program. Debugging can be the most difficult and time-consuming part of trying to make a program work. These difficulties can be minimized by using the techniques listed in this chapter.

CHAPTER 16 EXERCISES

1. In this exercise you are to use defensive programming. Modify the program given in chapter 9 so that it will handle errors in the data gracefully. The program reads a list of names and prints the list in reverse order.

2. Try to write a program that is completely correct before you submit it to the computer. Have a friend help you by studying your program for errors after you are convinced that it is free of errors. Record the time you spend preparing the program and record any programming errors you make. Your program should perform one of the following tasks:

(a) The program should read a series of integers followed by the dummy value 9999. Output the sum of the positive integers and the number of negative integers.

(b) The program should read and output a list of alphabetically ordered names. If a name is repeated in the data, it should be output only once.

Chapter 17

PS/7: FILES AND RECORDS

So far we have spoken about files of records and discussed the process of searching for particular records. This process was made more efficient by having the files sorted. We then looked at ways of sorting files of records. All sorting methods involve moving records around in the computer memory. In our sorting examples, we did not really deal with the situation of sorting records that consisted of more than the one field, namely the key field of the ordering. In our examples, then, moving the record meant only moving this one field. In most data processing applications, records contain a number of fields, and it is important to be able to write statements in a program to move all the fields as a single unit. We will be introducing the idea of a *record structure* which is a group of several fields designed to make file processing simple to program.

When large quantities of data have to be processed, it is impossible to store files of records completely within the main memory of the computer. It is usual to keep large files in secondary storage such as magnetic disk storage. We must then be able to read records from such a file and write records into it. We will be looking at the statements in Pascal that permit us to manipulate files in secondary storage.

RECORDS

A Pascal RECORD is a collection of several fields and is particularly suitable for records in a file. As a simple example, suppose that we want to describe each entry in the telephone book as a record. We would identify the entire record by the identifier CUSTOMER and the three fields as

        CUSTOMER.NAME
        CUSTOMER.ADDRESS
        CUSTOMER.PHONENUMBER

Here is a diagram showing the fields:

CUSTOMER

NAME	ADDRESS	PHONENUMBER

The field identifiers are a composite of their own identifiers, NAME, ADDRESS, and PHONENUMBER and the whole record's identifier, CUSTOMER. The composite is constructed by putting a dot, or period, between the record name and the field name.

The record structure would be declared this way.

```
VAR CUSTOMER:
RECORD
     NAME: PACKED ARRAY[1..18] OF CHAR;
     ADDRESS: PACKED ARRAY[1..23] OF CHAR;
     PHONENUMBER: PACKED ARRAY[1..8] OF CHAR
END;
```

This record structure consists of two levels of naming. At the first level we have the identifier of the record structure declared, namely CUSTOMER. The next level has three fields declared. Each of these has its own type. So it is possible to have each field with a different type. Here, all the fields are of type PACKED ARRAY..OF CHAR, but each has a different range. We might have used STRING variables but then we would have to input each item on a separate input line. Remember that when a STRING variable is read all the characters on the line up to the EOLN (the return) are read. A record structure is sometimes called the *layout* of a record.

MOVING RECORDS

One of the reasons for having record structures is that they make it simple to program the movement of a whole record from one place to another. When a move is to take place, the location that will receive the structure must be declared to have exactly the same set of fields. If we want to have two or more different records with the same layout we can describe the layout as a type as in

```
TYPE CUSTTYPE=
RECORD
     NAME: PACKED ARRAY[1..18] OF CHAR;
     ADDRESS: PACKED ARRAY[1..23] OF CHAR;
     PHONENUMBER: PACKED ARRAY[1..8] OF CHAR
END;
VAR CUSTOMER,WORKSPACE: CUSTTYPE;
```

The record WORKSPACE will have all the same fields, NAME, ADDRESS and PHONENUMBER. They will be referred to as WORKSPACE.NAME, WORKSPACE.ADDRESS, and so on. We say that the record structures CUSTOMER and WORKSPACE have the same record type.

To move the record CUSTOMER into the record WORKSPACE we need only write

        WORKSPACE := CUSTOMER;

This is equivalent to the group of assignment statements

        WORKSPACE.NAME:=CUSTOMER.NAME;
        WORKSPACE.ADDRESS:=CUSTOMER.ADDRESS;
        WORKSPACE.PHONENUMBER:=CUSTOMER.PHONENUMBER;

An entire record can be assigned to another by a single assignment statement only if one record has the same type as the other.

ARRAYS OF RECORDS

Just as other types such an INTEGER may form arrays, records may form arrays. Each member of the array of records has the same type. For the telephone-book records, an array of 100 such records could be declared by

        TELEPHONEBOOK: ARRAY[1..100] OF CUSTTYPE;

An array of records can be used for grouping records for sorting purposes. A procedure for sorting a group of CUSTOMER records that have been declared in the main procedure will be given. The records are to be sorted on the key PHONENUMBER. The array of records called CUSTOMER will be global to the procedure. The only parameter that the procedure has is NUMBEROFRECORDS. A WORKSPACE record is declared as a local variable with the type CUSTTYPE.

```
 PROCEDURE SORT(NUMBEROFRECORDS: INTEGER);
    (* SORT RECORDS BY PHONENUMBER *)
    VAR WORKSPACE: CUSTTYPE;
        I,J: INTEGER;
    BEGIN
        FOR I:=1 TO NUMBEROFRECORDS-1 DO
            FOR J:=1 TO NUMBEROFRECORDS-I DO
                IF CUSTOMER[J].PHONENUMBER >
                        CUSTOMER[J+1].PHONENUMBER THEN
                    BEGIN
```

```
                    (* SWAP CUSTOMER[J] AND CUSTOMER[J+1] *)
                    WORKSPACE:=CUSTOMER[J];
                    CUSTOMER[J]:=CUSTOMER[J+1];
                    CUSTOMER[J+1]:=WORKSPACE
              END
    END;
```

In this example we have an array that contains records. The records in this example contain arrays: the arrays of characters for names, addresses and phone numbers. In general a record can contain any type, including other records.

INPUT AND OUTPUT OF RECORDS

The record is a convenient form for moving the groups of fields around in the main memory of the computer. But we have not yet said how such structures may be read into or written out from the main memory. The input-output statements that we have had so far, the READ and WRITE, can be used to read or output individual fields of a record in exactly the same way as the values of individual variables are read or output. The next section will show how to transfer the record as a unit when the program has explicit declarations for files.

If you input records from the keyboard, each field is read independently. Here is a program that reads a set of at most 25 customer records, sorts them and outputs them:

```
(* READ, SORT BY NUMBER, AND OUTPUT CUSTOMER RECORDS *)
PROGRAM NUMBERS;
    TYPE CUSTTYPE=
        RECORD
            NAME: PACKED ARRAY[1..18] OF CHAR;
            ADDRESS: PACKED ARRAY[1..23] OF CHAR;
            PHONENUMBER: PACKED ARRAY[1..8] OF CHAR
        END;
    VAR WORKSPACE: CUSTTYPE;
        CUSTOMER: ARRAY[1..25] OF CUSTTYPE;
        I,J,NUMBEROFRECORDS: INTEGER;
        CH: CHAR;
    (copy procedure SORT here)
    BEGIN
        WRITE('NUMBER OF RECORDS=');
        READLN(NUMBEROFRECORDS);
```

```
(* READ RECORDS INTO ARRAY *)
WRITELN('NAME','ADDRESS':21,'PHONE':21);
FOR I:=1 TO NUMBEROFRECORDS DO
    BEGIN
        FOR J:=1 TO 18 DO
            BEGIN
                READ(CH);
                WORKSPACE.NAME[J]:=CH
            END;
        FOR J:=1 TO 23 DO
            BEGIN
                READ(CH);
                WORKSPACE.ADDRESS[J]:=CH
            END;
        FOR J:=1 TO 8 DO
            BEGIN
                READ(CH);
                WORKSPACE.PHONENUMBER[J]:=CH
            END;
        CUSTOMER[I]:=WORKSPACE;
        READLN
    END;
(* SORT RECORDS BY PHONENUMBER *)
SORT(NUMBEROFRECORDS);
(* OUTPUT SORTED ARRAY OF RECORDS *)
WRITELN;
WRITELN('LIST SORTED BY PHONE NUMBER');
WRITELN('PHONE','NAME':8,'ADDRESS':21);
FOR I:=1 TO NUMBEROFRECORDS DO
        WRITELN(CUSTOMER[I].PHONENUMBER,
            ' ',CUSTOMER[I].NAME,CUSTOMER[I].ADDRESS)
END.
```

Here is a sample display:

NUMBER OF RECORDS=5

NAME	ADDRESS	PHONE
JOHNSTON,R.L.	53 JONSTON CRES.	491-6405
KEAST,P.	77 KREDLE HAVEN DR.	439-7216
LIPSON,J.D.	15 WEEDWOOD ROAD	787-8515
MATHON,R.A.	666 REGINA AVE.	962-8885
CRAWFORD,C.R.	39 TREATHERSON AVE.	922-7999

LIST SORTED BY PHONE NUMBER

PHONE	NAME	ADDRESS
439-7216	KEAST,P.	77 KREDLE HAVEN DR.
491-6405	JOHNSTON,R.L.	53 JONSTON CRES.
787-8515	LIPSON,J.D.	15 WEEDWOOD ROAD
922-7999	CRAWFORD,C.R.	39 TREATHERSON AVE.
962-8885	MATHON,R.A.	666 REGINA AVE.

In this example we are referring to characters in the three fields of the record named WORKSPACE using the variable names WORKSPACE.NAME[J], WORKSPACE.ADDRESS[J], and WORKSPACE.PHONENUMBER[J]. In Pascal there is a way to avoid repetition of the record name by using the WITH statement. It has the form

```
WITH record name DO
   BEGIN
      statements referencing field name only
   END
```

In our program we could have used this set of statements instead of what we had

```
WITH WORKSPACE DO
   BEGIN
      FOR J:=1 TO 18 DO
         BEGIN
            READ(CH);
            NAME[J]:=CH
         END;
      FOR J:=1 TO 23 DO;
         BEGIN
            READ(CH);
            ADDRESS[J]:=CH
         END;
      FOR J:=1 TO 8 DO
         BEGIN
            READ(CH);
            PHONENUMBER[J]:=CH
         END
   END;
```

FILES IN SECONDARY MEMORY

In our discussion of files so far, we have had the files stored in the main memory. In most real file applications, the files are too large to be contained in main memory. The part of the file being processed must be brought into main memory, but the complete file is stored in secondary memory. The secondary memory may be magnetic tape or magnetic disk.

A file in secondary storage is a collection of values all of the same type. The collection is sometimes called a *dataset*. One item at a time may be transferred from the dataset to a structure in main memory, or from a structure in main memory to the dataset. The item that is transferred must be the *next* item in the sequence of records in the dataset. We say that the file can be read sequentially from the secondary memory to the main memory or written sequentially from the main memory to secondary memory. This kind of file is called a *sequential file*. It is not possible in standard Pascal at any moment to get access to an arbitrary item in the file; the next item in sequence is the only one that is available.

Since files in secondary storage are to be accessed sequentially, there must be a statement in the program that will position the file reader at the first item of the dataset. Before a file in secondary storage can be read, we must have a statement of the form

> RESET(file name,'directory name');

The file name is that used to refer to the file within the Pascal program. The directory name is the one used in the UCSD operating system directory of files. The directory name must end in .TEXT or .DATA and is enclosed in quotes. The names *may* be the same. We could write for example

> RESET(OLDFILE,'OLDFILE.DATA');

The file name OLDFILE would have to be declared at the beginning of the procedure by

> VAR OLDFILE: FILE OF CUSTTYPE;

In general, a file may be declared as a FILE OF any type, such as FILE OF INTEGER or FILE OF PACKED ARRAY[1..10] OF CHAR.

To read the next item from the file in secondary storage, we write statements of the form

> variable:=file name↑;
> GET(file name);

We can read records from OLDFILE into variables such as CUSTOMER whose type is CUSTTYPE using these statements.

> CUSTOMER:=OLDFILE↑;
> GET(OLDFILE);

We will explain the meaning of these statements in Chapter 19. They are UCSD Pascal's substitute for the single standard Pascal statement

READ(OLDFILE,CUSTOMER);

If a file is to be written instead of read, it must first be prepared for writing using the statement

REWRITE(file name,'directory name');

To write a record into such a file, we use statements of this form

file name$\uparrow$:=expression;
PUT(file name);

These are equivalent to the single standard Pascal statement (not available in UCSD Pascal)

WRITE (file name,expression);

As with input files, an output file must be declared as a FILE and can receive only values (expressions) of the type given following FILE OF.

Following RESET the file can be read but not written. Following REWRITE the file can be written but not read. Once a file has been written, the program can RESET the file and then read it. At the end of a program that reads or writes files the files must be closed. Files that have been read are closed by the statement

CLOSE(file name);

Files that have been written should be closed by

CLOSE(file name,LOCK);

if the file is to be saved on the disk after the programs ends. If you want to get rid of a file that has been read use

CLOSE(file name,PURGE);

The names of files used by a program may appear in the program heading statement. In all programs we have shown so far the input came from the keyboard and the output went to the screen. These "files" have the standard names INPUT and OUTPUT. In UCSD Pascal we do not need to mention that we are using these files. If we intend to use files named OLDFILE and NEWFILE our program heading might be

PROGRAM identifier(OLDFILE,NEWFILE);

FILE MAINTENANCE

As an example of reading and writing files we will program a simple file-maintenance operation. We will assume that there exists on the disk a file of CUSTOMER records called in the operating system directory OLDFILE.DATA, and we want to update this file by adding new customers. The information about the new customers is entered on the keyboard. Each input line corresponds to a *transaction* that must be *posted* in the file to produce an up-to-date customer file, which we will call NEWFILE in the program and NEWFILE.DATA in the disk directory. This is an example of *file maintenance*. The file OLDFILE is ordered alphabetically by CUSTOMER.NAME and the transactions must also be arranged alphabetically. This program will be very similar to the merge-sort program of Chapter 15, except that the records of the two files being merged are not in an array.

```
PROGRAM UPDATE (OLDFILE,NEWFILE);
    (* ADD NEW CUSTOMERS TO CUSTOMER FILE *)
    CONST DUMMY='ZZZZZZZZZZZZZZZZZZ';
    TYPE CUSTTYPE=
        RECORD
            NAME: PACKED ARRAY[1..18] OF CHAR;
            ADDRESS: PACKED ARRAY[1..23] OF CHAR;
            PHONENUMBER: PACKED ARRAY[1..8] OF CHAR
        END;
    VAR OLDFILE,NEWFILE: FILE OF CUSTTYPE;
        CUSTOMER,TRANSACTION: CUSTTYPE;
        J: INTEGER;
        CH: CHAR;

    PROCEDURE READTRANSACTION;
        BEGIN
            WITH TRANSACTION DO
                BEGIN
                    FOR J:=1 TO 18 DO
                        BEGIN
                            READ(CH);
                            NAME[J]:=CH
                        END;
                    FOR J:=1 TO 23 DO
                        BEGIN
                            READ(CH);
                            ADDRESS[J]:=CH
                        END;
                    FOR J:=TO 8 DO
                        BEGIN
                            READ(CH);
                            PHONENUMBER[J]:=CH
                        END
                END
        END
```

```
            END;

        BEGIN
            REWRITE(NEWFILE,'NEWFILE.DATA');
            RESET(OLDFILE,'OLDFILE.DATA');
            (* READ FIRST CUSTOMER RECORD FROM FILE *)
            CUSTOMER:=OLDFILE↑;
            GET(OLDFILE);
            (* READ FIRST TRANSACTION FROM KEYBOARD *)
            WRITELN('NAME','ADDRESS':21,'PHONE':21);
            READTRANSACTION;
            READLN;
            (* POST TRANSACTIONS TO CUSTOMER FILE *)
            WHILE(TRANSACTION.NAME<>DUMMY) OR
                    (CUSTOMER.NAME<>DUMMY) DO
                IF CUSTOMER.NAME>TRANSACTION.NAME THEN
                    BEGIN
                        (* WRITE TRANSACTION TO NEWFILE *)
                        NEWFILE↑:=TRANSACTION;
                        PUT(NEWFILE);
                        READTRANSACTION;
                        READLN
                    END
                ELSE
                    BEGIN
                        (* WRITE CUSTOMER TO NEWFILE *)
                        NEWFILE↑:=CUSTOMER;
                        PUT(NEWFILE);
                        (* READ NEXT CUSTOMER RECORD *)
                        CUSTOMER:=OLDFILE↑;
                        GET(OLDFILE)
                    END;
            (* ADD DUMMY RECORD TO END OF FILE *)
            NEWFILE↑:=CUSTOMER;
            PUT(NEWFILE);
            CLOSE(NEWFILE,LOCK);
            CLOSE(OLDFILE)
        END.
```

Here is the display:

NAME   ADDRESS   PHONE
(transactions one to a line)

ZZZZZZZZZZZZZZZZZZ   NULL   NULL

The DUMMY value of ZZ...Z alphabetically follows any legal names in the file. This value is used because in the merging loop, comparisons with DUMMY will force all legal names to be merged before the DUMMY value.

We can use the function EOF(OLDFILE) to determine when no more records can be read. The WHILE...DO test can be replaced by this:

WHILE (NOT EOF) AND (NOT EOF(OLDFILE)) DO

Notice that when EOF has no parameter it applies to the standard input file, the keyboard.

PASCAL TEXT FILES

The two standard files INPUT (the keyboard) and OUTPUT (the screen) are implicitly declared as

VAR INPUT,OUTPUT: FILE OF CHAR;

RESET(INPUT,'CONSOLE:') and REWRITE(OUTPUT,'CONSOLE:') are implicitly performed as the program begins execution. The program should not explicitly perform RESET or REWRITE for INPUT or OUTPUT.

A file which is declared as FILE OF CHAR is called a text file, and can equivalently be declared using the predeclared types TEXT or INTERACTIVE. Text files, such as INPUT and OUTPUT are special in that READ, READLN, WRITE and WRITELN can transfer values other than the file's type which is CHAR. In particular, INTEGER and REAL values can be read and INTEGER, REAL and string values can be written, and formatting can be specified. If F is declared as

VAR F: TEXT

then WRITE(F,'X IS',12:3) is a legal statement. The first parameter in any WRITE or WRITELN is a text file variable; if the parameter is omitted, the OUTPUT file is used. Similarly READ and READLN have as their first parameter a text file variable, which is taken to be INPUT if omitted. Text files other then INPUT and OUTPUT must have explicit RESET and REWRITE operations.

You may have noticed that when you enter Pascal programs using the UCSD operating system they are being stored as a workfile. The untranslated program has the type TEXT. This means that you could enter a file of data that is of type TEXT in exactly the same way as you enter a Pascal program. You can edit the data then all you want since it is not being read by your program until later. You may have found it rather frustrating that a single typing error in the data caused the Pascal program to terminate. For example, if a letter is typed instead of a digit, when the program is expecting an integer, the execution will cease and you cannot restart from where you left off. You must go back to the beginning. As a result we tend to resist programs where there is any sizable amount of data to be input.

When there is a lot of data the easiest approach is to use the UCSD operating system just as you do for entering programs. Of course you would not try to R(UN your data as if it were a program. You just store it as a named file and then that named file can be referenced and used in a Pascal program. If the file name is DATA you need a type declaration of the form

VAR DATA:TEXT;

Files of records may not be prepared in this way but must be created by being read in by a Pascal program. However, it is possible to have the Pascal program read from a TEXT file prepared in the way we described instead of having the input through the keyboard.

This way of operating, where the data is all prepared in machine readable form before the program starts to execute is similar to the mode of operating a computer known as *batch processing.* When transactions are entered on the keyboard one at a time and the program processes them before the next is entered, we call it *interactive processing.* Interactive processing is particularly appropriate when different responses are requested from the person at the console depending on what the computer does. In a true interactive situation, files are not processed sequentially but instead are accessed at random. To be processed randomly rather than sequentially, a file must be a file of records.

RANDOM ACCESS TO FILES

In UCSD Pascal it is possible to access disk files randomly. Any record can be read at random and any record may be written at random. In any disk file of records the records have an implicit address. The first record has address 0; it has *record number* 0. The second has record number 1, and so on. To position the read/write heads at a particular record you use the statement

SEEK (file name,record number);

Once you are in position you may read the record. When you read a record, you automatically move the access mechanism to the next record in the file so that if you wanted subsequently to write an updated record back in the same location you would have to perform another SEEK.

The question is: How do you know what the record number of a particular record in the file is in order to seek it? One way is to keep a directory for the file, like a telephone directory, which will give you the record number of any record you want. We would then search the directory for the record number by any of the means we have discussed for searching and then go by the SEEK to the complete record. As new records are added to the file new directory items are added to the directory. The directory may be kept sorted in order to speed up the search, using binary search, for example. But the file itself need not then be kept sorted. A search through a directory can be a lot faster than a search through a file because the directory can be kept in the high speed memory during the search. The directory can of course be stored as a separate, single-record file on the disk.

CHAPTER 17 SUMMARY

In this chapter we introduced programming language constructs for manipulating records and using files in secondary memory. The following important terms were discussed in this chapter:

Record - a collection of fields of information. For example, a record might be composed of a name field, an address field and a telephone number field.

RECORD type - the Pascal construct for records. For example, this declaration establishes a record type called DIRECENTRY with name, address and telephone-number fields.

```
TYPE DIRECENTRY =
RECORD
    NAME: PACKED ARRAY[1..18] OF CHAR;
    ADDRESS: PACKED ARRAY[1..23] OF CHAR;
    PHONENUMBER: PACKED ARRAY[1..8] OF CHAR
END;
VAR CLIENT: DIRECENTRY;
```

CLIENT is a variable whose type is a record.

Array of records - to declare an array of records of the record type DIRECENTRY we use the declaration:

```
VAR PHONEBOOK: ARRAY[1..50] OF DIRECENTRY;
```

This creates an array of 50 records where each record has the same fields as CLIENT. PHONEBOOK[5].NAME refers to the name field of the fifth record in the array.

Assigning records - if two record variables are of the same type as each other, one can be assigned to the other by a single assignment statement. For example, we can write

PHONEBOOK[5]:=CLIENT;

to assign the three fields of CLIENT to the corresponding three fields of PHONEBOOK[5].

Dataset - a file of information residing on secondary storage, typically on a disk or tape.

Sequential files - files that are always accessed (read or written) in order, from first item to second item to third item and so on.

Random access files - files in which any particular record is accessed directly by means of its record number. The records of a file are numbered sequentially starting from 0 for the first record.

RESET a file - means to prepare a file for reading by a program. A file in Pascal can be opened for input using:

RESET(file name,'directory name');

The directory name is the one used to list the file in the UCSD Pascal operating system's file directory. The directory name should end in .DATA or .TEXT. Notice that the directory name is enclosed in quotes. When RESET is executed the file is positioned to its first item (if any). The file can be read but not written.

REWRITE a file - means to prepare a file for writing by a program. A file in Pascal can be opened for output using:

REWRITE(file name,'directory name');

The file is positioned to write the first item and previous contents of the file are lost. The file can be written but not read.

READ - access the next (or first) value in a file. The READ statement has the form

READ (file name, variable);

In UCSD Pascal this READ is not available except for text files. Instead we use the equivalent two statements

variable:=file name↑;
GET(file name);

WRITE - add a record to a file. The WRITE statement has the form:

WRITE (file name, expression);

In UCSD Pascal this WRITE is not available except for text files. Instead we use the equivalent two statements

> file name↑:=expression;
> PUT(file name);

CLOSE - files that have been opened by RESET or REWRITE must be closed after processing is finished by

> CLOSE(file name[,option])

The LOCK option is used for newly written files that you want saved. The PURGE option for files you want deleted. Otherwise omit the option.

File declaration - a file that is used in a program can be declared using the form

> VAR file name: FILE OF type;

Program heading - programs that use permanent files in secondary storage must in Standard Pascal have the file names listed, separated by commas, in the program heading. In UCSD Pascal they may be so listed if you want. For example, if files named OLDFILE and NEWFILE are to be used the heading might be

> PROGRAM name(OLDFILE,NEWFILE);

File maintenance - means to keep a file up to date. This involves reading transactions and adding, deleting or modifying file records.

WITH statement - when a series of references is made to the fields of a single record, rather than referencing each field by its full name, namely

> record name . field name

We can use a WITH statement whose form is

> WITH record name DO
>   BEGIN
>   statements using field name only
>   END

This cuts down on the length of names and simplifies the program.

Text file - a file variable declared as TEXT, INTERACTIVE, or FILE OF CHAR can use the READ, READLN, WRITE and WRITELN operations usually associated with the standard input and output files.

Data preparation in advance - a file of data of type TEXT can be prepared and entered using the editing facilities of the UCSD Pascal system in much the same way as Pascal programs are entered. They are entered into the workfile and then stored as a named file which can be referenced in your Pascal program. This is read as a TEXT file using READ and READLN. Files of records cannot be prepared directly in this way.

SEEK a record - means to find a particular record in a file.

       SEEK(file name,record number);

will position the read/write head of the disk at the required record.

CHAPTER 17 EXERCISES

The exercises for this chapter are based on a data processing system to be used by Apex Plumbing Supplies. For each of its customers, Apex has a record with the fields:

Name	(20 char)
Address	(20 char)
Balance	(integer)
Credit limit	(integer)

These records are entered from the keyboard. However, they are to be transferred to a disk file. A sample of the data is shown:

ABBOT PLUMBING	94 N.ELM	3116	50000
DURABLE FIXIT	247 FOREST HILL	0	10000
ERICO PLUMBING	54 GORMLEY	9614	5000

  ...

The exercises for this chapter require you to write programs for various parts of the data processing system for Apex.

1. Enter data and create a master file for Apex Plumbing Supplies. You may use the UCSD Pascal editing method for this. First prepare a TEXT file then read this to prepare a file of records.

2. Write a program to read an old version of the master file for Apex, sort the file, creating a new master file that is guaranteed to be in alphabetic order according to the name field.

3. Write a program that takes an existing master file for Apex and creates a new master file by deleting or adding new customer records. For example, the transaction data entries for your program might be

DAVIS REPAIR	4361 MAIN	2511	10000
ERICO PLUMBING	DELETE	0	0

You can assume that the transactions are in alphabetic order. If the address field of the transaction specifies DELETE, the account is to be deleted from the file; otherwise it is an addition.

4. Write a program that reads the Apex master file and outputs the list of customers whose balances exceed their credit limits.

5. Write a program that reads the Apex master file and outputs a bill for each customer whose balance is greater than zero. For example, for the file record

> DAVIS REPAIR   4361 MAIN   2511   10000

your program should output

> TO: DAVIS REPAIR
>   4361 MAIN
>
> DEAR SIR OR MADAM:
>   PLEASE REMIT $25.11 FOR PLUMBING SUPPLIES.
>   THANK YOU,
>
>   JOHN APEX, PRES.
>   APEX PLUMBING SUPPLIES
>   416 COLLEGE ST.

6. Write a program that updates the master file using billing and payment transactions. A billing transaction is an entry of the form

> name   (columns 1-20)
> amount   (columns 41-50)

For each billing transaction, the balance of the account is to be increased by the specified amount. A payment transaction is an entry of the form

> name   (columns 1-20)
> amount   (columns 41-50)
> CR   (columns 51-52)

For each payment transaction, the balance of the account is to be decreased by the specified amount. The billing and payment entries are in order.

7. Organize the master file so that its records may be accessed randomly by creating a directory file for it. Repeat all the other exercises using random access.

Chapter 18

DATA STRUCTURES

In the last chapter we introduced the idea of records. By using these data structures we could move a group of items of data around in the computer as a unit. Also, we can have arrays of records.

All of the classifications, variables, arrays of single variables, records, and arrays of records are examples of what we generally call *data structures*. Just as we systematize our programs by attempting to write well-structured programs, we systematize the way in which data is stored. We structure data.

In this chapter we will describe other structural forms for data and give examples of how these structures are useful to us. We will describe data structures called *linked lists* and *tree structures*. There are many kinds of lists, for example, *stacks, queues, doubly linked lists*, and so on. Tree structures can be limited to *binary trees*, or may be more general.

Pascal contains a feature called *pointers* that can be used to implement linked lists but it is possible to implement all of these data structures without pointers using arrays instead. We will do this first and then show how Pascal pointers can be used.

LINKED LISTS

Suppose that we had a file of records stored in an array called DATA. The records are arranged in sequence on some key. For simplicity, we will consider that each record consists only of a single field which is the key to the ordering. We know that if the order is ascending and no two keys are identical, then

$$DATA[I+1] > DATA[I]$$

The difficulty with this kind of data structure for a file comes when a new item is to be added to the file; it must be inserted between two items. This means we would have to move all the items with a key higher than the one to be inserted, one location on in the array. For example, you can see what happens when we insert the word DOG in this list:

	before	after inserting DOG
DATA[1]	CAT	CAT
DATA[2]	DUCK	DOG
DATA[3]	FOX	DUCK
DATA[4]	GOOSE	FOX
DATA[5]	PIG	GOOSE
DATA[6]	-	PIG

Any list that is changing with time will have additions and deletions made to it. A deletion will create a hole unless entries are moved to fill the hole.

When the list changes with time we can use the data structure called the *linked list*. In the linked list each item has two components, the data component and the linking component or *link*. (We will be using Pascal pointers to implement links later.) We associate with each entry in the DATA array an entry in a second array of integers called LINK. The number stored in LINK[I] is the index of the next entry in the sequence of the DATA array. This means that the actual or *physical sequence* in the DATA array is different from the *logical sequence* in the list. Here is an example showing our previous list as a linked list. The start of the list is stored in the INTEGER variable FIRST.

		FIRST	3
DATA[1]	PIG	LINK[1]	0
DATA[2]	FOX	LINK[2]	4
DATA[3]	CAT	LINK[3]	5
DATA[4]	GOOSE	LINK[4]	1
DATA[5]	DUCK	LINK[5]	2
DATA[6]	-	LINK[6]	-

Here is a diagram of this:

You can follow the list by beginning with the value of FIRST, which is 3. The first entry will be in DATA[3]; it is CAT. By looking then at LINK[3] you find a 5 which is the index of the next list item, DATA[5], which is DUCK. You follow the list down until you reach a LINK whose value is 0; this is the signal that you have reached the end of the list. Other signals can be used, such as having a negative number.

INSERTING INTO A LINKED LIST

To see the merit of a linked list we must see how to insert new entries. We will add DOG in its proper list position. We will do this first by hand; afterwards we will have to program it for the computer. We will place DOG in DATA[6] since it is an available or free location. We must now change the values of certain of the links so that the new entry will be inserted. We must put a value into LINK[6] and change the value of the LINK of the entry before DOG, which is CAT, to point to DATA[6]. This means that LINK[3] must be changed to 6 and LINK[6] must be set to 5 so that the entry after DOG is DUCK, which is DATA[5]. The linked list then becomes:

		FIRST	3
DATA[1]	PIG	LINK[1]	0
DATA[2]	FOX	LINK[2]	4
DATA[3]	CAT	LINK[3]	6
DATA[4]	GOOSE	LINK[4]	1
DATA[5]	DUCK	LINK[5]	2
DATA[6]	DOG	LINK[6]	5

Here is a diagram:

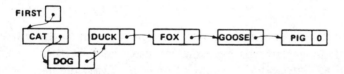

To add DOG, one LINK must be changed and one set. No movement of the existing items in DATA is necessary. This is surely an improvement over moving half the list, on the average, to insert a new entry. The cost of this improved efficiency of operation comes in having to reserve memory space for the LINK array. This array gives the structure of the list and is stored explicitly for a linked list. In an array, the sequence or structure is implicit; each entry follows its neighbor. We will use other kinds of structures that require us to store the structure information explicitly.

MEMORY MANAGEMENT WITH LISTS

With linked lists, some of the memory is used for structure information and some for data. For any list, as the list grows, we use more memory; as it shrinks, we use less. This means we must reserve enough memory to hold the longest list that we ever expect to have. But we should not waste memory. As we stop using certain elements of the array by deleting entries, we must keep track of where they are, so when additions occur we can reuse these same elements. To keep track of the available array elements we keep them together in a second linked list. The list of available array elements does not have any useful information in the DATA part, but it is structured as a list using values in the LINK part. We must keep track of the beginning of this list so we keep the index of its beginning in a INTEGER variable AVAILABLE.

Here is an array of 10 elements that stores our previous data items in a different set of locations and has the available space linked up:

	FIRST 10	AVAILABLE	7
DATA[1]	GOOSE	LINK[1]	9
DATA[2]	FOX	LINK[2]	1
DATA[3]	-	LINK[3]	6
DATA[4]	DUCK	LINK[4]	2
DATA[5]	-	LINK[5]	0
DATA[6]	-	LINK[6]	5
DATA[7]	-	LINK[7]	3
DATA[8]	DOG	LINK[8]	4
DATA[9]	PIG	LINK[9]	0
DATA[10]	CAT	LINK[10]	8

In these arrays there are two linked lists, one containing the actual data, the other containing elements available for use. Each list has a pointer to its start; each has a last element with a link of 0. Every element of the array is in one list or the other.

The next problem is to write a procedure for adding a new item to the list. We will develop the algorithm for this using step-by-step refinement.

PROCEDURE FOR INSERTING INTO A LINKED LIST

The first step is to construct a solution tree. We will presume the value to be added is in the variable NEWDATA:

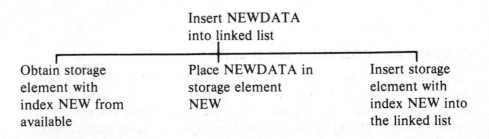

Obtain storage element with index NEW from available	Place NEWDATA in storage element NEW	Insert storage element with index NEW into the linked list

The expansion of the left branch of the solution tree requires us to find the index NEW of the first element of the list of available elements and remove the element from the list. Here is the program segment that does this:

    NEW:=AVAILABLE;
    AVAILABLE:=LINK[AVAILABLE];

The middle branch is also simple. It is

    DATA[NEW]:=NEWDATA;

We must expand the right branch still further:

Insert storage
element with
index NEW into
the linked list

|

IF NEWDATA goes first in list THEN
place element at beginning of list
ELSE find place to insert NEWDATA
and adjust links to make insertion

NEWDATA will go first in the list if either the list is empty or NEWDATA is less than the first element of the list. So we can write, "IF NEWDATA goes first in list," in this way:

IF (FIRST=NULL) OR (NEWDATA<DATA[FIRST]) THEN

We have assumed that NULL is a named constant whose value is zero. We can write, "Place element at beginning of list," in this way:

    BEGIN
        LINK[NEW]:=FIRST;
        FIRST:=NEW
    END

For the part of the program after the ELSE we need to examine the entries in the list and compare them with NEWDATA. The index of the element being compared we will call NEXT. The index of the previously compared element we will call PREVIOUS. We need to keep track of this previous element, because if

    NEWDATA < DATA[NEXT]

we must insert our element with index NEW between PREVIOUS and
NEXT. Here is the program segment for this:

```
BEGIN
    (* FIND PLACE TO INSERT NEW DATA *)
    PREVIOUS:=FIRST;
    NEXT:=LINK[FIRST];
    WHILE (NEXT<>NULL) AND (NEWDATA>=DATA[NEXT])DO
        BEGIN
            PREVIOUS:=NEXT;
            NEXT:=LINK[NEXT]
        END;
    (* ADJUST LINKS TO MAKE INSERTION *)
    LINK[PREVIOUS]:=NEW;
    LINK[NEW]:=NEXT
END
```

The whole procedure can now be written out. We are presuming that
DATA, LINK, FIRST, and AVAILABLE are global to this procedure. The
type of the entries in the list is ENTRYTYPE, which could be PACKED
ARRAY[1..5] OF CHAR for our example, but the procedure would also be
correct for other types such as INTEGER.

```
 (* INSERT NEW DATA INTO LINKED LIST *)
 PROCEDURE INSERTDATA(NEWDATA:ENTRYTYPE);
    VAR NEW,PREVIOUS,NEXT: INTEGER;
    BEGIN
        (* OBTAIN STORAGE ELEMENT FOR NEW DATA *)
        NEW:=AVAILABLE;
        AVAILABLE:=LINK[AVAILABLE];
        (* PLACE NEWDATA IN STORAGE ELEMENT *)
        DATA[NEW]:=NEWDATA;
        (* SEE IF NEW DATA GOES FIRST IN LIST *)
        IF (FIRST=NULL) OR (NEWDATA<DATA[FIRST]) THEN
            BEGIN
                LINK[NEW]:=FIRST;
                FIRST:=NEW
            END
        ELSE
            BEGIN
                (* FIND PLACE TO INSERT NEW DATA *)
                PREVIOUS:=FIRST;
                NEXT:=LINK[FIRST];
                WHILE (NEXT<>NULL) AND
```

```
                (NEWDATA> =DATA[NEXT])DO
            BEGIN
                PREVIOUS:=NEXT;
                NEXT:=LINK[NEXT]
            END;
            (* ADJUST LINKS TO MAKE INSERTION *)
            LINK[PREVIOUS]:=NEW;
            LINK[NEW]:=NEXT
        END
  END;
```

So far we have ignored a problem in our INSERTDATA procedure. The conditions for both the IF statement and the WHILE loop use an element of the DATA array which may have the index NULL (0). To avoid an out-of-bounds index, the DATA array should be declared with a lower bound of zero. DATA[0] should be given a value, although the value is not actually part of the list.

DELETING FROM A LINKED LIST

The process of deletion is very similar. We will just record the complete procedure.

```
(* DELETE SPECIFIED DATA FROM LINKED LIST *)
PROCEDURE DELETEDATA(OLDDATA:ENTRYTYPE);
  VAR PREVIOUS,OLD: INTEGER;
  (* FIND THE ITEM TO BE DELETED *)
  BEGIN
    OLD:=FIRST;
    WHILE DATA[OLD]<>OLDDATA DO
      BEGIN
        PREVIOUS:=OLD;
        OLD:=LINK[OLD]
      END;
    (* REMOVE ITEM FROM LIST *)
    IF FIRST=OLD THEN
        FIRST:=LINK[OLD]
    ELSE
        LINK[PREVIOUS]:=LINK[OLD];
    (* ADD STORAGE ELEMENT TO FREE LIST *)
    LINK[OLD]:=AVAILABLE;
    AVAILABLE:=OLD
  END;
```

Before using these two procedures we must set FIRST to NULL, set AVAILABLE to 1, and LINK[I] to I+1, with the exception of the last element which should have a NULL link.

RECORDS AND NODES

We have used links that are in separate arrays from the arrays that hold the actual data values. Sometimes we collect the data and the link to form a record. For example, we could use these declarations

```
TYPE NODE=
   RECORD
      DATA: ENTRYTYPE;
      LINK: INTEGER
   END;
   VAR LIST: ARRAY[1..MAXQUEUE] OF NODE;
```

Each item in a list is called a *node*. With these declarations, we refer to the data in node I as LIST[I].DATA and the link as LIST[I].LINK.

STACKS

In the preceding sections we showed how to insert and delete items for a linked list. The insertions and deletions could be anywhere in the list. In each case, as the list of data items was changed, a second linked list of available storage elements was maintained. A deletion from the list of data items resulted in an addition to the list of available elements; an addition in the data list produced a deletion in the available list. The actions involving the available storage list were much simpler. This is because the additions and deletions for it always were to the beginning of that list. A list that is restricted to having entries to or removals from the beginning only is called a *stack*. The situation is similar to a stack of trays in a cafeteria. When you want a tray you take it off the top of the stack; when you are through with a tray you put it back on the top. When a list is used as a stack, we often call the pointer to the beginning of the list TOP. When an entry is removed from the top we say we have *popped* an entry off. TOP must then be adjusted to point at the next entry. When we add an entry we say we have *pushed* it onto the stack.

Because a stack change only occurs at one end, it is convenient to implement a stack without using a linked list; an ordinary array will do. In our examples, a linked list is necessary for our stack of available storage elements because they are scattered all over. Stacks have other uses so we will show how a stack can be implemented using an array. We will call the array STACK. The bottom of the stack will be in STACK[1], the next entry in STACK[2], and so on. Sorry if our stack seems to be upside down! Here is a stack of symbols:

TOP   4

STACK[1]   +

STACK[2]   -

STACK[3]   +

STACK[4]   /

This sort of stack is often used in compilers for translating arithmetic expressions into machine language.

Before using the stack we initialize it to be empty by setting TOP to zero:

TOP:=0;

To add an item to the stack we can call the procedure PUSH:

```
PROCEDURE PUSH(SYMBOL:ENTRYTYPE);
    BEGIN
        TOP:=TOP+1;
        STACK[TOP]:=SYMBOL
    END;
```

To remove the top item from the stack we can call the procedure POP:

```
PROCEDURE POP(VAR SYMBOL:ENTRYTYPE);
    BEGIN
        SYMBOL:=STACK[TOP];
        TOP:=TOP-1
    END;
```

The variable TOP and the array STACK must be global to the PUSH and POP procedures. Stacks may be implemented in other ways than shown here.

RECURSIVE PROCEDURES

If we want to read a list of integers and output it in reverse order then we can program it this way using a stack.

```
(* Output numbers in reverse order *)
WHILE there are more numbers to read DO
    BEGIN
        Read number N;
        Push number N onto the stack
    END;
```

```
        WHILE the stack is not empty DO
          BEGIN
              Pop number N from the stack;
              Write number N
          END
```

Another way of programming this is by using a recursive procedure, which is a procedure that calls itself. In the execution of a recursive procedure there is an implicit stack.

```
 PROGRAM REVERSE;
    PROCEDURE OUTPUTINREVERSE;
        VAR N: INTEGER;
        BEGIN
          IF NOT EOF THEN
              BEGIN
                  READLN(N);
                  OUTPUTINREVERSE;
                  (* OUTPUT ANY OTHER NUMBERS *)
                  WRITELN(N)
              END
          ELSE
              WRITELN
        END;
    BEGIN
        OUTPUTINREVERSE
    END.
```

Here is a sample display:

```
5
10     (end of file pressed here)
10
5
```

The main program calls OUTPUTINREVERSE. This causes local variable N to be created and 5 is read into it. Next, OUTPUTINREVERSE calls itself, which creates a new local variable called N, which has 10 read into it. These two local variables are quite separate from each other even though they have the same name. Next, OUTPUTINREVERSE calls itself again, but finding that EOF is now true, it returns without reading. This return is to the activation of OUTPUTINREVERSE where N is 10. After 10 is output, the return goes back to the activation in which N is 5 and 5 is output. Then a return is made to the main program and execution is complete.

Each new recursive call to OUTPUTINREVERSE creates a new copy of local variable N. These variables are stacked in a LIFO manner (last in first out), so that each return finds the previous value of N. Because of this implicit creation of a stack of variables, we do not have to use an array to implement a stack.

QUEUES

Another specialized type of list is a *queue*. For it, entries are made at the end of the list, deletions are made from the beginning. Rather than search for the end of the list each time an entry is made, it is usual to have a pointer indicating the last entry. Queues involve using things in a manner referred to as, "First in first out" (FIFO) or, "First come first served" (FCFS). This is the usual way for a queue waiting for tickets at a box office to operate.

A queue is not as easy as a stack to implement using an array. It is always growing at one end and shrinking at the other. If an array is used, when the growth reaches the maximum limit of the array, we start it at the beginning again. Here is a queue of users of a computer waiting for service. We have a maximum of 8 elements. Five people are in the queue. The next person to be served is named GREEN.

FIRST 6	LAST 2
QUEUE[1]	GEORGE
QUEUE[2]	JOHNSTON
QUEUE[3]	-
QUEUE[4]	-
QUEUE[5]	-
QUEUE[6]	GREEN
QUEUE[7]	LINNEMANN
QUEUE[8]	JACOBS

Here are procedures used to ENTER or LEAVE this queue. We will use a constant named MAXQUEUE whose value is 8 so we can easily change the maximum size of the queue. Before using these procedures the queue can be initialized to be empty by setting FIRST to 1 and LAST to MAXQUEUE.

```
CONST MAXQUEUE=8;
PROCEDURE ENTER(NAME:ENTRYTYPE);
    BEGIN
        LAST:=LAST+1;
        IF LAST > MAXQUEUE THEN
            LAST:=1;
```

```
        QUEUE[LAST]:=NAME
END;

PROCEDURE LEAVE(VAR NAME:ENTRYTYPE);
    BEGIN
        NAME:=QUEUE[FIRST];
        FIRST:=FIRST+1;
        IF FIRST > MAXQUEUE THEN
            FIRST:=1
    END;
```

We have used wrap around or modulo arithmetic in that we wanted FIRST and LAST to keep increasing until they reach MAXQUEUE and then to wrap back to 1. The IF statements in the ENTER and LEAVE procedures make sure that wrap around occurs. There is a MOD operator that accomplishes wrap around by returning the remainder of dividing one integer by another. We can write

```
        FIRST:=(FIRST MOD MAXQUEUE)+1;
```

This means to set FIRST to one more than the remainder of FIRST divided by MAXQUEUE. As long as FIRST has a value of 1, 2 up to one less than QUEUESIZE, then this just adds one to FIRST. But if FIRST equals MAXQUEUE then MOD returns a value of zero which added to one causes FIRST to be assigned the value one. So we can shorten the ENTER and LEAVE procedures by using MOD.

Queues can be implemented by linked lists as well as by simple arrays. Queues are used in the programs called *operating systems* that operate multi-user computer systems. Different jobs requiring service are placed in different queues, depending on the demands they are making on the system's resources and the priority that they possess to be given service. Also, in programs that simulate other systems such as factories, queues are maintained to determine the length of time jobs are required to wait to be served when other jobs are competing for the same production facilities.

TREES

A linked list is an efficient way of storing a list that is changing with time, but it introduces an inefficiency in retrieval of information from the list. In Chapter 15 we saw that a binary search for an item in a list is much more efficient for long lists than a linear search. Unfortunately, there is no possibility of doing a binary search in a linked list; we must start at the beginning and trace our way through. There is no direct access to the middle of a linked list. It is for this reason that a more complicated data structure called a *tree* is used. We can get the efficiency of a binary search by having the elements linked into a *binary tree structure.*

To show how a binary tree is formed, we will look at the example of our list of names of animals:

$$
\begin{array}{rl}
3 & \rightarrow \text{CAT} \\
2 & \rightarrow \text{DOG} \\
  & \text{DUCK} \\
1 & \rightarrow \text{FOX} \\
  & \text{GOOSE} \\
  & \text{PIG} \\
  & \text{SNAKE}
\end{array}
$$

To do a binary search we should begin in the middle. (We have added SNAKE to the list so the list has a middle entry.) If we are looking for the name CAT we find that CAT < FOX, so we then discard the middle entry and the last half of the list. The next comparison is with the middle entry of the remaining list, namely with DOG. Since CAT < DOG we eliminate the last half of the smaller list. By this time, we are down to one entry, which is the one we are looking for. It took three comparisons to get there. A linear search for CAT would, as it happens, have taken only 1 comparison. On the *average*, the binary search takes fewer comparisons than a linear search. A short list is not a good example for showing off the efficiency of binary searching, but it is much easier to write out all the possibilities.

We will now look at the binary tree that would be used to give the same searching technique. Here it is:

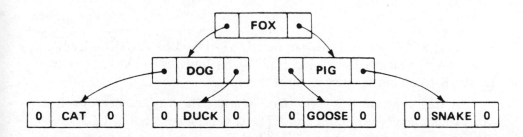

Each data element in the tree structure consists of three parts, the DATA itself and two links that we designate as LEFTLINK and RIGHT-LINK. The word FOX is in a special position in the tree, called the *root.* From FOX we have *branches* going to the left to DOG and to the right to PIG. In a sense, DOG is in the root position of a smaller tree, what we call the *left subtree* of the main tree. PIG is at the root of the *right subtree.* The words CAT, DUCK, GOOSE, and SNAKE are at the end of branches and are called *leaves* of the tree. All the data elements are in *nodes* of the tree; FOX is the *root node* and CAT is a *leaf node.* To search for an entry in a binary tree, we compare the element in the root node with the one we are seeking. If the root is the same, we have found it. If the root is larger we follow the LEFTLINK to the next entry; if smaller, we follow the RIGHT-LINK. We are then at the root of a smaller tree, a tree with half as many entries as the original. The process is then repeated until the looked-for data is found.

Here is our tree structure as it might be stored in three arrays called DATA, LEFTLINK, and RIGHTLINK. The variable ROOT holds the link to the root element. We have jumbled up the sequence to show that the actual order in the DATA array makes no difference. A zero link is used to indicate the end of a branch.

		ROOT	4
	DATA	LEFTLINK	RIGHTLINK
[1]	GOOSE	0	0
[2]	SNAKE	0	0
[3]	DOG	6	7
[4]	FOX	3	5
[5]	PIG	1	2
[6]	CAT	0	0
[7]	DUCK	0	0

Starting at ROOT, we find the root is in DATA[4]. LEFTLINK[4] leads us to DATA[3] which is DOG. RIGHTLINK[3] leads us to DATA[7] which is DUCK. You can see how it works.

A tree structure is a *hierarchical structure* for data; each comparison takes us one *level* down in the tree. The command language of UCSD Pascal has a tree structure; the COMMAND level is the root of the tree and when you press E(DIT you go down one branch to the edit level. From there pressing I(NSRT takes you down another level to the insert level. At each level there is a command which will take you back to the node that you came from one level up in the tree.

ADDING TO A TREE

To add a data item to a tree structure we simply look for the element in the tree in the usual manner, starting at the root. If the element is not already in the tree, we will come in the search to a link that is null (zero). This is where the element belongs. In our example, if we want to add COW, we would start at FOX, then go to DOG, then to CAT. At this point we would want to follow the right link of CAT, but we find a zero. If we stored the new entry in DATA[8], we would change RIGHTLINK[6] to 8 and set

DATA[8]   LEFTLINK[8]   RIGHTLINK[8]

COW   0   0

As we add items to a tree, the tree becomes lopsided; it is not well balanced. Searching efficiency depends on trees being well balanced, so that in an information retrieval data bank using a tree structure, an effort should be made to keep the tree balanced. We started with a balanced tree and it became unbalanced by adding a new item. If a tree is grown from scratch using the method we have described for adding a new entry, it is unlikely to be well balanced.

DELETING FROM A TREE

Removing an entry from a tree is a more difficult operation than adding an entry. The same method is used to find the element to be deleted, but then the problem comes. It is not difficult if both links of the element to be deleted are zero, that is, if it is a leaf. We just chop it off and make the link pointing to it zero. If only one link is zero it is similar to an ordinary linked list and deletion is similar to that. We just bypass it.

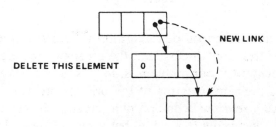

If neither link is zero in the element to be deleted, we must move another element into its position in the tree. In our original tree, if FOX is to be

deleted, it must be replaced by an element that is larger then all other elements in the left subtree or smaller than all the elements in the right subtree. This means that either DUCK or GOOSE is the only possible choice. The one to be moved must be deleted in its present position before being placed in its new position.

Remember, in a linked structure, we never move a data item from its physical location in the data array; we only change the links to alter its logical position.

LISTING A TREE IN ORDER

Trees are used where searching and updating are the main activities. Sometimes we must list the contents of a tree. We must be systematic about it and be sure to list every node. We will show how to list it alphabetically.

An algorithm for listing a tree alphabetically can be written in this way:

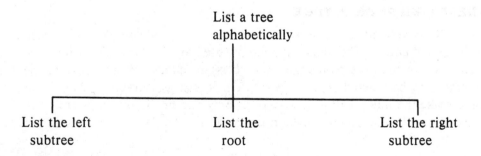

We see that we have described our algorithm in terms of three parts. The middle part, "List the root," is easy, but the other two require us to, "List a tree." This is exactly what our problem is, to "List a tree." We have defined the solution to a problem in terms of the original problem. This kind of definition is called a *recursive* definition of a solution. It seems rather pointless, as if we were just going in a circle, but it really is not. The reason it is not pointless is that the tree we are attempting to list when we say, "List the left subtree," is a smaller tree than the original tree when we said "List a tree." When we try to list the left subtree we get this solution:

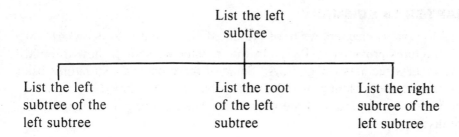

This time the left subtree of the left subtree has to be listed. It is smaller still. The algorithm is again repeated. Each application of the algorithm is on a smaller tree, until you reach a point where there is a zero link and there is *no* left subtree at all. Then the action of listing it is to do nothing: no tree, no listing. That is how recursive algorithms work. In programming terms, the algorithm calls itself over and over, each time to do a reduced task, until the task is easy to do.

In Pascal a procedure may indeed call itself as we saw in the example of displaying a list of numbers in reverse order. Here is a Pascal procedure for listing a tree in alphabetic order, given that its root is ROOT and its data and links DATA, LEFTLINK and RIGHTLINK are global variables.

```
PROCEDURE LISTTREE(ROOT:INTEGER);
    BEGIN
        IF LEFTLINK[ROOT]< >NULL THEN
            LISTTREE(LEFTLINK[ROOT]);
        WRITELN(DATA[ROOT]);
        IF RIGHTLINK[ROOT]< >NULL THEN
            LISTTREE(RIGHTLINK[ROOT])
    END;
```

Each time the procedure is entered for a new subtree, a different node is referred to by ROOT. For this job, a recursive procedure is very easy to program. It is much more difficult to program this job non-recursively. In a recursive algorithm, each time a program calls itself, a record must be kept of the point in the program where the procedure was called, so that control can return properly. Each new activation of the procedure gets new parameters and local variables; in this example there are no local variables but each activation of LISTTREE gets a different value of ROOT. As the procedure recursively calls itself, a list is built of the points of return. Each point of return is added on top of the stack of other points of return. Finding the way back involves taking return points, one after the other, off this stack. This is all set up automatically by the compiler.

CHAPTER 18 SUMMARY

In previous chapters we have presented arrays and records, which are data structures provided by PS/k. In this chapter we showed how to build up new data structures using arrays. Some of these new data structures use links to give the ordering of data items. The link (or links) for a given item gives the array index of the next item. The following important terms were discussed:

Linked list - a linked sequence of data items. The next item in the list is found by following a link from the present item. The physical order of a collection of items, as given by their positions in an array, is different from their logical order, as given by the links.

Inserting into a linked list - a new data item can be inserted by changing links, without actually moving data items.

Deleting from a linked list - a data item can be deleted by changing links, without moving data items.

Available list - the collection of data elements currently not in use.

Stack - a data structure that allows data items to be added, or *pushed*, on to one end and removed, or *popped*, from the same end. A stack does not require the use of links. A stack handles data items in a last-in-first-out (LIFO) manner.

Queue - a data structure that allows data items to be added at one end and removed from the other. A queue handles data items in a first-in-first-out (FIFO) manner.

Binary tree - a data structure in which each item or *node* has two links, a left link and a right link. The left link of a node locates another node and with it a subtree. Similarly, the right link locates a subtree. There is a unique beginning node called the *root*. If both links of a particular node are null, meaning they do not currently locate other nodes, then the node is called a *leaf*.

Recursive procedure - a procedure that calls itself. Each time the procedure is called, it is allocated new formal parameters and local variables.

CHAPTER 18 EXERCISES

1. The FLY-BY-NITE Airline company is computerizing its reservations system. There are four FLY-BY-NITE flights with the following capacities:

FLIGHT #1	5 seats
FLIGHT #2	5 seats
FLIGHT #3	8 seats
FLIGHT #4	4 seats

The information for passenger reservations is to be stored in a linked list. At some point during the booking period, the following diagram might represent the current passenger bookings.

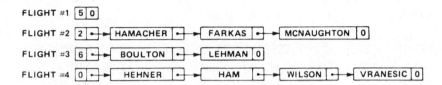

The above diagram shows the first element in each list holding the number of seats remaining. Each succeeding element holds the name of a passenger and either points to the next element or holds a 0 to indicate the end of the linked list.

In order to set up such a linked list system you will need two arrays. The first, called FLIGHT, will contain the four "first" elements. Each of these elements holds two pieces of information, the number of seats remaining and the location of the first passenger.

The second array called PASSENGER holds all the passengers. If all seats on all flights are taken, there will be CAPACITY=22 passengers. Hence PASSENGER will need a maximum of CAPACITY locations. Each element of the PASSENGER array contains two pieces of information, the passenger's name and the location of the next passenger, if any.

The PASSENGER array must be declared as an array of records in order to contain two different data types:

```
TYPE ENTRY=
  RECORD
       NAME: PACKED ARRAY[1..20] OF CHAR;
      LINK: INTEGER
  END;
VAR PASSENGER: ARRAY[1..CAPACITY] OF ENTRY;
```

This will designate each element of PASSENGER[J] to contain two parts:

PASSENGER[J].NAME and PASSENGER[J].LINK

Before any events happen, the free locations must be linked together. Arrange that each PASSENGER[J].LINK contains a value J+1, except PASSENGER[CAPACITY].LINK which contains a 0 as end of the list.

A variable AVAILABLE contains the location of the head of this chain of available locations. For the example given above, AVAILABLE contains 10 and PASSENGER could have these values:

PASSENGER[1]   PASSENGER[5]   PASSENGER[9]
  NAME HAMACHER NAME LEHMAN   NAME VRANESIC
  LINK 6   LINK 0   LINK 0

PASSENGER[2]   PASSENGER[6]   PASSENGER[10]
  NAME BOULTON   NAME FARKAS   NAME
  LINK 5   LINK 7   LINK 11

PASSENGER[3]   PASSENGER[7]
  NAME HAM   NAME MCNAUGHTON .
  LINK 8   LINK 0   .

PASSENGER[4]   PASSENGER[8]   PASSENGER[22]
  NAME HEHNER   NAME WILSON   NAME
  LINK 3   LINK 9   LINK 0

The reservation system is to accept four types of transactions:

Type 1 is a request for a reservation. The data entry contains the code word RES, name of the passenger, and the flight number.

Type 2 is a request to cancel a reservation. The data entry contains the code word CAN, name of passenger, and the flight number.

Type 3 is a request to display the number of seats remaining on a specified flight. The data entry contains the code word SEATS and a flight number.

Type 4 is a request to display a passenger list for the flight indicated. The data entry contains the code word LIST and a flight number.

Each type of transaction is to be handled by a procedure. PASSENGER, FLIGHT and AVAILABLE are global variables; all other variables are local to the procedure in which they are used. Here are descriptions of the procedures:

ADD(WHO,NUMBER). Adds passenger WHO to flight NUMBER. If that flight is filled, a message is displayed to that effect. ADD uses a location in PASSENGER and must update AVAILABLE.

CANCEL(WHO,NUMBER). Cancels the reservation made in the name of WHO on flight NUMBER. The location in PASSENGER is returned to the free storage pool. AVAILABLE must be updated.

INFO(NUMBER). Displays the number of seats remaining on flight NUMBER.

DISPLAY(NUMBER). Displays a passenger list for flight NUMBER.

The data should simulate a real reservation system in that input of type 1, 2, 3, 4 should be intermixed. It would seem reasonable to assume that most cancellations would be made by persons holding reservations. However, people being what they are, you should not assume too much. In order to get your system off the ground, several reservation entries should be first.

Write and test each procedure as a main procedure before putting the procedures together. Write DISPLAY first and call it from ADD or CANCEL to help in debugging. Be sure to test "odd" situations as well as the obvious ones.

2. The INSERTDATA and DELETEDATA routines in this chapter use zero as the value of NULL. Lines such as

IF(FIRST=NULL) OR (NEWDATA<DATA[FIRST]) THEN

cause an out-of-bounds array index when FIRST=NULL unless the DATA array allows a zero subscript. Rewrite INSERTDATA and DELETEDATA so NULL can be any negative value.

3. The INSERTDATA procedure in this chapter assumes that there are always enough elements to hold all items. Modify it to output an error message when there is not enough room for a new item. The DELETE-DATA procedure assumes that the item to be deleted is actually in the list. Modify it to output an error message when the item to be deleted is not in the list.

Chapter 19

PS/8: POINTERS AND FILE BUFFERS

In this chapter we introduce PS/8, which has features of Pascal that are helpful in organizing data structures and managing the reading and writing of files. These are pointers and file buffers.

POINTERS

We have been looking at linked lists and have shown how this kind of data structure could be implemented in Pascal using the array structure. The Pascal language provides a data structure that is designed to suit the processing of linked lists. Each element of the linked list is defined as a record and, within the record, one of the fields is a pointer to the next element in the linked list. Suppose that our list element consisted of a single data item and a link, and that the link to the first item in the list was stored in the variable FIRST. FIRST would be of a *pointer type* as would the LINK of each list item. The LINK of the last item in a list has the value NIL. NIL is a reserved word in Pascal and is the special pointer value that refers to no value at all.

In a program which uses these Pascal facilities for handing linked lists we would have to have definitions and declarations of this kind:

```
TYPE ENTRYTYPE=STRING[5];
     DATALINK= ↑LISTRECORD;
     LISTRECORD=
         RECORD
             DATA: ENTRYTYPE;
             LINK: DATALINK
         END;
VAR FIRST: DATALINK;
    ITEM: ENTRYTYPE;
```

The definitions of the DATALINK and LISTRECORD types are interlocking (a characteristic of linked lists). We say that the data structures are recursive because in their definitions they refer to each other. The vertical arrow (↑) in the definition of the DATALINK type indicates that it is a pointer type pointing to values of the type LISTRECORD. (Sometimes the symbol used is just the head of the arrow ˆ.) Then with the definition of the type LISTRECORD we see that the LINK field of the RECORD type has type DATALINK. The data part of the list element is of type ENTRYTYPE which has been defined here. We can store values such as the strings DOG, CAT, FOX, etc. in the data part.

In addition we need to define FIRST as a pointer type of the same type, DATALINK, as each of the LINK parts of the list elements. The variable ITEM will contain a data item of the same type as those in the linked list.

We will now give a procedure for searching the list to find if the data in ITEM is in the list. If it is we will set the place where it can be found in the pointer type variable PLACE. If it is not in the list PLACE will be set to NIL.

In the procedure we will use the notation

> LOCATION↑

which means the list element which is pointed to by the pointer in LOCATION. The DATA field for this element is LOCATION↑.DATA. Here is the procedure:

```
PROCEDURE LOCATE(ITEM:ENTRYTYPE; FIRST:DATALINK;
                VAR PLACE:DATALINK);
  VAR LOCATION:DATALINK;
  BEGIN
    LOCATION:=FIRST;
    PLACE:=NIL; (* VALUE IF ITEM NOT FOUND *)
    WHILE(PLACE=NIL) AND (LOCATION<>NIL) DO
      IF LOCATION↑.DATA=ITEM THEN
        PLACE:=LOCATION
      ELSE
        LOCATION:=LOCATION↑.LINK
  END;
```

If the ITEM is not in the list then LOCATION ends with the value NIL. Once LOCATION becomes NIL, then LOCATION↑.DATA is meaningless because LOCATION does not point to a list element. It is tempting to rearrange the statements and write the WHILE condition as

WHILE(LOCATION↑.DATA<>ITEM) AND (LOCATION<>NIL) DO

But this would cause an error when the ITEM is not in the list, because LOCATION would become NIL.

MEMORY MANAGEMENT WITH POINTERS

Our example procedure LOCATE shows how pointers can be used in representing lists. We follow the FIRST pointer to the first item and then we locate successive items by pointers within previous items. This means, as in the previous chapter, that the items can be scattered about, not necessarily in the same place. But pointers provide still more flexibility than we had in the last chapter, where we used arrays to hold the list items. All the items for the list had to be in one array and we had to know the maximum number of items so we could declare the bounds of the arrays.

With pointers we do not need to know when we are writing the program how many items might be in a list, because the items are allocated by a predeclared procedure NEW in this way:

NEW(pointer);

The NEW procedure finds space for the item and sets the value of the pointer to point to this space.

Suppose that we wanted a procedure to insert a data item NEWDATA into our linked list, assuming that the data items in our list are ordered alphabetically. As before the main program must have the type definition and variable declarations that we have shown. Here is the procedure

```
PROCEDURE INSERTDATA(NEWDATA:ENTRYTYPE);
    VAR PLACE,PREVIOUS,NEXT: DATALINK;
        FOUND: BOOLEAN;
    BEGIN
        (* OBTAIN STORAGE ELEMENT FOR NEWDATA *)
        NEW(PLACE);
        PLACE↑.DATA:=NEWDATA;
        NEXT:=FIRST;
        FOUND:=FALSE;
        WHILE(NOT FOUND) AND (NEXT<>NIL)DO
            IF NEWDATA<NEXT↑.DATA THEN
                FOUND:=TRUE
            ELSE
                BEGIN
                    PREVIOUS:=NEXT;
                    NEXT:=NEXT↑.LINK
                END;
```

```
      (* STORE LINK FOR NEWDATA *)
      PLACE↑.LINK:=NEXT;
      (* ADJUST LINKS TO MAKE INSERTION *)
      IF NEXT=FIRST THEN
          FIRST:=PLACE
      ELSE
          PREVIOUS↑.LINK:=PLACE
  END;
```

You can see that memory management is done for you automatically by the NEW procedure. There is no need to keep a linked list of available locations as we did when we used arrays to store linked lists. This kind of memory allocation is said to be *dynamic allocation*. Only as much memory as is needed at any time has to be reserved for the storage of a linked list. When you use arrays their size must be declared at the time the program is compiled. But with pointers the memory, as needed, is requested at execution time.

It would be a good idea if you return any unused memory locations to the system so that they could be used again. In Standard Pascal this is done by calling the predeclared procedure DISPOSE by

DISPOSE(pointer to element no longer needed);

The procedure would be used whenever a data item is deleted from a linked list and its memory location no longer needed. Unfortunately DISPOSE has not been implemented in UCSD Pascal. This means that space cannot easily be reused. Read your computer manuals for details of an approximation to DISPOSE.

USING POINTERS

In principle we never need to use pointers; we could use arrays instead as we did in the last chapter. However, pointers provide two main advantages. First, they are somewhat more efficient than arrays, for example

A[I].DATA:=VALUE

is slower to execute than

P↑.DATA:=VALUE

Second, they allow memory to be traded off from one kind of item to another. For example, suppose a program first needs to store many items of type T and then gradually needs to store fewer of these items but more items of type U. This is easy to accomplish using pointers by creating items of types T and U as needed using NEW and then deleting them with

DISPOSE (or its equivalent) when they are no longer needed. But with arrays, this would be quite difficult.

Just as arrays can contain various types (including records and other arrays), pointers can point to various types. Elaborate data structures, including trees, can be built up using pointers, records and arrays.

Sometimes a WITH statement can simplify a program that uses pointers. For example, instead of

```
LOCATION↑.LINK:=NEXT;
LOCATION↑.DATA:=NEWDATA
```

we could write

```
WITH LOCATION↑ DO
    BEGIN
        LINK:=NEXT;
        DATA:=NEWDATA
    END
```

Within the WITH statement, the value of LOCATION should not be changed. For example, the BEGIN...END should not include the statement LOCATION:=PREVIOUS.

FILE BUFFERS

As a file is read into memory, data items pass from the file to intermediate storage called the *file buffer*. File buffers are similar to items located by pointers, for example, the file buffer for file F is F↑. Suppose that an input file is declared by

```
TYPE FILEITEM=
    RECORD
        (field declarations)
    END;
VAR F: FILE OF FILEITEM;
    V: FILEITEM;
```

In this case the data items in the file are records. In order to read this file, assuming that it has been RESET, in standard Pascal we would use the statement

```
READ(F,V);
```

The READ is a predeclared procedure in standard Pascal which really consists of two more basic Pascal statements. These are the ones we have used in Chapter 17:

```
V:=F↑;
GET(F)
```

In these F↑ means "the buffer associated with file F". The first statement assigns the current contents of the file buffer to variable location V. Note that V has been declared to be of the same data type as the data items in the file. The statement GET(F) is an invocation of the procedure GET which places the next data item on file F, if any, in the buffer associated with file F, namely F↑. If there are no more items in the file then F↑ becomes undefined, in a way that depends on the particular Pascal implementation, and EOF(F) becomes true. Attempting to execute GET(F) when EOF(F) is true is an undefined operation.

The RESET operation, which must be performed on a file F before any GET statement is executed, resets the file to the first position. The file buffer F↑ is assigned the first value in the file, if any; if none exists, F↑ is undefined. EOF(F) becomes false unless the file is empty in which case EOF(F) becomes true.

When a file F is opened for output by a REWRITE statement the present contents of the file are discarded and EOF(F) becomes true. The standard Pascal predeclared procedure

> WRITE(F,expression)

is equivalent to these two more basic Pascal statements (which are the ones we used in Chapter 17)

> F↑:=expression;
> PUT(F)

Here the value of the expression is assigned to the buffer associated with file F and then by the PUT procedure the contents of the buffer are appended to the end of the file. EOF(F) must be true before the PUT and remains true after. When writing has taken place the value of F↑ becomes undefined.

In UCSD Pascal a file type INTERACTIVE is defined. It is similar to a TEXT file except that for such files a READ statement is equivalent to

> GET(F);
> V:=F↑;

The sequence of the two operations is reversed. The files corresponding to the keyboard (INPUT) and the screen (OUTPUT) are automatically typed as INTERACTIVE. This is essential to interactive operation since when a READ statement is executed you are expected to type in something on the keyboard. The GET statement fills the input buffer with what you type and the assignment moves it to the variable's location.

FILE MERGE USING BUFFERS

In previous chapters we showed how to merge two sorted files to make a third sorted file. The following program merges the files MASTER and TRANSACTION to form the NEWMASTER file. The items in these files are of a record type that is ordered by a field called KEY.

```
PROGRAM MERGE(MASTER,TRANSACTION,NEWMASTER);
(* MERGE MASTER AND TRANSACTION FILES *)
    TYPE ITEM=
        RECORD
            KEY: type of key;
            other fields
        END;
    VAR MASTER,TRANSACTION,NEWMASTER: FILE OF ITEM;
        BEGIN
            RESET(MASTER,'MASTER.DATA');
            RESET(TRANSACTION,'TRANS.DATA');
            REWRITE(NEWMASTER,'NEWMASTER.DATA');
            WHILE(NOT EOF(MASTER)) AND
                    (NOT EOF(TRANSACTION)) DO
                IF MASTER↑.KEY < TRANSACTION↑.KEY THEN
                    BEGIN
                        (* COPY MASTER ITEM *)
                        NEWMASTER↑:=MASTER↑;
                        GET(MASTER);
                        PUT(NEWMASTER)
                    END
                ELSE
                    BEGIN
                        (* COPY TRANSACTION *)
                        NEWMASTER↑:=TRANSACTION↑;
                        GET(TRANSACTION);
                        PUT(NEWMASTER)
                    END;
            (* COPY REST OF MASTER OR TRANSACTION FILE *)
            WHILE NOT EOF(MASTER) DO
                BEGIN
                    NEWMASTER↑:=MASTER↑;
                    GET(MASTER);
                    PUT(NEWMASTER)
                END;
            WHILE NOT EOF(TRANSACTION) DO
```

```
        BEGIN
            NEWMASTER↑:=TRANSACTION↑;
            GET(TRANSACTION);
            PUT(NEWMASTER)
        END;
        CLOSE(MASTER);
        CLOSE(TRANSACTION);
        CLOSE(NEWMASTER,LOCK)
    END.
```

This procedure uses MASTER↑.KEY to access the KEY field in the master file's buffer. The statement

NEWMASTER↑:=MASTER↑;

copies the entire record in the master file's buffer to the new master file's buffer.

CHAPTER 19 SUMMARY

In this chapter we introduced programming language features called pointers and file buffers. Pointers are particularly suited for constructing efficient linked lists and they allow dynamic allocation of variables. A file buffer is the intermediate storage that items on a file are read into or written from. The following important terms were discussed in this chapter:

Pointer - In Pascal each pointer can point to an item of only one type, for example pointer P can locate only values of type T:

VAR P: ↑T;

This declaration of P creates a pointer but P does not yet point to a value. Pointers to the same type can be compared for equality and assigned. For example if Q is also a pointer to T then P=Q determines if P and Q locate the same item or are both NIL. After Q:=P, Q locates the same item as P (or is also NIL). After Q↑:=P↑, the item pointed to by Q has the same value as the item pointed to by P.

NIL - any pointer can be assigned or compared to the special pointer value NIL.

NEW - a predeclared procedure that creates an item.

NEW(P)

creates an item of type T, where P is of type ↑T (pointer to T). P points to the new item.

DISPOSE - a predeclared procedure that frees storage located by a pointer. Given that P locates an item,

> DISPOSE(P)

frees the storage used by the item. DISPOSE has not been implemented in UCSD Pascal.

File buffer - given file F declared as FILE OF T, then F↑ is the intermediate storage for the file.

PUT - The statement PUT(F) causes the buffer value F↑ to be appended to file. EOF(F) must be true before PUT(F) is executed and remains true afterwards.

GET - The statement GET(F) causes the buffer value F↑ to receive the next value in the file if any. EOF(F) must be false before GET(F) is executed. EOF(F) becomes true if the file contains no more values, in which case F↑ becomes undefined.

INTERACTIVE file - a UCSD Pascal file type for which a READ(V) statement is equivalent to the sequence of statements

> GET(INPUT);
> V:=F↑;

A normal standard Pascal TEXT file READ statement is equivalent to the two statements in the reverse order.

CHAPTER 19 EXERCISES

1. Rewrite the DELETEDATA procedure of Chapter 18 using pointers.

2. Using the description of binary trees from Chapter 18, write procedures that insert an item into an alphabetically ordered tree and that list the tree in order. Use pointers to represent the tree.

3. Using pointers computerize the FLY-BY-NITE airline company described in exercise 1 of Chapter 18.

4. Define a record called PERSON that has fields for the person's name, sex, father, spouse, first-born, and younger sibling. These last four fields will be pointers to this same record type. Assuming that a collection of such records has been appropriately interconnected using these pointers, write four procedures which accept a pointer to such a record and (a) output the person's children, (b) output the person's ancestors, (c) output the person's descendants and (d) output the person's patriarchal descendant family tree.

Chapter 20

SCIENTIFIC CALCULATIONS

Most of the applications that we have discussed so far in this book are connected with the use of computers in business or in the humanities. We do business applications on computers because of the large numbers of each calculation that must be done. A single payroll calculation is simple, but if a company has thousands of employees, computer processing of payroll is warranted. Computers were originally developed with scientific and engineering calculations in mind. This is because many scientific and engineering calculations are so long that it is not practical to do them by hand, even with the help of a pocket calculator.

Often the scientific laws describing a physical situation are known in the form of equations, but these equations must be solved for the situation of interest. We may be designing a bridge or aircraft or an air-conditioning system for a building. A computer can be used to calculate the details of the particular situation.

Another important use of computers in science is to find equations that fit the data produced in experiments. These equations then serve to reduce the amount of data that must be preserved. Science as a word means knowledge. The object of scientific work is to gather information about the world and to systematize it so that it can be retrieved and used in the future. There is such a large amount of research activity now in science that we are facing an *information explosion*. We have talked about retrieving information from a *data bank* and computers will undoubtedly help us in this increasingly difficult and tedious job. But the problem of *data reduction* is of equal importance.

In this chapter we will try to give some of the flavor of scientific calculations, but we will not be including enough detail for those people who will need to work with them. We will give only an overview of this important use of computers.

EVALUATING FORMULAS

To solve certain scientific problems we must substitute values into formulas and calculate results. For example, we could be asked to calculate the distance traveled by a falling object after it is dropped from an airplane. A formula that gives the distance in meters traveled in time t seconds, neglecting air resistance, is

$$d = 4.9t^2$$

Here the constant 4.9 is one-half the acceleration due to gravity. Here is a program to compute the distance at the end of each second of the first 10 seconds after the drop:

```
PROGRAM FALL;
    (* OUTPUT TABLE OF DISTANCE FALLEN VERSUS TIME *)
    VAR DISTANCE,TIME: REAL;
        I: INTEGER;
BEGIN
    TIME:=0;
    (* LABEL TIME-DISTANCE TABLE *)
    WRITELN('TIME','DISTANCE':16);
    FOR I:=1 TO 10 DO
        BEGIN
            TIME:=TIME+1;
            DISTANCE:=4.9*TIME*TIME;
            WRITELN(TIME:10,DISTANCE:12)
        END
END.
```

The output for this program is

TIME	DISTANCE
1.00000	4.90000
2.00000	1.96000E1
3.00000	4.41000E1
4.00000	7.84000E1
5.00000	1.22500E2
6.00000	1.76400E2
7.00000	2.40100E2
8.00000	3.13600E2
9.00000	3.96900E2
1.00000E1	4.90000E2

This example outputs a table of values of DISTANCE for different times. Calculation of tables is an interesting and historic scientific use of computers. Scientific calculations are usually done using REAL variables. In the output the distances and times are given with six digits in the fraction part, one digit to the left and five to the right of the decimal point. Not all these digits are *significant*; the constant 4.9 in the formula is only expressed with two digits. We must realize then that only about two digits of the distance traveled are significant.

The calculations are carried out in the computer keeping 6 digits, but this does not imply that they are meaningful. Even if the constant in the formula were entered to 6-digit precision, we would not necessarily have 6 significant digits in the answer. Because computers represent REAL numbers only to a limited precision, there are always what are called numerical errors. These are not mistakes you make but are inherent in the way that REAL numbers are represented in the computer. When two REAL numbers are multiplied, the product is rounded off to the same precision as the original numbers; no more digits in the product would be significant. As calculations proceed, the rounding process can erode the significance even of some of the digits that are maintained. We usually quote numerical errors by saying that a value is, for example,

$$19.25 \pm 0.05$$

This means that the value could be as high as 19.30 or as low as 19.20. If the error were higher, say 0.5 instead of 0.05, then the values could range between 19.75 and 18.75. In this case the fourth digit in the value is certainly not significant, and you would say instead that the value was

$$19.2 \pm 0.5$$

Or we might round it off instead of truncating the insignificant digit, and write

$$19.3 \pm 0.5$$

The estimation of errors is an important job that is done by *numerical analysts*. If you are doing numerical calculations, you should be aware of the fact that answers are not exact but have errors.

PREDECLARED MATHEMATICAL FUNCTIONS

Scientific calculations require mathematical functions that are not commonly used in business calculations. For many of these functions, programs have already been written for Pascal; they are predeclared in the compiler. For example, suppose for our falling-body calculation we wanted to compute the times when the body reached different distances. To calculate the time, given the distance, we use this form of the same formula:

t = the square root of (d/4.9)

Now we need to be able to calculate a square root. This can be done by using the built-in function for square root, which is called SQRT. We would write in the program:

TIME := SQRT(DISTANCE/4.9);

Other predeclared functions available to Pascal for scientific calculations are connected with trigonometry. They include SIN and COS. These give the values of the sine and cosine, when the argument of the function is in radians. ARCTAN(X) gives the angle in radians whose tangent is X. The natural logarithm is obtained by using LN, the exponential by using EXP.

GRAPHING A FUNCTION

Frequently a better understanding of a scientific formula can be had if you draw a graph of the function. In the first example of this chapter we evaluated a function at regular intervals. It is possible to use these values to plot a graph on the screen. We could, for instance, plot a distance-time graph for the falling object. We will show a way to plot a graph on the screen without using the UCSD graphics.

When you draw a graph of X versus Y you usually make the X-axis horizontal and have the Y-axis vertical. The values of X, which is the independent variable, increase uniformly; the corresponding values of Y are obtained by substituting X into the function Y=f(X). When we plot a graph in text mode the lines of output text are uniformly spaced, so we will use the distance between lines to represent the uniform interval between the Xs. This means that the X-axis will be vertical and the Y-axis horizontal.

We represent the Y-value corresponding to the X of a particular output line by displaying an asterisk in the position that approximates its value. We use 31 columns to represent the range of Ys. If the lowest Y-value that we must represent is YMINIMUM and the highest is YMAXIMUM, then the 31 output positions must represent a range of

YRANGE = YMAXIMUM - YMINIMUM

To find the position for a value Y we compute an INTEGER variable YPOSITION from

YPOSITION:=ROUND(30*(Y-YMINIMUM)/YRANGE)+1;

The value 1 is added to put YMINIMUM in the first position. We are assuming YRANGE is not zero so that we can divide by it. To form a string of characters for display, we replace the blank in the YPOSITION position of a string of blanks by an asterisk. We first create a string variable called BLANKS that holds a string of blanks. The line of characters to be displayed, which is a packed array of characters, we call YLINE. We put an X-axis on our graph if it is in the proper range. To do this we place a vertical bar (or exclamation mark) in the line of blanks and call the new variable BASICLINE. The axis is placed in the position where a zero value of Y would be placed. The axis does not appear at all if 0 is less than YMINIMUM or greater than YMAXIMUM. Here is the program segment for forming the BASICLINE. Here instead of 31 output positions we assume a number given by a constant WIDTH. Then it can be easily changed if we want a wider or narrower graph.

```
BASICLINE:=BLANKS;
ZEROPLACE:=ROUND((WIDTH-1)*(0-YMINIMUM)/YRANGE)+1;
IF(ZEROPLACE>=1) AND (ZEROPLACE<=WIDTH) THEN
    BASICLINE[ZEROPLACE]:='!';
```

For each line we set YLINE to BASICLINE and then place an asterisk in the proper position. This is done by

```
    YLINE:=BASICLINE;
    YLINE[YPOSITION]:='*';
```

We do not display a Y-axis, but we list the X-values corresponding to each line opposite the line.

A PROCEDURE FOR PLOTTING GRAPHS

Here is the complete procedure for plotting a graph from N pairs of REAL values of X and Y stored in arrays of those names. The values of X are uniformly spaced. The actual names of the variables to be plotted will be given as arguments XNAME and YNAME, which are of type NAME. The calling statement would be of the form

```
    GRAPH(X,Y,N,XNAME,YNAME);
```

We will call a procedure to find YMAXIMUM and YMINIMUM. It will be called MINMAX.

```
(* PROCEDURE TO PLOT A GRAPH *)
PROCEDURE GRAPH(X,Y:TABLE; N:INTEGER ;
                XNAME,YNAME:NAME);
  CONST WIDTH=31;
  TYPE LINE=PACKED ARRAY[1..WIDTH] OF CHAR;
  VAR BLANKS,BASICLINE,YLINE: LINE;
      YMINIMUM,YMAXIMUM,YRANGE: REAL;
      ZEROPLACE,YPOSITION,I: INTEGER;

(* FIND SMALLEST AND LARGEST IN TABLE *)
```

```
PROCEDURE MINMAX(VALUE:TABLE;N:INTEGER;
           VAR MINIMUM,MAXIMUM:REAL);
BEGIN
    MINIMUM:=VALUE[1];
    MAXIMUM:=VALUE[1];
    FOR I:=2 TO N DO
        BEGIN
            IF VALUE[I]<MINIMUM THEN
                MINIMUM:=VALUE[I];
            IF VALUE[I]>MAXIMUM THEN
                MAXIMUM:=VALUE[I]
        END
END;

BEGIN
    (* FIND RANGE OF Y TO BE PLOTTED *)
    MINMAX(Y,N,YMINIMUM,YMAXIMUM);
    YRANGE:=YMAXIMUM-YMINIMUM;
    (* FORM STRING OF WIDTH BLANKS *)
    FOR I:=1 TO WIDTH DO
        BLANKS[I]:=' ';
    (* PLACE X-AXIS MARK IN BASICLINE *)
    BASICLINE:=BLANKS;
    ZEROPLACE:=ROUND((WIDTH-1)*
            (0-YMINIMUM)/YRANGE)+1;
    IF(ZEROPLACE>=1) AND (ZEROPLACE<=WIDTH) THEN
        BASICLINE[ZEROPLACE]:='!';
    (* LABEL GRAPH *)
    WRITELN(' GRAPH OF ',YNAME,' VERSUS ',XNAME);
    WRITELN(' MINIMUM OF ',YNAME,YMINIMUM:10:2);
    WRITELN(' MAXIMUM OF ',YNAME,YMAXIMUM:10:2);
    (* PREPARE AND OUTPUT LINES OF GRAPH *)
    FOR I:=1 TO N DO
        BEGIN
            YPOSITION:=ROUND((WIDTH-1)*
                (Y[I]-YMINIMUM)/YRANGE)+1;
            YLINE:=BASICLINE;
            YLINE[YPOSITION]:='*';
            WRITELN(X[I]:5:2,' ',YLINE)
        END
END;
```

USING THE GRAPH PROCEDURE

We now give the program that can be used to plot the function of x,

$$y = x^2 - x - 2$$

between the values x=-2 and x=3. We plot it at intervals of x that are 0.2 wide. There are 26 points in all. Here is the program:

```
(* PLOT THE FUNCTION Y=X*X-X-2 *)
PROGRAM CURVE;
   CONST TABLESIZE=50;
       INTERVAL=0.2;
       POINTS=26;
   TYPE TABLE=ARRAY[1..TABLESIZE] OF REAL;
       NAME=PACKED ARRAY[1..10] OF CHAR;
   VAR X,Y: TABLE;
       I: INTEGER;
       XNAME,YNAME: NAME;
   (copy GRAPH procedure here)
   (* COMPUTE VALUES FOR X AND Y ARRAYS *)
   BEGIN
       FOR I:=1 TO POINTS DO
           BEGIN
               X[I]:=-2+(I-1)*INTERVAL;
               Y[I]:=X[I]*X[I]-X[I]-2
           END;
       XNAME:='X        ';
       YNAME:='Y        ';
       GRAPH(X,Y,POINTS,XNAME,YNAME)
   END.
```

Unfortunately it is not easy to show the output for this program in this book as the type setting process uses a variable space for characters whereas on the screen each character takes the same space. You will have to try this on your computer to see what it looks like. The graph as displayed requires more than the 24 lines that you have on the screen so that as the bottom half is being displayed the image on the screen will scroll up. You can stop the scrolling by pressing some key (or keys). For the Apple this is CTRL-S. If you want the scrolling to continue press CTRL-S again. If you run this example you will notice that as the graph crosses the X-axis the exclamation mark is replaced by an asterisk. It crosses twice, at

x = -1.00   and at
x = 2.00

We say that $x = -1$ and $x = 2$ are the roots of the equation

$$x^2 - x - 2 = 0$$

The function $(x^2 - x - 2)$ becomes zero at these values of x. This graphical method is one way of finding the roots of an equation. We will look later in this chapter at another way of finding roots that is numerical rather than graphical.

FITTING A CURVE TO A SET OF POINTS

In the last sections we have seen how to compute a set of points of corresponding X and Y values from a formula and then to plot a graph of these points. In some scientific experiments we measure the value of a variable Y as we change some other variable X in a systematic way. The results are displayed by plotting X and Y. If there is a theory that relates the values of X to Y in a formula or equation, then we can see how well the results fit the theoretical formula.

One way would be to compute the values of Y for each X from the formula. The measured values could be called Y(experimental) and the calculated ones Y(theoretical). The differences between corresponding values

Y(experimental) - Y(theoretical)

are called *deviations* of experimental from theoretical values.

We have spoken so far as if it were possible to compute the proper theoretical value that corresponds to each experimental value. This is the case if the formula has no other variable in it. Frequently there are other variables in the formula that can change. For example, here is the formula for V, the velocity of an object at time T, given that its initial velocity is VINITIAL and its acceleration is A.

V := VINITIAL + A*T

If we measured the velocity of an object that has a uniform acceleration we could plot a graph between V and T. Theoretically, the graph should be a straight line, but the experimental points are scattered. It is possible to draw a line by eye that is placed so that the deviations of points from the line are small. Since some deviations, V(experimental)-V(theoretical), are positive and some negative their sum might be small even though individual deviations were large. To get a good fit we minimize the sum of the squares of the deviations rather than the sum of the deviations. The squares of the deviations are always positive. We choose as the best straight line the one that makes the sum of the squares of the deviations the least.

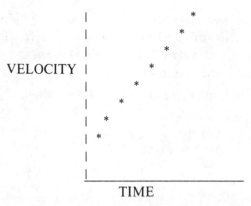

TIME

This is called *least-squares fitting* of a curve (here a straight line) to experimental points. This process can be done very efficiently by a computer. Most computer installations provide standard procedures for least-squares fitting, so that scientists do not have to write their own.

Sometimes no theoretical curve is known. We can still fit our data to an equation. We choose an equation that has a form resembling our data. If there is no theory we say it is an *empirical* fit, meaning that it is an equation based on the observations.

SOLVING POLYNOMIAL EQUATIONS

The graph that we plotted as an example was of the function

$$y = x^2 - x - 2$$

This is a *polynomial* function of x. The places where the graph crosses the x-axis are the *roots* of the equation

$$x^2 - x - 2 = 0$$

This is a second-degree equation since the highest power of the unknown x is the second power. It is a *quadratic equation.* There are general formulas for the roots of a quadratic equation. For the equation

$$ax^2 + bx + c = 0$$

the two roots x1 and x2 are given by the formulas

$$x1 = (-b + \sqrt{b^2 - 4ac})/(2a) \quad \text{and}$$

$$x2 = (-b - \sqrt{b^2 - 4ac})/(2a)$$

Most students of mathematics know these formulas. If the quantity $(b^2 - 4ac)$ inside the square root sign is positive, all is straightforward. If it is negative, then the formula requires us to find the square root of a negative number, and we say the roots are *complex*. This means, in graphical terms, that the curve does not cross, or touch, the x-axis anywhere. It is either completely above or completely below the x-axis. There is no use looking for values of x where the function is zero.

Here is a procedure for finding the roots of a quadratic equation.

```
(* FIND ROOTS OF A*X*X+B*X+C=0 *)
PROCEDURE ROOTS(A,B,C: REAL);
   VAR TEST,ROOT1,ROOT2,SQROOT: REAL;
   BEGIN
       TEST:=B*B-4*A*C;
       IF TEST >= 0 THEN
          BEGIN
              SQROOT:=SQRT(TEST);
              ROOT1:=(-B+SQROOT)/(2*A);
              ROOT2:=(-B-SQROOT)/(2*A);
              WRITELN(' ROOTS ARE',ROOT1:14,ROOT2:14)
          END
       ELSE
          WRITELN(' ROOTS ARE COMPLEX')
   END;
```

In this procedure the formulas for finding the roots do not provide values that are accurate under various circumstances. For example, if ROOT1 is nearly zero because B and SQROOT are very close in value, a better approximation to it can be obtained by working out ROOT2 and using the assignment:

```
       ROOT1:=C/(A*ROOT2);
```

to compute ROOT1. This relationship holds in general so it can always be used. Can you see why it is true?

For equations that are polynomial in x of degrees higher than two, the method for finding the roots is not as easy. For an equation of degree three or four, there is a complicated formula for the roots. For larger degrees there are no formulas and we must look for the roots by a *numerical method.*

The secret of any search is first to be sure that what you are looking for is in the right area, then to keep narrowing down the search area. One method of searching for roots corresponds to the binary search we discussed in Chapter 15. First we find two values of x for which the function has different signs. Then we can be sure that, if it is continuous, the graph will cross the x-axis at least once in the interval between these points. The next step is to halve the interval and look at the middle. If there is only one root in the interval, then in the middle the function will either be zero, in which case it is the root, or it will have the same sign as one of the two end points. Remember they have opposite signs. We discard the half of the interval that is bounded by the middle point and the end with the same sign and repeat the process. After several steps we will have a good *approximation* to the location of the root. We can continue the process until we are satisfied that the error, or uncertainty, in our root location is small enough. There is no point in trying to locate it more accurately than the precision with which the numbers are stored in the computer. A numerical analyst could determine the accuracy of the calculated answer.

SOLVING LINEAR EQUATIONS

Computers are used to solve sets of linear equations. If we have two unknowns, we must have two equations to get a solution. We can solve the set of equations

$$x-y=10$$
$$x+y=6$$

to get the result $x=8$, $y=-2$. To solve the equations we first eliminate one of the unknowns. From the first equation we get

$$x=y+10$$

Substituting into the second eliminates x. It gives

$$(y+10)+y=6 \text{ or } 2y=-4 \text{ or } y=-2$$

Then substituting back gives

$$x=-2+10 \text{ or } x=8$$

This process of elimination can be carried out a step at a time for more equations in more unknowns. Each step lowers the number of unknowns by one and the number of equations by one. A computer program can be written to perform this job, and can be used to solve a set of linear equations. What we must provide is the coefficients of the unknowns and the right-hand sides of the set of equations. A common method is called the *Gauss elimination method.*

COMPUTING AREAS

Another numerical method that is relatively easy to understand is the calculation of areas by the *trapezoidal method.* Suppose we have a curve of $y=f(x)$ and we want to find the area between the curve and the x-axis and between lines at $x=X1$ and $x=Xn$.

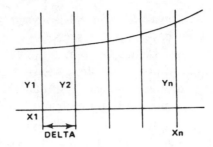

We will divide the distance between X1 and Xn into intervals of size DELTA. In the drawing we have shown four intervals. The area of the first section, thinking of it as a trapezoid, is

(Y1+Y2)*DELTA/2

The total area under the curve is approximated by the sum of all the trapezoids. The total area of the trapezoids is

(Y1+Y2)*DELTA/2+(Y2+Y3)*DELTA/2+...
(Y[n-1]+Yn)*DELTA/2

If we factor out DELTA the formula becomes

((Y1+Yn)/2+Y2+Y3+... +Y[n-1])*DELTA

This is half the sum of Y1 and Yn plus the sum of the other Ys multiplied by the width of the trapezoids. As DELTA is made smaller, the sum of the areas of the trapezoids comes closer and closer to the area under the curve. It is a better and better approximation. There is, however, a limit to the accuracy that can be obtained, due to the precision of the REAL numbers. Here is a program segment to compute the area if the Ys are stored in an array:

```
SUM:=(Y[1]+Y[N])/2;
FOR I:=2 TO N-1 DO
    SUM:=SUM+Y[I];
AREA:=SUM*DELTA;
```

CHAPTER 20 SUMMARY

This chapter has given an introduction to the use of computers in scientific calculations. Generally, these calculations are done using REAL numbers. The scientist needs to know the accuracy of the final answers. The answers may be inaccurate because of:

Measurement errors - the original data was collected by measuring physical
quantities, such as length or speed. These measurements can never

be perfect and an estimate of the measurement error should be made.

Round-off errors by the computer - a given computer stores REAL numbers with a particular precision, typically 6 decimal digits of accuracy. Calculations using REAL numbers will be no more accurate than the number of digits of precision provided by the computer. They could even be less accurate due to the cumulative effect of round-off. (Note: sometimes the programmer can choose between "single-precision" REAL, giving typically 6 digits of accuracy and "double-precision" REAL, giving typically 14 digits accuracy.)

Truncation errors in repeated calculations - some calculations, such as searching for the roots of a polynomial equation, produce approximations that are successively closer to the exact answer. When the repeated calculation stops, we have a truncation error, which is the difference between the final approximation and the exact answer (ignoring errors due to measurement and round-off).

The number of digits of accuracy in a particular answer is called its number of *significant figures*. The scientist needs to know that the computer produces a particular answer with enough significant figures for his purposes.

Pascal provides predeclared functions that are useful in solving scientific or mathematical problems. The function SQRT takes the square root of a non-negative number. The functions SIN, COS and ARCTAN operate on or return angles in radians. LN takes the natural logarithm of a number, and EXP raises e to a specified power.

This chapter presented the following typical scientific and mathematical uses of computers.

Evaluating formulas - a computer can produce tables of numbers, for example tables of navigational figures used on sailing boats.

Graphing functions - a computer can plot a particular function using the display screen. Graphs can be obtained using the UCSD graphics package or by using the ordinary text mode display.

Fitting a curve to a set of points - data points from an experiment can be read by a program and used to determine an equation (a curve) that describes the data.

Solving polynomial equations - a polynomial equation such as

$$x^3 + 9x^2 + 6x - 23 = 0$$

can be solved by a program that reads the coefficients (1, 9, 6 and -23).

Solving linear equations - a set of equations such as

$$2x + 9y = 7$$

$$10x - 4y = 2$$

can be solved by a program that reads the coefficients of the unknowns (2, 9, 10 and -4) and the right sides of the equations (7 and 2).

Areas under curves - a program can find the area under a given curve by using the heights of the curve at many points. Essentially, the program slices the area into narrow strips and adds up the areas of the strips. This process is sometimes called numerical integration or quadrature.

CHAPTER 20 EXERCISES

1. One jet plane is flying 1083.7 kilometers per hour; another jet plane, chasing it from behind, is flying 1297.9 kilometers per hour. What is the relative speed of the second plane, that is, how fast is it catching up to the first plane? The speed of the first plane is known to an accuracy of ±5 km/hr and the speed of the second is known to an accuracy of ±0.5 km/hr. How accurately can we calculate the relative speed? How many significant figures are there in the first plane's speed, the second plane's speed and the relative speed?

2. Use the graphing procedure given in this chapter to plot the function SIN(X) for X varying from zero to three in steps of one tenth.

3. Use the graphing procedure given in this chapter to plot the function X*SIN(X) for X varying from 0 to 12 in steps of 0.25.

Appendix 1:

SPECIFICATIONS FOR THE PS/k LANGUAGE

PS/k is a sequence of subsets of the Pascal language that has been developed for the purpose of teaching computer programming. PS/k is based on the SP/k subsets of PL/1 designed at the University of Toronto, and this appendix is an adaption of a technical report by Richard C. Holt and David B. Wortman for the SP/k subset.

Since PS/k is a compatible subset of UCSD Pascal, PS/k programs can be run under any compiler that supports UCSD Pascal. The extensions to Standard Pascal implemented in the UCSD Pascal for strings of characters and graphics are included in PS/k so that any programs that include these extensions would *not* run on a compiler that supports only Standard Pascal as defined by Jensen and Wirth in the "Pascal User Manual and Report".

In the interest of making Pascal more suitable for pedagogic purposes, PS/k restricts or eliminates some Pascal features. The following features are eliminated: GOTO statements, sets (powersets), variant records and subprograms as parameters.

We will specify PS/k by giving a list of included features. Language features introduced by subsets PS/1 to PS/8 are summarized in the following table.

Subset   Features Introduced

PS/1 Characters: letters, digits and special characters
       Constants: integer, real and character string
       Expressions: +, -, *, /, div, mod, trunc, round
       Simple output: write, writeln
       Predeclared functions: abs, sin, cos, arctan, ln, exp, sqrt

PS/2 Identifiers and variables
       Declarations: integer and real

Assignment statements (with integer to real conversion)
Simple input: read
Real to integer conversion: trunc, round

PS/3 Comparisons: $<$, $>$, $=$, $<=$, $>=$, $<>$
Logical expressions: AND, OR, and NOT
Selection: if-then-else, case
Repetition: while, repeat and for loops
Paragraphing
Boolean variables and constants
Type definitions

PS/4 Arrays (including multiple dimensions)
Subranges
Named types

PS/5 Characters and strings
Character string comparison
Enumerated types
Predeclared functions: eof, eoln, ord, chr, succ, pred

UCSD Pascal extensions for strings
Predeclared functions: copy, concat, pos
Predeclared procedures: insert, delete

PS/6 Procedures and functions
Calling and returning
Actual and formal parameters
Global and local variables
Arrays and character strings as parameters

UCSD Pascal extensions for graphics
Predeclared procedures: initturtle, textmode, grafmode, move, turn,
moveto, turnto, pencolor, fillscreen, clearscreen, wchar, wstring
Predeclared functions: turtlex, turtley, turtleang

PS/7 Records
Files with read, write, reset, rewrite and eof

PS/8 Pointers
Dynamic allocation: new
File buffers

The following sections give detailed specifications for each subset. In describing the subsets, we will use this notation:

[item] means the item is optional

{item} means the item can appear zero or more times

Note that square brackets are used around the index of an array in the language itself and here are used as non-terminal symbols to indicate that an item is optional. You will just have to try not to confuse these two uses as we have run out of different kinds of brackets. Sometimes we call a non-terminal symbol a *meta-symbol*. A meta-symbol is part of the *meta-language* which is used to describe the syntax of the actual language, which in our case is PS/k. When presenting the syntax of language constructs, items written in *upper case* letters, for example,

PROGRAM

denote keywords; these items must appear in PS/k jobs exactly as presented. Items written in *lower case* letters, for example,

statement

denote one of a class of constructs; each such item is defined below as it is introduced.

PS/1 : EXPRESSIONS AND OUTPUT

We now begin the specification of the first subset.

A *character* is a letter or a digit or a special character.

A *letter* is one of the following:

A B C D E F G H I J K L M N O P Q R S T U V W X Y Z
a b c d e f g h i j k l m n o p q r s t u v w x y z

Some implementations do not have lower case letters.

A *digit* is one of the following:

0 1 2 3 4 5 6 7 8 9

A *special character* is one of the following:

+ - * / ( ) = < > . : ; , [ ] { } ↑ ? %
b (blank)
' (apostrophe or single quote)

Implementations may make the following substitutions for these special characters:

[becomes (.
] becomes .)
{ becomes (*
} becomes *)
↑ becomes @ (or ˆ)

Some implementations may not have all these special characters or may have additional special characters.

An *unsigned integer* is one or more digits (without embedded blanks), for example:

4 19 243 92153

An *unsigned real* can take two forms. One form consists of two or more digits with a decimal point. At least one digit, which may be 0, must precede and must follow the decimal point. The other form consists of a mantissa followed by an exponent part (without embedded blanks). The *mantissa* must be one or more digits with an optional decimal point. If there is a decimal point, at least one digit must precede it and follow it. The *exponent* part must have the letter E, followed by an optional plus or minus sign followed by one or more digits. The following are examples of real constants.

5.16 50E0 0.9418E24 1.0E-2

An *unsigned number* is an unsigned integer or an unsigned real. Unsigned numbers cannot contain blanks and cannot be split across lines.

A *literal* (or *character string*) is a single quote (an apostrophe), followed by one or more occurrences of non-single-quote characters or twice repeated single quotes, followed by a single quote. The following are examples of literals:

'FRED' 'X=24' 'MR. O''REILLY'

In PS/1, an *expression* is one of the following:

unsigned integer
unsigned real
literal
+expression
-expression
expression + expression
expression - expression
expression * expression
expression / expression
expression DIV expression
expression MOD expression
(expression)
predeclared function designator

Real and integer values may be combined in expressions. When an integer value is combined with a real value using +, - or * the result is a real value. Two integers combined with +, - or * yield an integer result.

The / operation can have real and integer operands and always returns a real result. The DIV and MOD operations must have integer operands. DIV produces an integer result, which is division with truncation toward zero. MOD produces an integer result which is the remainder of the DIV operation.

Evaluation of expressions proceeds from left to right, with the exceptions that multiplications and divisions have higher precedence than (i.e., are evaluated before) additions and subtractions and that parenthesized sub-expressions are evaluated before being used in arithmetic operations. The following are examples of legal expressions.

-4+20   2*8.5   (4.0E+01 -12.0E1)/-2

The values of these three expressions are, respectively, 16, 17.0, and 4.0E1.

Character strings cannot be used in arithmetic operations.

A PS/1 *predeclared function designator* is one of the following:

ABS(expression)
SQR(expression)
SIN(expression)

```
COS( expression )
ARCTAN( expression )
LN( expression )
EXP( expression )
SQRT( expression )
ROUND( expression )
TRUNC( expression )
```

The ABS, SQR, SIN, COS, ARCTAN, LN, EXP, and SQRT mathematical functions accept a single integer or real expression as an argument and except for ABS and SQR produce a real result. For ABS and SQR the result has the same type as the parameter. ROUND and TRUNC accept a real expression and produce an integer result. Appendix 3 gives a more detailed description of PS/k predeclared functions.

A PS/1 *statement* is one of the following:

```
WRITE(output-item {,output-item})
WRITELN[(output-item {,output-item} )]
PAGE (OUTPUT)
```

A PS/1 *program* is:

```
PROGRAM identifier;
    BEGIN
        statement{;statement}
    END.
```

Standard Pascal requires you to place (INPUT,OUTPUT) after the identifier in the PROGRAM heading; UCSD Pascal does not.

Remember that the notation {item} means optional repeats, so statement {;statement} means one or more statements separated by semicolons. The following is an example of a PS/1 program:

```
PROGRAM DEMO;
    BEGIN
        WRITELN(2, ' PLUS ', 3, ' MAKES ', 2+3)
    END.
```

The output from this example is: 2   PLUS   3   MAKES   5

Each *output-expression* is one of the following:

(a) e

(b) e:width

(c) e:width:fractional digits   (only for REAL value "e")

where "e" is an expression value to be output and "width" is the field width to hold the value.

If e is a literal (string) and the width is not given, then the width is taken to be the number of characters in the string. If the width is given then the displayed item is the string value padded with blanks on the left to the specified width.

If e is an integer value then it is output right-justified in a field of "width" characters. If width is not given then the field width is just enough to hold the integer.

If e is a REAL value then it is output right-justified in a field of "width" characters, where the default width is just enough to hold the number with a sign, and 5 digits to the right of the decimal point. Forms (a) and (b) cause the REAL value to be output with its exponent value. Form (c) causes output without the exponent in fixed point form; for example, 1.7324E1:6:2 causes this to be output: b17.32.

There will be a slight difference in the handling of certain aspects of the PS/1 subset by different implementations. The maximum number of characters on a display screen may be as small, say as 40, or as large, say as 80. The maximum magnitude of integers depends on the implementation but is usually at least 32767, which is common for minicomputers and microcomputers. The maximum magnitude of real numbers depends on the implementation, but is probably at least 1E36. Some implementations of Pascal, use the first character of each output line for carriage control of a printer; for such systems, the first character of each line can be a blank.

PAGE(OUTPUT) starts a new page in the output.

PS/2: VARIABLES, CONSTANTS, INPUT AND ASSIGNMENT

We now begin the specifications of the second subset, PS/2.

An *identifier* is a letter followed by letters or digits. An identifier cannot contain embedded blanks. UCSD compilers use only the first eight characters of each identifier. With these compilers, identifiers can be longer than eight characters, but characters after the first eight are ignored. Identifiers cannot contain blanks and cannot be split across lines.

An identifier cannot be the same as one of the Pascal *keywords*:

AND	END	NIL	SET
ARRAY	FILE	NOT	THEN
BEGIN	FOR	OF	TO
CASE	FUNCTION	OR	TYPE
CONST	GOTO	PACKED	UNTIL
DIV	IF	PROCEDURE	VAR
DO	IN	PROGRAM	WHILE
DOWNTO	LABEL	RECORD	WITH
ELSE	MOD	REPEAT	

Predeclared identifiers including REAL, INTEGER and WRITE can be redeclared to have new meanings, but this is poor programming style which causes confusion.

A PS/2 *program* is:

```
PROGRAM identifier;
    [constant declaration]
    [variable declaration]
    BEGIN
        statement {;statement}
    END.
```

A *constant declaration* is:

```
CONST identifier = constant;
    {identifier = constant;}
```

A *variable declaration* is:

```
VAR identifier {,identifier} : type;
    {identifier {,identifier} : type;}
```

A *type* is one of the following:

```
INTEGER
REAL
```

A *statement* is one of the following:

```
WRITE(output-item {,output-item} )
WRITELN[(output-item {,output-item} )]
```

```
PAGE(OUTPUT)
variable := expression
READ(variable {,variable})
READLN[(variable{,variable})]
```

An identifier declared using the CONST construct is a *named constant.* It takes the value of the *constant* which must be a literal (string) or an optionally signed value, The value is an unsigned number or a named constant representing a number.

An identifier declared using the VAR construct is a variable. (There are no arrays in PS/2.)

In Pascal all variables must be declared.

In PS/2 an expression may contain variables as well as constants.

Real values may not be directly assigned to or read into integer variables. Real values may be converted to integer values in order to be assigned to integer variables by using either the ROUND or TRUNC functions. Integer values may be assigned to or read into real variables with automatic conversion.

In PS/2 each item in the data (the input stream) read by the READ statement must be an unsigned number optionally preceded by + or -. Consecutive items must be separated by blanks or ends of lines. One number is read for each item in the READ statement.

Any number (real or integer) can be read (and will be automatically converted if necessary) into a real variable. Only an integer can be read into an integer variable.

Any number of blanks and line ends can appear between symbols, e.g., between constants, keywords, identifiers, operators +, -, *, / and the parentheses (and). When constants, keywords or identifiers are adjacent, for example, the adjacent keywords WHILE and NOT, they must be separated by at least one blank or end of line.

A *comment* consists of the characters (* followed by any characters except the combination *) followed by the characters*). A blank cannot appear between the (and * or between the * and). Comments can appear wherever blanks can appear. In general, it is good practice for comments to appear on separate lines or at the ends of lines. Comments cannot appear in the data. UCSD compilers allow braces {...} to enclose comments as well as the convention (*...*) used in this book.

PS/3: LOGICAL EXPRESSIONS, SELECTION AND REPETITION

A *condition* is one of the following:

> TRUE
> FALSE
> NOT condition
> condition AND condition
> condition OR condition
> comparison
> (condition)
> Boolean variable

A condition is sometimes called a *BOOLEAN expression.*

A *comparison* is one of the following:

> expression < expression
> expression > expression
> expression = expression
> expression < = expression
> expression > = expression
> expression < > expression (< > means "not equal to")

A PS/3 *type* is one of the following:

> INTEGER
> REAL
> BOOLEAN

Variables declared to have the BOOLEAN type are called *BOOLEAN variables.* BOOLEAN variables can be operands in the logical operations of AND, OR and NOT. Real or integer values cannot be operands in logical operations. The AND operator has higher priority than the OR operator. Boolean variables can be compared and assigned. Boolean values cannot participate in numeric operations. They cannot be read in or output.

The operations are evaluated in order according to these four precedence classes:

> first: NOT
> second: * / DIV MOD AND
> third: + - OR
> fourth: = < > > = < = < >

Operations in the same class are evaluated from left to right. Parenthesized subexpressions are evaluated first.

Unfortunately, the Boolean operations (AND, OR, NOT) have higher precedence than comparisons, so comparisons should be parenthesized when Boolean operations are involved, as in

IF (J> =1) AND (J< =12) THEN...

A PS/3 *statement* is one of the following:

WRITE(expression {,expression})
WRITELN[(expression {,expression})]
PAGE(OUTPUT)
variable := expression
READ(variable {,variable})
READLN[(variable{,variable})]

IF condition THEN
  statement
[ELSE
  statement]

WHILE condition DO
  statement

FOR identifier := expression TO expression DO
  statement

FOR identifier := expression DOWNTO expression DO
  statement

BEGIN
  statement {;statement}
END

CASE expression OF
  case-label{,case-label}:statement
    {;case-label{,case-label}:statement}
END

If a list of statements is wanted in a THEN, ELSE or CASE clause or as the body of a loop, these must be enclosed in BEGIN...END. The list of statements inside BEGIN...END are separated by semicolons. Note that THEN, ELSE, DO, BEGIN and OF are *not* followed by semicolons.

Each label for a case statement must be an optionally signed integer constant; this constant can be an identifier defined as a CONST. (In a later subset, PS/5, case labels will be allowed to have character or enumerated-type labels.) If the expression in the CASE statement does not evaluate to one of the case labels, control goes to the next statement after the case statement.

In the FOR loop, the index variable (identifier) must have been declared as an integer variable. Each expression is evaluated once before execution of the loop begins. The body (statement) of the loop is executed once for each value in the range defined by the two expressions in increasing order for TO and decreasing order for DOWNTO. There are zero repetitions if the first expression exceeds the last for TO (or the last exceeds the first for DOWNTO). (In a later subset, PS/5, FOR loop index variables are allowed to be of character or enumerated types.) The value of the index variable must not be changed during the loop's execution. After the execution of the loop the value of the index variable should not be used (the remaining value if any depends on the particular implementation).

The following is an example of a PS/3 program.

```
PROGRAM PS3;
    VAR N,X,TOTAL: INTEGER;
    BEGIN
        TOTAL:=0;
        WRITE('N=');
        READLN(N);
        WRITELN('ENTER ',N,' INTEGERS');
        WHILE N>0 DO
            BEGIN
                READ(X);
                TOTAL:=TOTAL+X;
                N:=N-1
            END;
        WRITELN(' TOTAL IS ',TOTAL)
    END.
```

Paragraphing rules are standard conventions for indenting program lines. A set of paragraphing rules can be inferred from the method used to present PS/k constructs.

Comments that are on separate lines should be indented to the same level as their corresponding program lines. The continuation(s) of a long program line should be indented beyond the line's original indentation. If the level of indentation becomes too deep, it may be necessary to abandon indentation rules temporarily, maintaining a vertical positioning of lines.

PS/4: ARRAYS, SUBRANGES AND NAMED TYPES

Named types (type identifiers) can be defined.

A PS4 *program* is:

> PROGRAM identifier;
>   [constant declaration]
>   [type declaration]
>   [variable declaration]
>   BEGIN
>   statement{;statement}
>   END.

A *type declaration* is:

> TYPE identifier=type;
>   {identifier=type;}

Each declared identifier in a type declaration names a type. The definition of "type" is expanded to include arrays, subranges and named types (type identifiers).

A *type* is one of the following:

> INTEGER
> REAL
> BOOLEAN
> type-identifier
> constant..constant   (subrange type)
> ARRAY[type{,type}] OF type

A *type-identifier* is an identifier declared to name a type in a type declaration.

A *subrange type* has the form constant..constant. For PS/4, each *constant* is an optionally signed value, the value being an unsigned integer or a named constant that has an integer value. (In PS/5, subranges are expanded to allow constants that are characters, Booleans and enumerated values.)

An *array type* has the form ARRAY[type{,type}] OF type. The square brackets here are special symbols that must appear in the Pascal program; they are not meta brackets. The type appearing in brackets must be a subrange type (possibly named). The type appearing after OF can be any type including an array.

An element of an array A is referred to as A[expression{,expression}] where the square brackets are Pascal special symbols. Each expression must be within the subrange of the corresponding type in the array's type definition. Entire arrays may be assigned, but comparison, reading and output are only possible element by element.

PS/5: CHARACTERS, ENUMERATED TYPES AND STRINGS

The definition of "type" is expanded to include:

> CHAR
> (identifier{,identifier}) (enumerated type)
> PACKED ARRAY[type] OF type

The predeclared type CHAR is introduced. A CHAR variable has as its values a character (a letter, digit or special character). Such a value is written as a literal string containing a single character, that is, a single quote, followed by the character, followed by another single quote, for example 'A'. If the character value is a quote, it is written a four quotes, namely ''''. CHAR values can be compared and assigned.

Each CHAR value C has a unique corresponding ordinal value ORD(C) which is a non-negative integer. If I is the integer value ORD(C) then CHR(I) has the character value C. In most implementations,

$$ORD('0')=ORD('1')\text{-}1=ORD('2')\text{-}2...=ORD('9')\text{-}9.$$

SUCC(C) of character value C is the next character value, if any, after C. PRED(C) is the previous character value if any.

An *enumerated type* has the form (identifier{,identifier}). Each identifier is a newly defined value; it names a member of an enumerated set. For example (BLEU,BLANC,ROUGE) defines the type whose values are the three colors in the French flag. Enumerated types can be assigned and compared but not read or written. ORD, CHR, SUCC and PRED can be applied to enumerated types. For example, ORD(BLEU) is 0 and SUCC(BLEU) is BLANC. These functions can also be applied to Boolean; ORD(FALSE)=0 and SUCC(FALSE)=TRUE.

The following are *scalar types*: INTEGER, BOOLEAN, CHAR and enumerated types. Scalar types can have subranges; these can be array index types. Case labels can be of scalar types. FOR loop index variables can be of scalar types.

Arrays can be PACKED meaning that the implementation may try to use less space for the array at the possible cost of slower access time. In some implementations, PACKED has no effect on either space or type.

A literal (string) of length n, where n is two or more characters, e.g., 'ABC', has the special type

> PACKED ARRAY [1..n] OF CHAR

Values of this array type for a particular n can be compared (=, >, <, >=, <=, <>) according to the alphabetic ordering of the collating sequence of the underlying character set. No other arrays can be compared.

The input stream read by the predeclared procedure READ is a file of characters, divided into lines. When there are no more characters to be read in the file, EOF becomes true. When there are no characters to be read on a particular line, EOLN becomes true. A character variable C can be read, for example by

READ(C)

In contrast to reading numbers, this does *not* skip preceding blanks and ends of lines. If the next character is a blank then C is assigned the value blank. If the last character on the line is read, then EOLN becomes true and the READLN predeclared procedure should be called. When READLN is called without parameters, it skips any remaining characters on the line and the end of line allowing the next line to be read.

Note that READ(I) when reading the last number in the data does not make EOF become true when the integer is followed by blanks. READLN can have parameters:

READLN(variable{,variable})

This is defined to mean

{READ(variable);} READLN

This reads each of the variables, then skips the remaining characters of the line and skips the end of line, allowing the next line to be read.

In UCSD Pascal there is a predeclared data type STRING which is roughly equivalent to

PACKED ARRAY[1..80]OF CHAR

The principal difference is that the length of the array is adjusted to the length of the string assigned to the array. The maximum length of string that can be stored is 80 characters. If a maximum of length N characters is required, use the type STRING[N]. N may be chosen smaller than 80 to conserve memory space. Variables of type STRING can be read provided that the string to be read ends an input line. In comparisons between STRING variables the shorter string is effectively padded on the right with blanks to make them equal in length. When STRING variables are output, the field used is just the width needed to hold the number of characters in the value of the variable.

The LENGTH built-in function has as its argument a character string expression and yields as a value: the number of characters in the string.

There are several other predeclared functions for use with string variables: strings may be joined using CONCAT, certain positions of strings copied by means of COPY, and the position of a certain string pattern within a string may be determined by POS.

There are also two predeclared procedures for use with string variables: a string may be inserted into another string using INSERT, and a deletion from a string may be produced by DELETE.

PS/6: PROCEDURES AND FUNCTIONS

A *subprogram* is a procedure or function. The form of a program is extended to allow the definition of these.

A PS/6 *program* is:

        PROGRAM identifier;
            [constant declaration]
            [type declaration]
            [variable declaration]
            {subprogram declaration}
            BEGIN
                statement{;statement}
            END.

A *subprogram declaration* is one of the following:
        procedure declaration
        function declaration

A *procedure declaration* is:

        PROCEDURE identifier
            [([VAR]identifier{,identifier}:type-identifier
            {;[VAR]identifier{,identifier}:type-identifier})];
            [constant declaration]
            [type declaration]
            [variable declaration]
            {subprogram declaration}
            BEGIN
                statement{;statement}
            END;

A *function declaration* is:

        FUNCTION identifier
            [(identifier{;identifier}:type-identifier
            {;identifier{,identifier}:type-identifier})]:
                type-identifier;
            [constant declaration]
            [type declaration]
            [variable declaration]
            {subprogram declaration}
            BEGIN
                statement{;statement}
            END;

The identifiers declared in the optional list following the subprogram name are *formal* parameters. The call to a subprogram consists of the subprogram's identifier followed optionally by a parenthesized list of expressions (no parenthesized list occurs when the subprogram has no formal parameters). These expressions are the *actual parameters.* The number and type of actual parameters must correspond to the formal parameters.

A formal parameter declared with VAR is a *variable* formal parameter; those declared without are *value* formal parameters. Functions may have value formal parameters but not variable formal parameters. A value formal parameter behaves like a variable local to the subprogram that is initialized to the value of the actual parameter. A variable formal parameter behaves like the actual parameter with a new name; the corresponding actual parameter must be a variable (i.e., it must be able to change its values). It cannot be a constant or a result of an operation or a function call. If the actual parameter is an array element, the array indices are evaluated at call time and do not change.

Formal parameters must have a type given by a type identifier such as INTEGER or REAL. If the parameter is an array (or record), a user-defined type must be declared in the calling program.

Elements of a packed array may not be used as arguments of subprograms. This should be particularly noted with regard to the predeclared procedure READ.

Functions should not have side effects, meaning they should not change (or cause to change) any but local variables or variables local to subprograms that they call directly or indirectly. No reading or writing should be done.

A function is called when its identifier with actual parameter list appears in an expression. A procedure is called when its identifier with actual parameter list appears as a statement.

A function is given a value by an assignment within it that assigns a value to its identifier. (Full Pascal but not PS/k allows names of subprograms to be parameters.)

PS/7: RECORDS AND FILES

The definition of *type* is expanded to include records and files:

RECORD
    identifier{,identifier}: type
    {;identifier{,identifier}: type}
END

    FILE OF type

A record is an aggregate consisting of several fields, with an identifier defined for each field. The types of the fields are not restricted to be scalar and can be previously defined records and arrays. Arrays of records are also allowed. (Full Pascal but not PS/k allows records to have variants.) A variable V of a record type with field F has this field referred to as V.F. A record can be PACKED.

A new statement allows fields in records to be referenced by field name only:

    WITH variable{,variable} DO
        statement

Each *variable* must be of a record type. Usually the statement will be BEGIN...END. Within the statement references to fields of the record are by field name only. For example, if R is the record variable and R.F is a field, then within the statement F can be written instead of R.F.

A file is a sequence of values of its type that can be read or written. If F is a variable whose type is FILE OF T then

    F↑:=e;
    PUT(F);

appends a value e of type T to the end of F and

    v:=F↑;
    GET(F);

reads the next (or first) value of F into variable v of type T. Before a file F is written it must be cleared to be an empty file:

    REWRITE(F,'directory name')

The directory name is the one used in the UCSD operating system file directory. It should end in .DATA or .TEXT. Before a file can be read, it must be reset to its beginning:

    RESET(F,'directory name')

REWRITE and RESET are predeclared procedures.

Files that exist beyond the execution of a program are called *external*. Files created by a program and not kept afterwards are called *local*. External files may be listed in the program header which has the form

PROGRAM identifier(identifier{,identifier});

In standard Pascal the parenthesized list usually contains INPUT and OUTPUT as these are the standard files for reading and writing. For example, if INPUT, OUTPUT and F are to be used then the header in standard Pascal is

PROGRAM identifier(INPUT,OUTPUT,F);

The files INPUT (keyboard) and OUTPUT (screen) need not be included in UCSD Pascal. They are automatically included. In fact no files need to be included in UCSD Pascal.

There is a predeclared function EOF that takes a file variable as its parameter. When reading file F, EOF(F) is true when there are no more items beyond the item most recently read from the file. When a file is RESET, EOF(F) becomes false unless the file is empty. After REWRITE and WRITE, EOF(F) is true. Reading when EOF is true is undefined (depends on the implementation).

There is a predeclared type TEXT that is defined as FILE OF CHAR. In UCSD a type similar to TEXT files but suitable for interactive operation is INTERACTIVE. INPUT and OUTPUT are predeclared INTERACTIVE files. There is an implicit RESET(INPUT) and REWRITE(OUTPUT) before a program begins execution. INPUT and OUTPUT must have no other RESET or REWRITE operations.

TEXT and INTERACTIVE files other than INPUT and OUTPUT can have the same READ, READLN, WRITE and WRITELN procedure usages as do INPUT and OUTPUT, except that the file identifier is the first parameter in the procedure call. These files can be reset and rewritten.

Files other than TEXT and INTERACTIVE files can only be read or written using the forms with GET and PUT.

Implementations do not usually support files of files, records of files, pointers to files or arrays of files.

PS/8: POINTERS AND FILE BUFFERS

The definition of type is expanded to include pointers:

↑type-identifier

For example, variables P and Q are pointers to record type R.

TYPE R=RECORD...END;
VAR P,Q: ↑R

P is made to point to a *dynamically* created variable of type R by executing the statement

NEW(P)

P can be made to point to no variable by assigning it the NIL value:

P:=NIL

When P is pointing to a variable, this variable has its space released in standard Pascal by the statement

DISPOSE(P)

In UCSD Pascal DISPOSE is not implemented but an approximation to its operation may be obtained by using MARK and RELEASE (see your computer reference manuals for this). When P has value NIL or points to a variable, Q can be assigned the same pointer value:

Q:=P

P↑ denotes the variable pointed to by P. For example, when P and Q are pointing to variables, Q↑:=P↑ assigns the variable pointed to by P to the variable pointed to by Q. If P is not pointing to a variable then P↑ is meaningless. Most implementations do not allow pointers to files.

Pointers can be used to create recursive data structures. For example, NEXT in a PERSON record type points to another variable of type PERSON.

TYPE LINK=↑PERSON;
    PERSON=
        RECORD
            ...
            NEXT: LINK
        END;

For each file variable F, there is a *buffer variable* for F that is denoted F↑. When file F is being read, F↑ gives the value of the next item that will be read. When file F is being written, F↑ gives the next value to be appended to the file. For FILE OF T and v of type T we read a record by the statements:

```
v:=F↑;
GET(F)
```

The GET procedure advances the file so that F↑ locates the next value in the file if any exists. If there are no more items in the file then F↑ becomes undefined (implementation dependent) and EOF(F) becomes true. When a file is RESET, F↑ locates the first value (if any) in the file. Attempting to GET(F) when EOF(F) is true is undefined.

For FILE OF T and e of type T is to write a record we use the statements:

```
F↑:=e;
PUT(F)
```

The PUT procedure appends the value in F↑ to the end of the file; F↑ becomes undefined. PUT is defined only when EOF(F) is true.

The particular type FILE OF CHAR is predeclared as type TEXT. For these files reading and writing is accomplished by READ or READLN and WRITE or WRITELN. Files of type INTERACTIVE, which is a type available in UCSD Pascal, are similar to files of type TEXT, except that, if F is such a file, READ(F,v) is equivalent to

```
GET(F);
CH:=F↑;
```

Appendix 2:

THE SYNTAX OF PS/k

This is the syntax of full Pascal with expressions omitted and these Pascal features eliminated: GOTO statements, label declarations, sets, variant records and subprograms as parameters.

Notation:

      [item] means the item is optional

      {item} means the item repeated zero or more times.

A *program* is:

      PROGRAM identifier(identifier{,identifier});

          [constant declaration]

          [type declaration]

          [variable declaration]

          {subprogram declaration}

          BEGIN

              statement {;statement}

          END.

A *subprogram declaration* is one of the following:

      procedure declaration

      function declaration

A *procedure declaration* is:

      PROCEDURE identifier

          [([VAR]identifier {,identifier}: type-identifier

          {;[VAR]identifier {,identifier}: type-identifier})];

          [constant declaration]

          [type declaration]

          [variable declaration]

          {subprogram declaration}

          BEGIN

              statement {;statement}

          END;

A *function declaration* is:

      FUNCTION identifier

```
        [(identifier {,identifier}: type-identifier
        {;identifier {,identifier}: type-identifier})] :
            type-identifier;
    [constant declaration]
    [type declaration]
    [variable declaration]
    {subprogram declaration}
    BEGIN
        statement {;statement}
    END;
```

A *constant declaration* is:
```
    CONST identifier=constant;
        {identifier=constant;}
```

A *type declaration* is:
```
    TYPE identifier=type;
        {identifier=type;}
```

A *variable declaration* is:
```
    VAR identifier {,identifier}: type;
        {identifier {,identifier}: type;}
```

A *type* is one of the following:
```
    INTEGER
    REAL
    BOOLEAN
    CHAR
    STRING
    (identifier {,identifier}  (enumerated type)
    constant..constant  (subrange type)
    [PACKED] array-type
    [PACKED] record-type
    [PACKED] FILE OF type
    ↑ type
    type-identifier
```

An *array-type* is:
```
    ARRAY[type{,type}] OF type
    (square brackets are special symbols here)
```

A *record-type* is:
```
    RECORD
        identifier {,identifier}: type
      {;identifier {,identifier}: type}
    END
```

A *statement* is one of the following:

      WRITE([file name,] output-item {,output-item})
      WRITELN[([file name,]output-item {,output-item})]
      READ([file name,] variable {,variable})
      READLN[([file name,] variable {,variable})]
      PAGE(OUTPUT)
      variable:=expression

      BEGIN
      statement{;statement}
      END

      IF condition THEN
          statement
      [ELSE
          statement]

      CASE expression OF
          constant {,constant}: statement
          {;constant {,constant}: statement}
      END

      WHILE expression DO
          statement

      REPEAT
          statement {;statement}
      UNTIL expression

      FOR variable:=expression TO expression DO
          statement

      FOR variable:=expression DOWNTO expression DO
          statement

      WITH variable {,variable} DO
          statement

      procedure-identifier[(expression {,expression})]

      (empty statement--contains nothing)

Appendix 3:

PREDECLARED PASCAL FUNCTIONS AND PROCEDURES

FUNCTIONS

For these predeclared functions, the parameter may be real or integer. The result is real.

SIN(x)　　- sine of x radians.

COS(x)　　- cosine of x radians.

ARCTAN(x)- arctangent of x in radians.

LN(x)　　- natural logarithm of x.

EXP(x)　　- e to the x power.

SQRT(x)　- square root of x.

For these functions a real parameter produces a real result; an integer parameter produces an integer result

ABS(x) - absolute value of x.

SQR(x) - x squared (x*x).

For these functions the arguments must be real; the result is integer.

ROUND(x)- the integer part of the number rounded.

TRUNC(x)- the integer part of the number truncated.

These functions have a Boolean value.

EOF [(file name)]　- value is false unless the end of the file has been reached.

EOLN [(file name)]　- value is false unless the end of the current line of the file has been reached.

If no parameter is given for these two functions the INPUT file is the one that they refer to.

This Boolean function requires an integer parameter:

ODD(x)　- value is true if x is an odd integer.

For these functions the parameter must be a *scalar type*, that is, integer, Boolean, char, or enumerated type (or any subrange of such a type):

SUCC(x) - has a value which is the successor to x in the ordering.

PRED(x) - has a value which is the predecessor of x in the ordering.

The ORD function is used with parameter of a *scalar type*.

ORD(x) - yields an integer value corresponding to the ordinal value of the character in the set of characters. The actual value of a character may vary from one compiler to another but alphabetic characters are always in alphabetical order.

CHR(x) - yields a character value corresponding to the integer x. This is the inverse function of ORD, so CHR(ORD(C))=C for any character C.

The following functions are associated with UCSD Pascal variables of type STRING.

CONCAT(string,string{,string}) - yields a string which is the concatenation of all the string parameters.

COPY(string,start,length) - yields a substring of string, beginning at the start position and going for length characters.

POS(pattern string,source string) - yields an integer which gives the position of the first match, from left to right, of the pattern string in the source string. If there is no match POS has a zero value.

The following functions are associated with UCSD Pascal Turtle Graphics.

TURTLEX - yields an integer, the x-coordinate of the turtle expressed in some distance units.

TURTLEY - yields an integer, the y-coordinate of the turtle expressed in some distance units.

TURTLEANG - yields an integer the angle in degrees that the turtle's direction makes with the horizontal (to the right) measured counterclockwise.

PROCEDURES

The following predeclared procedures are associated with the UCSD Pascal variables of type STRING.

INSERT(string to be inserted,destination string variable,position of insertion) - causes one string to be inserted into another, the destination string, beginning at the given position.

DELETE(destination string variable, position of first character to be deleted, number of characters to be deleted) - causes a deletion from the destination string of the given number of characters starting at the given position.

The following predeclared procedures are associated with the UCSD Pascal Turtle Graphics.

INITTURTLE - causes the Turtle Graphics package to be initiated: the screen is cleared, pen color set to none, and the turtle placed at the center of the screen facing right along the horizontal.

PENCOLOR(color) - causes the pen color to be set to the given color. Available colors are, for black and white display, NONE, WHITE and BLACK. For color display GREEN, VIOLET, ORANGE and BLUE as well as BLACK and WHITE 1 and 2.

TEXTMODE - causes display to be set to text mode to display lines of text.

GRAFMODE - causes display to be set to graph mode to display line graphics.

CLEARSCREEN - clears graphic display.

FILLSCREEN(color) - fills screen with given color. If color is REVERSE the negative graphic image is displayed.

MOVETO(x,y) - moves turtle to point on screen whose coordinates are x and y.

MOVE(distance) - moves turtle distance units in the direction it is pointing.

TURN(angle) - turns turtle from present direction through angle degrees counterclockwise.

TURNTO(angle) - turns turtle to point in direction given by angle.

WCHAR(character) - displays a single character starting at turtle's present position.

WSTRING(string) - displays a string of characters horizontally starting at the turtle's present position.

The following predeclared procedures are associated with storage allocation using pointers.

NEW(pointer) - creates an item of type T where the pointer is of type ↑T. The pointer points to the new item.

Appendix 4:

SUMMARY OF PASCAL INPUT/OUTPUT FEATURES

BASIC FILE HANDLING

PUT(f) appends the value of buffer variable f↑ to the file f. EOF(f) must be true before the PUT and remains true after. The value of f↑ becomes undefined.

GET(f) advances the file position; buffer variable f↑ is assigned the next value in the file if any. If none exists, f↑ is undefined. EOF(f) must be false before the GET.

RESET(f,'d') resets the file position to the first position; file buffer f↑ is assigned the first value in the file if any. If none exists, f↑ is undefined. EOF(f) becomes false unless the file is empty in which case EOF(f) becomes true. The d in the statement is the name of the file in the UCSD operating system directory. It is enclosed in quotes.

REWRITE(f,'d') discards the present contents of the file if any. EOF(f) becomes true. A PUT(f) but not a GET(f) can be executed next.

Note: The standard files INPUT and OUTPUT are implicitly declared and RESET(INPUT) and REWRITE(OUTPUT) are performed automatically. The Pascal program must not RESET or REWRITE the INPUT or OUTPUT files.

BASIC READING AND WRITING

For a file variable f declared as FILE OF t, where t is not CHAR, reading of variable v of type t is accomplished by:

    v:=f↑;
    GET(f)

Writing of the value of expression e of type t is accomplished by:

    f↑:=e;
    PUT(f)

If you want to access a file of records randomly use

    SEEK(file name, record number)

This will position the read/write head of the disk at the record whose number is given. The first record of a file is record 0, the second is record 1, and so on. The GET or PUT operations advance the read/write head one record so that after reading a record and updating it in memory it cannot be written in the same location in the file without another SEEK.

TEXT FILES

There is a predeclared type TEXT defined as FILE OF CHAR. The standard files INPUT and OUTPUT are variants of TEXT files known as INTERACTIVE files. The input and output statements of READ and WRITE including READLN and WRITELN can be used with TEXT and INTERACTIVE files.

TEXT files are divided into lines. If when reading TEXT or INTERACTIVE file f the last character of a line of the file is read, EOLN(f) becomes true.

    WRITELN[(f)] completes the current line of file f;
       the next line can then be written.

    READLN[(f)] skips the rest of the current line of file f;
       the next line can then be read.

When f is omitted, OUTPUT is assumed for WRITELN, INPUT for READLN.

    READLN and WRITELN can have multiple parameters.

    WRITELN(f{,output-item}) is defined as:

       {WRITE(f,output-item);} WRITELN(f)

    READLN(f{,variable}) is defined as:

       {READ(variable);} READLN(f)

As before the file parameter f is optional.

For TEXT files the variable of a read must be of type CHAR, REAL or (subrange of) INTEGER. If REAL, preceding blanks and line ends are skipped and an optionally signed number value (unsigned integer or unsigned real) is read. If INTEGER, the same action is taken but the input value must be an integer.

For TEXT files the *output-item* must have one of the forms

(a) e

(b) e:width

(c) e:width:fractional digits (only for REAL value "e")

where "e" is an expression value to be output and "width" is the field width to hold the output value.

If e is a literal (string) and the width is not given, then the width is taken to be the number of characters in the string. If the width is given then the item is the string value padded with blanks on the left to the specified width.

If e is an integer value then it is right-justified in a field of "width" characters. If width is not given then the field width equals the number of digits in the integer.

If e is a REAL value then it is right-justified in a field of "width" characters. Where the default width is just what is required to hold the number with 5 digits to the right of the decimal and a blank in front if the number is positive. Forms (a) and (b) cause the REAL value to be printed with its exponent value. Form (c) causes output without the exponent in fixed point form with the specified number of fractional digits. For example, 1.7324E1:6:2 causes this to be printed: b17.32 (where b means blank).

PAGE[(f)] starts a new page in file f (OUTPUT file is used to refer to the screen display).

Files of type INTERACTIVE are similar to those of type TEXT except that the two parts of the READ operation are reversed. READ(f,v) for an INTERACTIVE file is equivalent to:

        GET(f);
        v:=f↑;

Appendix 5:

COLLATING SEQUENCE

The order determining comparisons among character values is determined by the character collating sequence of the implementation. For most implementations, ORD(C) for character value C returns the numeric value of the representation of C. For most implementations

$$ORD('0')=ORD('1')-1=ORD('2')-2...=ORD('9')-9$$

Fortunately, the following holds for most collating sequences.

'A'<'B'<'C'...<'Z'
ORD('A')<ORD('B')<ORD('C')...<ORD('Z')

We will give three common encodings of the characters. Most unprintable characters are not given. Various characters may vary from implementation to implementation.

ASCII: Used on most microcomputers and minicomputers.

0:		(null character)
4:		(EOT: end of transmission)
8:		(backspace)
9:		(tab)
10:		(line feed)
12:		(form feed)
13:		(carriage return)
32:	b	(blank)
33:	!	
34:	"	(quotation marks)
35:	#	
36:	$	
37:	%	
38:	&	
39:	'	(apostrophe or single quote)
40:	(	
41:	)	

42:	*	
43:	+	
44:	,	(comma)
45:	-	
46:	.	
47:	/	
48-57:	0 to 9	
58:	:	
59:	;	
60:	<	
61:	=	
62:	>	
63:	?	
64:	@	
65-90:	A-Z	
91:	[	
92:	\	(reverse slant)
93:	]	
94:	↑	
95:	_	(underscore)
96:	`	(reverse single quote)
97-122:	a to z	
123:	{	
124:			(vertical bar)
125:	}	
126:	~	(tilde)

Appendix 6:

SYNTAX DIAGRAMS
FOR STANDARD PASCAL

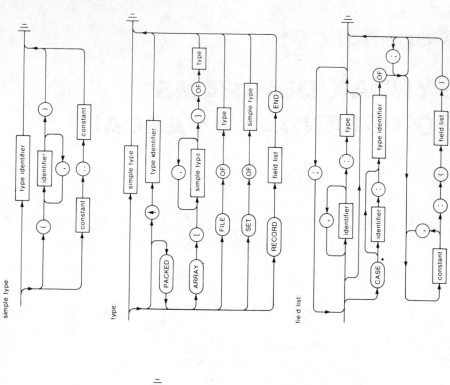

simple type:

type:

field list:

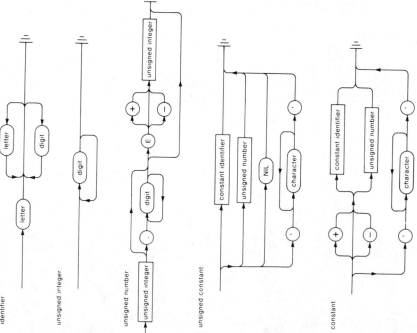

identifier

unsigned integer

unsigned number

unsigned constant

constant

*Variant records not in PS/k

simple expression:

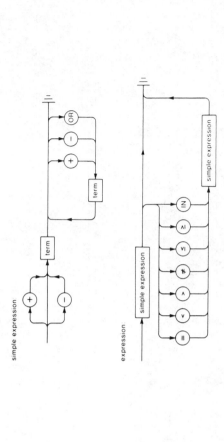

expression:

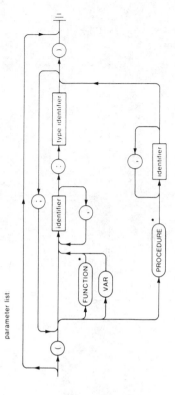

parameter list:

*Subroutines as parameters not in PS/k

variable:

factor:

term:

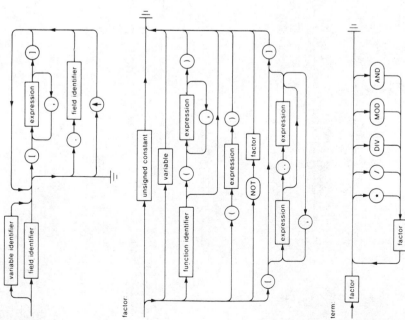

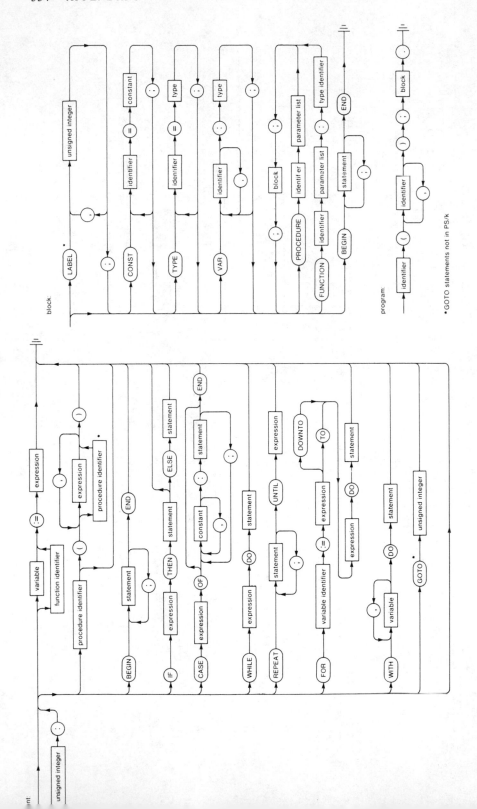

block:

program:

* GOTO statements not in PS/k

INDEX